D1237561

A SURVEY OF
PERSIAN
HANDICRAFT

A SURVEY OF PERSIAN HANDICRAFT

A PICTORIAL INTRODUCTION TO THE CONTEMPORARY FOLK ARTS AND ART CRAFTS OF MODERN IRAN

JAY GLUCK
SUMI HIRAMOTO GLUCK

Editors

CARL J. PENTON

Associate Editor

Published under the Auspices of
THE BANK MELLI IRAN

SURVEY OF PERSIAN ART
Tehran—New York—London—Ashiya, Japan
2535—1977

Editorial Advisory Board

The late Phyllis Ackerman
The late Leó Bronstein
Reza Alavi
Iran Ala Firouz
Alireza Heydari
Khodadad Raffi
Farangis Shahrokh (Yeganegi)
Yahya Zoka

All material from its archives (used by arrangement)
© Copyright A Survey of Persian Art, Japan
Rights reserved in Iran to Bank Melli

ALL RIGHTS RESERVED. NO PART OF THIS WORK MAY BE REPRO-
DUCED IN WHOLE OR IN PART, TEXT OR ILLUSTRATIONS, EXCEPT FOR
REASONABLE EXCERPTS BY BONAFIDE REVIEWERS, WITHOUT PER-
MISSION IN WRITING FROM THE PUBLISHERS OR THE BOARD OF
EDITORS.

NK
1041
.S87
1977
c.1

FOREWORD

Supporting and reviving Iranian arts and handicrafts have ever been the subject of my particular care and interest, for these lively, charming creations are brilliant reflections of the endless fecundity of the Iranian nation's eminent culture, and have always assumed a lofty status within the context of our people's artistic creativity and spiritual life.

Notwithstanding their affiliations with particular periods, Iranian handicrafts bear witness to remote, esteemed memories legated to us throughout the centuries and eras of our history, thus encompassing a pure, explicit expression of all the apparently dissimilar epochs, yet, without any pretense, reminding us of the effort and love devoted by Iranian artists and craftsmen to the perpetuation of their skills.

Handicrafts are crystallizations of a nation's reminiscences and represent equivalents of folkloric proverbs and dances, which, likewise, are remnants of many forgotton rites and events. This is why the continuation of bird and beast patterns decorating prehistoric pottery may be seen on carpets and textiles woven by today's villagers. This is also why these crafts are revered by contemporary Iranians, and why their expansion and revival are imperative in view of the respect due to original Iranian traditions. Handicrafts also bear economic and social significance. Once rediscovered, such objects acquire their true value and status. Their commerce creates possibilities for their manufacture, thus providing means for the expansion of simple, unspoilt crafts pursued by humble, tradition-oriented artists who have never considered art as an independent subject apart from the context of life.

By adorning objects of everyday use, craftsmen bestow beauty and joy on life, provide for warmth and appreciation towards existence, disseminate motifs and colors among all things everywhere, and, in their useful creativity, make objects endowed with the deep love of Iranians for beauty and decoration.

Such an occupation can, on one hand, provide a valuable, meaningful activity for the leisure time of women and men living in villages and small cities, and, on the other hand, bear economic fruits which, in the long run, may considerably expand other economic pursuits such as tourism.

Moreover, handicrafts are but small industries in which a proper balance has been achieved between economic practicality and inherent beauty. In other words, they embody the unity of human values with material and economic considerations, which is considered by many thinkers throughout the world as an ideal requirement for the happiness of all mankind.

I am delighted that the Bank Melli Iran has, on the occasion of the fiftieth anniversary of the Pahlavi Dynasty, commissioned the publication of this significant work on Iranian handicrafts and hope that through similar initiatives by other organizations, the preservation and expansion of all the manifestations of Iranian arts and culture may come to be regarded as a national duty, considering that knowledge and appreciation of the various aspects of the civilization and culture of this land will demonstrate and establish the true essence and roots of our nation, as well as its eminent status in human civilization.

FARAH PAHLAVI

UWEC McIntyre Library

DISCARDED
EAU CLAIRE, WI

PREFACE

By YOUSEF KHOSHKISH

INVOLVEMENT in a lavish art book such as this may at first glance seem to be out of line for a bank, but a good reading of the now rare,fine editions of the early travelers will illustrate our purpose. These ancient books, printed on fine rag paper and bound in leather, are today considered works of art in themselves as well as important research tools for art historians and anthropologists. But in their day they were intended as primary sources for those concerned with economic questions. While a historian of textiles, let us say, will scour Tavernier's or Chardin's *Voyages* for contemporary data on Kashan weaves or cotton prints, the readers for whom the books were intended were equally interested in the same facts— but in order to learn what they might import themselves, or what need they might profitably fill as exporters with minimal competition from the local market. Such data was of the utmost importance to the bankers of that day who would finance their activities. And even further back in time, that epitome of the "romantic traveler," Marco Polo, was writing not just an autobiography of his most wondrous life, but an important economic source book for the merchant society in which he lived.

The purpose, then, of this present book is manifold. As modern Iranians we are still much the Persians of old who could understand—as we still do—our king of 2,500 years ago when he inscribed in ageless stone at Persepolis, "All that I have made here that is beautiful I have done through the love of God." And we can today understand the words of our own Shahan-shah, "It is in artistic creations...that Iran expresses her most essential character...her most precious contribution." Yes, we take pride in our artistic creations, our arts and crafts, and keep a place for them in our everyday life—for what Persian will call a house a home unless he has a hand-knotted carpet or handsome tea-glass holders to serve his treasured guests, as we do here even at our prosaic bank.

But while such pursuit of classic pastimes might be supported by modern psychotherapists as essential for the well-being of the harried executive, our immediate motive behind this book is the purely ulterior one of presenting to the world a catalogue of exportable crafts products. A more long-range purpose is to document an important aspect of technological capital— the craftsmanship of our people. Take a people with a high level of crafts technology and a rising expectancy outstripping the production capacity, and you have a nation ready to enter the modern industrial era. This was true of the first European states in the Industrial Revolution, with the highly skilled pioneer Americans, and with the first people in Asia to enter the twentieth century, the Japanese. Yet the Japanese still hand loom fine brocades in the shadow of ancient Kyoto's modern textile mills, just as the British yet weave timeless tweeds and hand paint fine porcelains, and America's craftsmen add tens of millions annually to the G.N.P. hand-customizing automobiles and in the process pioneer technological improvements which in future years may find their way to the assembly lines of Detroit. The prototype machine, whether Whitney's cotton gin or NASA's first space capsule, must be a product of the handcraftsman. A Japanese automobile maker who had named his product after our own ancient deity was dubious of a suggestion that he assemble and eventually manufacture his trucks in Iran. He was given a red carpet grand tour of the country with little evidence that he was professionally impressed—until he strolled through the Isfahan bazaar shopping for souvenirs and entered the metal workers' lane. He stood for a long time watching the youths manipulate their tools and form the full but pliant metals into shining utilitarian works of art. Enwrapped in thought, he sighed, "Yes, I see now that we can make cars here. Good cars!" And he and we together do today, as do also many others.

Aside from these practical considerations, however, there is still another, less tangible motive for our interest in the present work. There is a "philosophical"—even a spiritual—aspect to handicraft. The spiritual health and greatness of a people is directly reflected in its art. Arts and crafts cross-fertilize each other—in fact, without good craft there can be no good art. These truths have always worked at the center of the Persian tradition to produce beauty on every level of life, from its work-a-day side to its highest moments, from spoons to mosques. We feel that this tradition of beauty is still as active a part of Iran's life as ever—or should be. And if this book helps to stimulate "good art" as well as good commerce, we will be able to congratulate ourselves indeed.

Certainly no nation can surpass us in our rising expectations, instilled in us through half a century of inspired and, by true definition, revolutionary leadership by the Pahlavi Dynasty. Two Shahanshahs, with whom we have been doubly blessed by Providence and no less by the continued support of the people, have been aware of our great traditions harking back millennia to the dawn of civilization, to the very dawn of civilized consciousness. Reza Shah the Great, on the eve of his ushering in the Pahlavi Era, sat in audience in the building (preserved today in our headquarters compound as the Management Club) to hear Arthur Upham Pope's lecture extolling the greatness of Persian art and pleading for support for a conscious renaissance. A few days later before the Sheikh Lutfullah Mosque in Isfahan, the soon-to-be Shahanshah ordered his personal funds dispensed to restore the venerable building, and soon after ordered his architects to take inspiration from it in building his Marble Palace—now the Pahlavi Museum—using the finest traditional craftsmen available. His Majesty ordered the first Bank Melli building, still our central office, to be built in a purely Persian style. For five decades quality control has been exercised over exports of our most characteristic artcraft and second foreign currency earner after oil, the Persian carpet. And in this our Golden Jubilee year Their Imperial Majesties set fashion standards by utilizing traditional textiles in their couture.

This then is our tradition, of which we are justly proud. And here we present a catalogue of this, our traditional pride. It is also a Jubilee Progress Report on the state of our greatest asset and intangible capital, our native craftsmanship.

EDITOR'S PREFACE

By JAY GLUCK

'SEARCH for the soul of the country, look for the folk arts, the traditional artcrafts," admonished the late Arthur Upham Pope and the late Léo Bronstein on the eve of my first departure for Iran in 1958. They were only repeating what they had said several years earlier countless times in lectures at the Asia Institute.

Tehran in 1958 was as ever bubbling with Iranian hospitality—but served on English or German chinaware, seated at Iranian tables or in deep French armchairs and carried from host to warmer host in American cars, there was little if anything to suggest this was the country one had come to know through the treasures in the *Survey of Persian Art*. In an audience with His Imperial Majesty came the next admonition, "Leave Tehran and see the villages," as His Majesty spoke animatedly and affectionately of the artistic and indomitable soul of his people. He summed up the material value of art when his gaze swept the *khatam* marquetry walls of his study, "A people who can do this, can do anything they set their hearts and minds to."

Enriched by the experience of the organic architecture, some of it pure abstract sculpture that served also as homes, the simple rustic floor coverings of felt and flat weaves and coarse tribal tufted weaves, I returned from a long visit to villages on the Qazvin plain and belabored Iranian friends with my reborn enthusiasm. Hesitatingly they brought the Caspian namads back out which they had tucked away to honor the visit of the foreigner, spread *jajims* again and put back saddlebags stuffed as cushions.

Looking back now after almost a generation, it was an exciting time to be in Tehran, and subsequent visits over the next several years provided a front seat at the quiet cultural revolution then under way. The modern painters returned from the art schools of Paris and New York, designers from London. The "Amlash" finds of 1000 B.C. burst upon the international art world proving again, as the Luristan discoveries had thirty years earlier, the ageless contemporaneity of Persian art. Leyly Matine-Daftary opened the first gallery to show contemporary Persian art. It was at first indistinguishable from a minor show in Greenwich Village, except that there were stuffed saddlebags to sit on. But the scene changed rapidly as the newly returned artists rejected the poor imitation of Europe their parents filled their homes with and seized upon the warm colors and patterns they had obviously been happy with on childhood vacations to the countryside. The first collectors of folk arts were these modern artists and it soon showed in their work, much of which soon developed a solid tripod base of originality, nationality and universality. The art writers, Assad Behroozan and Karim Emami, who themselves lived simply in carpeted and cushioned rooms and modestly collected fine weavings, regaled the artists and helped them find new direction. Parviz Tanavoli, Hushang Kazemi, Zenderudi, Tabataba'i, Varizi, Oveysi, Iran Darroudi, Matine-Daftary and others quickly led the development of what must be the first truly original art revival in Asia since the war. Kazemi and Behroozan preached the movement from the pulpits of their classrooms in the new College of Decorative Arts.

It was almost time to bring the crafts products themselves back to regular use, Maison d'Iran was opened by Mehdi Boushehri, Afsaneh Baghai (later Mrs. Hoveida), Rosey Malek, Vali Meshkati, Farrokh Gaffary and Matine-Daftary in the basement of Tehran's leading modern art galley, Borghese. The "organic" modest modernity of the anonymous rural products soon drew more attention than the lively experiments hung in the main gallery—and doubtlessly influenced them. But the logistics of marketing, despite the superb taste of the originators, were too much and the enterprise closed in Tehran, but took root in Paris.

Then Mehdi Ebrahimian returned from school in Paris and in the turmoil of delays in developing the Hotel Shah Abbas from its ancient caravanserai base, he landed the job to do the interiors and burst forth with his ideas of restoration, not of the monument itself but virtually of the whole spirit of his native Isfahan. He collected restorers, salvaged parts of old houses.

It was obviously time for something like a state Handicrafts Organization to do what Maison d'Iran found a small private group could not do in such an immense and varied nation. Farangis Shahrokh, known better to the world of handicrafts as Mrs. Yeganegi, was the right person in the right place at the right time, and she writes on the following pages of the birth of that vibrant group. It was fortunate that just at that time there were a few young Iranians either just returned, or in one case just visiting, who joined her. Certainly Mohammad Naraghi stands out. A brilliant designer, burning with a revolutionary ardor and an artistic patriotism that infected all around him, he was also a capable businessman and somehow with it all a very human being. He haggled like a bazaar merchant over prices— in order to raise them, to undo the degenerative downward spiral that had forced handicrafts to cheapen in impossible competition with machine-made goods. Coaxing craftsmen to show him their best, then estimating how much more money they would need to do even better, he would get it for them. Some of the most exciting items in this book come from the first exhibition of the Handicrafts Center in 1966 which he brought in, or were developed by him later when he went on his own in the basement of the Borghese and his later shops. His tragic, senseless death in 1972 was a loss to the nation and to the art world.

At this time, with the reissue of the *Survey of Persian Art*, Pope and Ackerman moved to Shiraz with their beloved Asia Institute and immediately began projecting future volumes. On his first visit in 1926 Pope had photographed a number of contemporary crafts. He was fascinated by the endurance of the carpet crafts and the manifold uses of the tough and beautiful weaves and the continuity of the arts of architectural decoration, as he was equally puzzled by the apparent demise of pottery. He had long planned a volume on the arts of today, as the subtitle of the *Survey* indicates, "...*From Prehistoric Times to the Present*."

Preparatory work on the Folk Art volume continued sporadically in Shiraz and the team gradually materialized, as we enumerate in the *Afterword*, where we acknowledge the cooperation of the host of people involved.

As impossible to categorize as it would have been to work without it, has been the support and sincere interest of Messrs. Yousef Khoshkish and Mahmoud Rais of the Bank Melli, of whom we could have asked no greater backing in everything we asked of them.

A standard of selection was set early with Pope and Ackerman, which was confirmed in 1976 with Bronstein, to draw a line, however arbitrary, between the basic arts and crafts of the people, and their developed forms in the industrial arts and fine arts.

It is arbitrary, perhaps too much so. But to our pleasant surprise, there is just too much going on in the contemporary arts and crafts in Iran to cover in a single volume. Arts rise and fall with eras, differ in each. We bemoan the loss of some, but let us rejoice at what lives and embrace and encourage it for the good of our own mortal souls. Honor the artists and give them the wherewithal to continue on their missions. The Awards for Handicraft Excellence initiated in 1975 by Her Imperial Majesty are a major first step in this, as has been the development of the Handicrafts Organization and its numerous commercial spinoffs.

The recipients of the first Awards for Excellence in Handicrafts are:

1975: Soghra Kabiri of Zovin, weaving (her prize-winning work is on page 182); Ms. Zarkhatun Baluchi of Baluchistan, needlework (p. 257); Mr. Majid Nematian of Sanandaj, woodwork (p. 351); Mr. Salman Durandesh of Tehran, glass (p. 99); and Mr. Ashout Boghassians of Tabriz, silver engraving.

1976: Mr. Abadis Hagopian of Tehran, silver engraving (p. 130); Mr. Mohammad Johari of Isfahan, steel figurines (p. 147); Mr. Mohammad Gholam Rezai of Yazd, weaving (p. 209); Mr. Reza Aghai Meibodi of Meibod, stone paste pottery (p. 77); and Mr. Jalal Kamran Haghighi of Zanjan, silver filigree (p. 125).

Special awards for contributions to the development of handicrafts were also made to Mr. Mohammed Naraghi (posthumously) and Ms. Farangis Yeganegi in 1975, and to Ms. Ada Jahanbani and Mr. Ali Kerimi in 1976.

For ourselves, seeing the craftspeople of Iran at work, we offer that this book be

DEDICATED TO
THE CRAFTSWOMEN OF IRAN
Who invented and developed the most characteristic crafts
the stuff from which any renaissance must grow

CONTENTS

FOREWORD. HER IMPERIAL MAJESTY FARAH PAHLAVI . *Page* 3

PREFACE. YOUSEF KHOSHKISH 6

EDITOR'S PREFACE. JAY GLUCK 8

THE SIGNIFICANCE OF PERSIAN HANDICRAFTS.

    The late ARTHUR UPHAM POPE 13

HANDICRAFT, THE ART OF THE PEOPLE. *The late* LÉO BRONSTEIN. . 17

HISTORY OF THE HANDICRAFTS CENTER. FARANGIS (YEGANEGI) SHAHROKH . 24

STONE. 29

POTTERY. JAY GLUCK 41

GLASS. 97

METALWORK. JOHN W. WERTIME 113

   NOTE ON *QALAMZANI*: LUTFULLAH HONARFAR. . . . 128

   ENAMEL. LUTFULLAH HONARFAR 161

   JEWELRY. IRAN ALA FIROUZ 169

TEXTILE. IRAN ALA FIROUZ *and* SUMI GLUCK 177

   NOTE ON THE WEAVING OF VELVET. JASLEEN DHAMIJA . . . 210

NEEDLEWORK. IRAN ALA FIROUZ 217

BASKETRY. JAY GLUCK *and* KHOSROW PIR 265

RUSTIC FLOOR COVERINGS. *The late* ARTHUR UPHAM POPE . . 273

   NAMAD FELT MATS. JASLEEN DHAMIJA, NIKKI KEDDIE *and* KHOSROW PIR . 277

   FLAT WEAVES. 289

   TUFTED WEAVES. C. GRIFFIN NELSON 321

   NOTE: NATURAL DYESTUFFS. KHOSROW PIR 322

WOODWORK: 345

   KHATAM-KAR. LUTFULLAH HONARFAR 361

   MUSICAL INSTRUMENTS. FOZIEH MAJD *and* MEHDI KAMALIAN . 369

PAINTING. ALI KERIMI 377

ARCHITECTURAL DECORATION. *The late* ARTHUR UPHAM POPE, THE EDITORS . 384

AFTERWORD. 409

   ACKNOWLEDGEMENTS 411

INDEX 413

Frontispiece:
Royal Family Portrait
Seated,
  His Imperial Majesty Mohammad Reza Pahlavi
  Her Imperial Majesty Farah Pahlavi
Standing rear, H.I.H. Crown Prince Reza
Standing left, H.I.H. Princess Farahnaz
Standing right, H.I.H. Prince Alireza
Seated center, H.I.H. Princess Leyla
    Photo by Yervand, SAYE, Tehran

The cover
Limited edition 2535 copies (total,
including Persian 1355, English 1180)
Bound in handloomed cotton *qalamkar*
block printed in natural colors by
Meshkat, Isfahan. Design by Carl J.
Penton using stock antique blocks
in style of Safavid book cover

Ordinary edition dust jacket, design
of Kurdish *chikh tapak*, tent surround
courtesy of Hajji Aziz Sanjavi

Published February 22, 1977 — 3 Esfand 2535 — to Commemorate Fifty Years of the Pahlavi Dynasty

Photos not otherwise credited are by Tadashi Yanagimoto, archives photographer, Survey of Persian Art.
A = Above, B = Below, *l* = left and *r* = right.
Johann Elbers: 33B, 35AB, 37AB, 46*l*, 54AB, 69AB, 70B, 71B, 73A, 78B, 79B, 82B, 83A, 85B, 96, 97*l*, 104*lr*, 108 all, 222A*r*, 223, 230*r*, 231, 232B*lr*, 238B, 239B*lr*, 240B, 243, 255A, 275, 299AB, 326*lr*, 344A*r* B*lr*, 348AB, 349AB, 369, 371 all, 372 all, 373*lr*, 374*r*, 375 all, 376*lr*, 395.
Iran Ala Firouz: 169*lr*, 174A, 271A, 312*l*, 336.
Carol and James George: 126, 138, 180, 198*l*, 265*r*, 296*lr*, 334*r*, 388 all, 394 all, 396, 403B*l*
Cellin Gluck: 114, 385 all, 386 all.
Garet Gluck: 120, 217
Jay Gluck: 46*r*, 50, 52, 58, 60, 62*r*, 64, 66, 70A*l*, 72, 77B, 80, 90, 92AB*l*, 93A, 116, 122B*l*, 136A, 154, 179, 212, 214, 284, 291*l*, 302, 308B*l*, 332, 334*l*, 342*r*, 346, 350A, 352, 353A*l*, 354, 356, 358AB*l*, 364, 374, 378*l*, 379B*l*, 387A, 391B*r*, 392, 398A, 400, 404
Hiromichi Inouye: 176*l*, 312*r*
Nikki Keddie: 32 all, 34A*lr*, 36AB, 122A*l*, 182, 196, 218*lr*, 270*l*, 378*r*
Khosrow Pir: 44 all, 45 all, 48*lr*, 170, 177, 190*lr*, 194 all, 200 *lr*, 202, 222*l*, 228B*lr*, 256*l*, 260B*r*, 265*l*, 277, 278*lr*, 280*lr* 282*lr*, 286*lr*, 321, 338, 360 all
Arthur Upham Pope: 273
Parviz Tanavoli: 156, 158, 344A*l*
Survey of Persian Art: 38A, 68, 148*lr*, 164*lr*, 166, 289, 290, 330
Musée Iran Bastan: 62*l*, 270*r*
Los Angeles County Museum: 250*l*
Ancient Iranian Cultural Library: 230*l*

Typeset in Monotype 12 point Times New Roman by Ishi Type Center, Osaka, Japan
Color and monochrome plates and printing by Hanshichi Shashin Insatsu, Tokyo, Japan

THE SIGNIFICANCE OF PERSIAN HANDICRAFTS

By the late ARTHUR UPHAM POPE

THE PERSIANS even today are masters of elegance, clear and crisp detail and jewel-like color, as evidenced by their modern applied miniatures and the tribal flat weave carpets alike, and by numerous other crafts as well. These fine miniatures have appeal to us, if only to our dilettantism. But it is the less familiar village and tribal art that is more basic to the national soul that has taken a longer time to overcome our cultural prejudices, both of us—non-Iranians and worldly, sophisticated upper-class Iranians.

For a long while the Western world regarded this primitive and folk art as inferior, an undeveloped art paralleling the meager condition of prehistoric and contemporary rural living —always on its margin of existence, with no leisure for planned artistic expression. Shapes were dictated by bare necessity. Ornament was random and meaningless, except where some crude symbol warned of some evil that had to be propitiated, as referring to some extremely simple fact or observation paralleling the crude simplicity of life. Little by little as civilization dawned, and economic social life grew more complex and the skill of the potters and the other artisans increased, the interest of the population also became diversified. The potters and decorators responded with new patterns that began to have meaning. As the society became more differentiated, some mere agricultural toilers began in part to expand into a class of artisans. Leaders as chiefs emerged with superior powers, resources and prestige. Standards and demands improved and the new and outstanding individuals began to command for themselves the products of the best workers. Accordingly, there grew an official class of superior artists who satisfied the more exclusive demands of the privileged few. Such was the emergence of court art, the steadily increasing expansion and refinement of the simplest arts of the earliest and simplest man.

All this plausible speculation was sharply challenged when, some 80-odd years ago, the French missions to Persia excavated at Susa some pottery of superior quality—almost as thin and light as paper, thoughtfully and ingeniously ornamented with patterns of great verve and beauty. The work was not that of a special group at the service of the few ruling classes, but an art that included the whole community. In short, a true communal and folk art. This mature and highly sophisticated pottery emerged about 3500 B.C. These patterns were invariably ornamented with recognizable natural phenomena—mountains, pools, reeds, water, running dogs, and other significant but less conventional figures. These signs evidently implied a language. They were symbolic appeals to the infinite powers for help by sympathetic magic, all showing want for water, with water birds and running clouds, water accumulation on the mountains with pools and reeds, all conceived and drawn with great emotion, much as they still are today in the woven goods of Kurdistan, Khurasan and Azarbaijan, among others.

These decorated vessels were the product of the whole community—their interest, beauty and communicability were products of the common mind. In various forms, they were the basis of all art and although elaborately expanded and undeveloped, these arts had their nourishing roots in the general character of the human intelligence, its experience and needs, and resources and emotional response to figures and patterns. These responses, of course, were infinite and as the wealth increased, the whole range of patterns, abstract and functional, was expanded to fill the expanding notions of the progressively less finite, known universe.

Primitive people had their own varied needs, their own faith and their own magic. They also needed material implements, weapons, accoutrements and with amazing ingenuity and skills that surprise and challenge us today, they continued to process a great variety of carefully fashioned objects. Simplicity, directness and feeling has characterized their work. In making these varied arts and crafts—instruments, rugs, weapons, ornaments—these folk arts often borrowed schemes and specific forms from the more elaborate court art and which they rendered in simpler forms, but their source in the court arts is obvious. Also the court arts borrowed many primitive patterns, more powerful and expressive patterns than were used generally, and were thereby enriched and invigorated. Court designs were always in danger of an overcomplication amounting to confusion and fussiness which the primitive arts avoid in favor of the strong and the simple and the immediate, deepened by emotional and magical symbols that frequently give to the simplest form a compelling, almost mysterious power and appeal. A power that has held its appeal, as we will see on the following pages, for several thousand years so much so that the primitive pictorial language we see emerging on the early painted pottery† is still present in the flat woven carpets of Azarbaijan.† The puzzling two-headed unidentifiable birds of the Luristan bronzes† still gaze at us Janus-like from the carpets of the southern Caucasus [or the copper mirrors of that most ancient copper center, Kerman†]. And the gardens and fish and wild ibex and other more comprehensible symbols of an earthly paradise which gamboled on the ancient pottery still retain the ability to transform the floor of the humblest abode into that very paradise when a carpet patterned with them is spread.†

298, 299
Survey, Pls. 25-72
139

324, 325, 327

In any case the ultimate source is the mind or spirit of the artist, whether court favorite of the artisans' bazaars of Isfahan or simple tribeswoman at her loom or her pottery tournet. These are the creative forces that have made Iran what it has been, but it could not have been done except on the basis of the character and life of the people themselves.

Over forty years ago* I came to Persia as a pilgrim. I had for more than twenty years been passionately fond of some of the great Persian carpets which I knew in museums and from a few Western books, but back of any achievement of such superb creations, there must be people, people with minds, hearts, imagination, poetry, genuine nobility. That Persia I wanted to see, and started on the long trip from San Francisco to Isfahan, a five weeks' journey.

You all know with what ecstasy the pilgrim greets the first gold glint of the dome of Imam Reza as he comes over the distant hills. It was the same for me as I came up out of hot and dusty Iraq to Qasr-i Shirin and there in the brilliant spring sunshine was a great wall of mountains behind which another blue wall and another higher still, and capping it all, fifty miles of gleaming snow white peaks. I was, of course, enraptured. There, beyond, lay the great Persia of my dreams and I would soon be there. I would soon see the land of the great artists, the great poets, the many saints and the noble architecture that could not be transmitted by a few poor photographs.

But I also had a sense of mission, not that I thought that I could accomplish anything, but I thought that the most elementary sense of honor required that someone in the Western world should undertake to remind that Western world of its vast and unpaid debt to Persia's contribution to civilization. I knew something of the history of the contribution of Persian art in the way of textiles, carpets, metalwork, miniatures, the art of the garden, all of which had brought enlightenment and the finest kind of happiness to Europeans who could appreciate it. I resolved that if anyone would listen to me, I would tell the Persians how great their art had been in the eyes of the wisest and best of Europeans. I knew the history of the last two centuries of Persia—all the grim disasters, the misrule, the economic collapse due to the industrialization of Europe and the shifting of the lines of commerce, then how Persia was all but murdered by the hideous Afghan invasion, and of her efforts to recover. And most of all,

Arthur Upham Pope
*The Past and Future
of Persian Art*
Ed., trans., Issa Sadiq
Tehran, 2535 (1976)

I had been thrilled by some first-hand accounts of what Reza Shah—still then Reza Khan—had undertaken in order to rescue his country from heartless exploitation. I felt that the Persians had never had a chance for a long time and that this powerful and heroic figure with his sense of justice for all and his enthusiasm for the real Persia would mark the beginning of a great renaissance, because Persia of all lands in history has suffered the most agonizing disasters—and yet, after each dreadful disaster has come the bursting of a glorious renaissance. Not one single renaissance like the European fifteenth century, but a half a dozen times from Achaemenid times through Reza Shah.

So the first chance I got—thanks to the warm and farsighted patronage of Hossein Ala, of precious memory, and with the brilliant young Issa Sadiq as translator—I gave an address to a group of notables, including Reza Khan and the leaders of Persian society. I spoke with all the fire and fury that I could command to tell the Persians that they had a most glorious history and a tradition of infinite worth and that they had, apparently for the moment, forgotten the key to their own treasure.[1] Could I perhaps make some suggestions how that combination lock could be opened up and Persia once more enter into the possession of her own vast historic treasures? Yes, I found that the awareness of the dignity and beauty of calligraphy was still alive, thus Persian taste was still acute and discriminating in many things.

For detailed history see
Survey, pp. 2879–83,
3249–99

But then the question was how to alert the world to this vast treasure that had only been partially explored and understood, how thus to encourage it so it would not die. It was necessary to carry the news of these Persian treasures to as many people as possible. So, we started a series of exhibitions from Philadelphia in 1926 to London in 1931, where we gathered together fourteen million dollars worth of superb works of art which put a new light on the history of Persian aesthetic achievement.[2] And in Leningrad in 1935 we concentrated on Persian art and its relations to other cultures, an exhibition which in magnitude and magnificence has perhaps never been equalled, with more than 25,000 objects on view. We followed this with an exhibition in New York in 1940, meanwhile undertaking to wrap it all up in the *Survey of Persian Art,*[3] which for its comprehensiveness, its system and coherent exposition has frequently been spoken of as the most important single work in the history of culture. Yet even this was only a beginning for we had not yet dealt with the art of the most recent century, nor with the arts of the tribes and the artcrafts of the bazaars which still continued to be and which had always been the font of the great art.

Third Edition
Published
Under the Auspices of
THE SHAHBANU FARAH
FOUNDATION, 2535–1977
with supplementary volumes

I realize that Persians today are making resolute and intelligent efforts to revive their ancient arts. In such as the National Fine Arts Schools in Tehran and Isfahan—revived by Reza Shah who put as much importance to them as he did to technical schools—talented students are put to the severe discipline of such as painting miniatures in the Persian manner, with its almost impossible demands on a sure eye, delicate touch and lovely imagination—portrait and landscape painting come later. Miniatures and illuminations are painted not only on paper, but also on parchment, leather, ivory, wood and mother-of-pearl. There is no sharp dividing line between high art and simple decoration, just as there is no sharp distinction between art and craft. The fine painter may practice his repertoire of design elements and perfect his approach to a particular design, much as a musician practices scales, by turning out almost mass-produced pen boxes and decorative objects for sale—frequently unsigned as he will consider them not good enough to bear his name. Similarly a young decorative crafts painter of miniatures on bazaar jewelry may improve his style and range of design and concept and work his way on up to pen boxes and the tops of *khatam-kar* boxes and eventually books and the ultimate framed panels.

Unlike the Western artist, the artist of the East does not laboriously copy from a model but rather concentrates all he has seen, known and can imagine about his subject in one fresh and poetic composition as organized yet controlled as a musical composition. The subjects are mostly legends from Persian history and poetry and have never been truly contemporary in terms of reflecting an experienced reality, any more than they are today. But to develop this repertoire the artist cannot just visualize it and transfer it to paper or ivory or a box top, so he does his finger exercises much as our pianists will and repeats and repeats many versions and variations on the theme until he has developed it to a point where he could risk a final work he might venture to consider art. These finger exercises are products of his craftsmanship and, more often than not, products for the market.†

That they may not enjoy at present a good market is due to the common fallacy that the work of art is excellent in proportion to its age, as if the mere rolling by of the years endowed an object with artistic merit. If so, the common stones by the roadside ought to be loveliest of all creative things. The beauty of a work of art is not derived from the years that have passed over it but from the understanding, skill and inspiration of some serious hard-working person. Nor are things that are expensive necessarily beautiful. The mere display of vast wealth is regarded by aristocrats always as vulgar and ridiculous. Theoretical soundness precedes practical success, and as long as so many workers and buyers alike in this country, and often abroad for that matter, also consider that art is measured by the skill and labor and fineness of the work rather than fundamental qualities of color and design, just so long will craftsmen be laboring at painful trifles and like mammoths laboring mightily producing only mice.

It is not true, for example, that the best rug has the greatest number of knots to the inch. There are rugs with more than two thousand which are aesthetically worthless whereas some of the great carpets in the world, those monumental so-called Dragon carpets from the Caucasus region, are very frequently less than eighty to the inch. And there is more art as well as sheer delight in some of the coarse tribal carpets of the Shiraz bazaar than in most of the tightest knotting in the carpet salons along Ferdowsi. Not more skill and time but understanding and inspiration are what create great art. Skill and patience are necessary for the execution of a great conception, but to substitute skill and labor for taste and sincere feeling is to enfeeble art at its source.

In all undertakings for the encouragement of art the absolute essential must never be forgotten, and that is the constant and severe insistence upon the highest standards, any admission of poor, shoddy or ill-conceived work is sheer poison, and little can be held out for the future unless those in whose hands the responsibility lies are riveted in their resolution to insist on high quality. Such improvement in the standard of workmanship will result not only in increased happiness to the workers but a marked improvement in the standard of living.

If Persia is true to her own traditions, generously helps in the acquisition of knowledge and all creative programs (the two basic components of art) that will be submitted for the approval of the Persian people, she can make good the promise of her immortality—that no vicissitudes can extinguish the great Iranian spirit. And if that can be united to patience and dedication, Persia will again enter into a period of greatness and renewed service to the world. Without the vision of beauty, the fullest and happiest life is not possible.

Khodah Hafez, Iran—

Arthur Upham Pope

---

* [Editor's note: The preceding is the last thing written by Arthur Upham Pope, having been dictated and tape-recorded during the late summer of 1969; intended as introduction to a volume on the folk arts of modern Iran for the *Survey of Persian Art*, planned by Dr. Pope and the present editors, and which has been in part (and by arrangement) incorporated into this book. A slightly expanded version, including his more personal observations of interest to Iranians was prepared for the Persian translation.]

HANDICRAFT
THE ART OF THE PEOPLE

By the late LÉO BRONSTEIN

IN speaking of the general tendencies of any civilization, one easily risks falling into the emptiness of imaginative phraseology. The personal quality in each individual creation, intangible in the last analysis, and the essential variations which the complexity of the material life of a people introduces into that civilization, force us to be constantly on guard against lapsing into generalizations. Yet there is, nevertheless, one sphere where generalization is permissible, where it is almost required, and even induced by the facts themselves. This is the sphere in which all artistic cultures, no matter how varied they may be in their final expression, stylistically and technically, no matter how distant they may be, one from the other in their physical geographical locations, participate in the same universal psychological source of man's creations.

Thus the only thing that remains for me to tell you in this respect are my old generalities (to be for sure "modernized" or brought scholarly up to date)—alas.

Generalities such as, to start with, the distinction to be made between a "popular art" and "the art of the people," this real in-depth folk art (both of them often in interaction, interfunction, hence the resulting conceptual confusion).

Popular art: The art of a temporary, localized semihistorical success, art and success promoted and often imposed by fashion or by the *dominating taste* of a privileged social (or/and imposed) stratum in a given society, and imitated often by the not-privileged. Random examples: the Hollywood-style's distortion and vulgarization of the *jazz* and *rock* music (this really depth-folk art in its ethno-social origins) by the "popular" television shows; or the official academic obsession about the Safavid art works, and their mass production—albeit by hand—for today's nostalgia market.

These two terms "popular" and "folk art" being parallel with the terms-definitions used by today's linguistic philosophers (Chomski, Sapir, etc.) as "deep deep structure" of language (its semantic-syntactical level, the level I call clumsily, but correctly, the *what-of-now* level) and "surface structure" of the visual *vocabulary,* my "what" level.

Now, what would be in the final (or primal) analysis, the substance and the structuring of this "deep deep structure" in our visual-linguist "universe of discourse"?

In my own old vision this: the Iranian "deep deep structure" (its *visual folk* structure) is the *particularly Iranian synthesis* of two primordial (historically verifiable) principles of visual "language," both universal, human, and individual (and both as psycho-historical presence of communication and expression): the *principle* of "stability" and the principle of "mobility." The "stable" quality is where the forms are clearly defined, seriated, stable, each individual and distinct from the other; the "mobile" quality is where the forms appear to the visual consciousness indissolubly attached to each other, one continuing the other, and together forming a kind of collective ensemble, a dynamic whole.

We might say that art through the ages has passed through great cycles, in which sometimes one, sometimes the other of these tendencies has been dominant. In some rare historic achievements, both tendencies have united to create an art at once complex and of supreme harmony.

Iran, as well as all other strongly individualized cultures of the classical Near East, is an extremely complicated structure, composed of multiple ethnic and political levels, each level representing more or less a new era of a dominating aristocracy of conquerors or newcomers, each level with its own artistic ideology, often, it is true, influenced by the immediately preceding level. The latter, changing in status from oppressor to oppressed, will be mingled partly with the totality of dominated masses and will increase by its contribution the existing treasure of "the art of the people." The presence of each of the two universal tendencies, "stable," "mobile," and above all their relative proportions, or the hegemony of one of them (when this is materially controllable), will enable us at least to indicate to which of the two large currents of Asia—the northern or the southern, or both—the analyzed period or "level" would appertain.

Where the multileveled structure of ancient Iran is concerned, we can distinguish (always grosso modo speaking, for want of space) at first two chief components: the Elam–Anzan cultural zone (modern Fars–Khuzistan); and the Zagros, or more precisely the Luristan zone.

Does all this mean that the "mobility" of Luristan directly contributed to the further and fundamental development of Iranian art? It would be more than imprudent to postulate this categorically. Nevertheless, the strong individuality of Luristan art and its organic affinity with other artistic cultures indicate a deep consciousness of "popular art" (in the sense of accumulated ethnico-political levels), which certainly must have passed the limits of a local artistic manifestation. Be that as it may, the ancient Iran, the entire history of which might be said to be a progressively acquired synthesis of the two primordial tendencies, seems to be more fundamentally characterized by the northern contribution.

Yet when, later on, the great Sasanian reconstruction of the Iranian empire took place, it was the aesthetic formula of the southern continuum which seems to have guided the official royal and feudal art, just as it had done in Achaemenid times, and, probably, for the same reasons. But towards the last period of that civilization we can see a new style, with tangible northern affinities, come more and more to light. And it is in the near-Caspian provinces, the very crucible of Iranian destiny, that this double aspect of the deep Iranian traditions was most intensively fulfilled—at first in its feudal-aristocratic form (under local rulers), and then in its popular form with the infiltration of Islam under the latter's altogether revolutionary (dissenting) aspect: Shi'ism.

We know how deeply Iranian was Shi'ism, if not in its "external" origin (Arabic ethnically and politically) certainly in its immediate diffusion, acceptance, and development. And we can already guess how profoundly connected in its "inner" origin it must have been with the lowest levels of the Iranian social, economic, and ideological structure. Can we possibly—against the teaching of history—imagine that this Iranian Islamic renaissance (which spread all over the Islamic world) did not affect the corresponding artistic ideology of the period?

Indeed it was in those northern or close-to-northern Iranian regions (which included all the culturally fertile zones of southern Caucasus and northeastern Iran), and at the very heart of this renaissance, both cultural and political (the formation of great Iranian feudal monarchies between the ninth and eleventh centuries: the Samanids, the Buyids, etc.), that the "synthesis," the peculiar Iranian "equilibrium" was reached under the hegemony of the "mobile" law.

The Iranian Islamic "style" was born: the interlacing and systematically "deforming" animal-human, animal-and-plant style of the so-called Gabri pottery, and related to it formally, all the ceramic art of other Iranian schools. The ceramic arts have, almost more than any others, their roots in the life of the people, and maintain intimate connections with almost every phase of their daily existence through practically all levels of society. Of course, it is not here meant to suggest a direct dependence of subsequent Iranian art upon this "popular" style of pottery.

It is sufficient only to aver the presence of the same formal tendency, but differently expressed. For instance, we have the "mobility" (animals-plants, human beings-plants) of the twelfth and thirteenth century ceramics; the same "mobility" in some North Iranian thirteenth century stone reliefs; in East Iranian wood carving; in sixteenth and seventeenth century carpets with their complicated abstract perspective formed by interlaced ornamental levels of color and design—reflected also in garden design and mosaic faience tilework; and perhaps also in the architecture, the mobility of the ogive; and certainly in the mobility of the people and the resultant mobile art of the nomad among whom, homologically, clothes and horse trappings are what architecture is to the urbanite (and should be analytically investigated as such). The personality of Iran was formed, and all the subsequent periods of Iranian artistic destiny were the epic deeds of the same personality—this and no other. But we must not forget the essential synthetic character of this personality: in all the artistic achievements or inventions of Islamic Iran there was an effort to attain a perfect fusion of the two antithetical psycho-historical tendencies. The effort at fusion is, basically, the whole imagery of Persia and her science of ornamentation. Fusion—the festivity of color, the elegance of line, the delightful brilliance of *ensemble*; the formula of despair is enveloped in an atmosphere of peace and resignation which makes it more profound and more human—the "it" may be a carpet, a miniature, a revetment, a pot.

However, the art of Iran in recent centuries has undergone a gradual, and what seems today to be a final decadence; it is often said that it no longer created, but merely repeated, unintelligently. This is not quite true. We can sometimes see the "decadent" eighteenth–nineteenth century art imposing creatively—so powerful is the great tradition, the instinctive awareness of and the instinctive fidelity to it!—its never forgotten formula of "mobile" synthesis on the most energetic and by this time most welcomed formula of European "stable" three-dimensionality.

Here again, it would seem, the explanation must be sought in some historical necessity. We can notice in history this very curious phenomenon: *the decadence of an imperial civilization usually coincides with the renaissance of its deeply rooted popular ideology,* an ideology submerged under the upper levels of the huge sociological structure. This historical phenomenon of decadence must have formed the physiognomy of the late Sasanian dynasty, as again even at the latter quarter of the last century and first quarter of this with the decline of the Qajars.

The real greatness of the past is gone. Still, having once been so universal and so new, hence inexhaustible by virtue of its synthetic essence, is it possible that this grand art will not be reborn? Iran gave birth, without realizing it, to a unique aesthetic form; it remains for Iran to find it again, but in full consciousness of its worth.

But one cannot organize or judge our images without loving them (to hate them would mean to make them visually disappear or be nonexistent). I love, that is, I exercise "volition-affection" toward my images; which is to say that visually, the images-among-themselves-and-I are mutually attracted. I "deform" them, accordingly, so that their emotion-volition, liberated from the anatomic external limitation of these images, might take possession of them more freely also, and so fulfill their desire for union and fusion. Their (images-and-I) narrow embrace becomes then the very shape or the contour of a "new" image-idea, an image-whole, an image-"monster": an idea-ornament. The ornament is then born. For ornament is "affection-volition" of perspective: the "stability" of judgment in it becomes the "mobility" of desire.

For the space of Iranian painting—and even more so the even less seemingly representational decorative arts of the carpet and textiles, the garden and faience architectural revetment, architecture and pottery—is neither a two-dimensional space nor a three-dimensional. It is not a three-dimensional space in the sense that Greece and Rome, through Europe's novel teaching since the Renaissance, have accustomed us to "judge" and to enjoy space-imagery: The articulated automation-system, closed and "logical," of space "which walks by itself," the technique of "correct" perspective, of "natural" relief, of chiaroscuro, etc.

The Iranian space is much more intense than that: it is neither two nor three-dimensional; it is about to become three-dimensional. Iran's charm and power, its "limitations" also—the "deformative," "illogical" absurdities of Iran's space construction—come from this aboutness. Hence its affinities with our own modern space-conception, which is about to overcome the impositions of an articulated and closed three-dimensionality. Hence also its neighborliness to the Romanesque experience. For Iranian space is also dominated by volition-emotion. But its particularity, its uniqueness, consists in the ultimate alliance between this "volition"-image and the pure, naïve first "image"-idea: alliance. And that is how a psycho-plastic depth or perspective was created in Iran. Within this magic world you are not—you cannot be—placed in front of the organized space images, as if in front of a "system which walks by itself," but you are within it, among the images. You are not, therefore, aware of it. You are about to be so. Iranian "mentality" is not a struggle against "judgment," but it is the will to "judge" (not for reconciliation's sake as in China, but for the plenitude of the eye's awareness); it is the effort to "judge" and, the same time, the impossibility of so doing. This is the "secret" of Iranian pictorial space. Within or "among" this romantic, and in appearance, so cheerful imagery (pure radiant pigments, secure outlinings, etc.), very strange things happen; strange and "illogical" things, because new and at the same time future things, things about to be totally "real." We can watch the sudden and tense "rigidity" of an evolving or moving image "rigidity": the plastic reflex of what we saw is about to be true, the immediate and not the mediated or "mnemonic" movement). Elsewhere, there will be here and there a sudden fusion of space and time, neither a two-dimensional nor three-dimensional universe, but a mobile in-between universe, an *about to be,* more plenary than the simply plastic universe of the eye: "ornament."

But why did not Iran overcome this uneasy limitation of "about"? Why did not Iran include the fullness of the judgment-perspective in the fullness of its visual equilibrium, and thereby create its own final space formula? This new formula, if invented, could have been as complete as that of Europe's Renaissance three-dimensionality (Brunelleschi, Alberti, Masaccio, etc.), more complete and richer, perhaps, because more dramatically matured through its stage of "about": not only the formula in-front-of-a-thing-which-walks-by-itself, but also the formula "within-the-thing."

Iranian "mentality," as was shown to us, is not a struggle against "judgment." It is the will, the effort to "judge," the nostalgia-memory of "judgment"; and at the same time it is the impossibility of exercising "judgment," the some-thing-against-it preventing.

This obstruction, what is it? To our question, why, granted that Europe and Iran, West and East, belong to the same historical current of visual realization, why did Europe create its formula of three-dimensionality, whereas the Near East, the East in general, did not. This time we propose a hypothesis:

Because the West discovered the "machine" and the East did not. Iran knew the tool, but not the machine. Iran belonged to the cyclic mentality of tool-facture (the feudal collective mentality) and not of machine-facture (the "capitalistic" collective mentality). A tool being, as it is usually formulated, "the continued hand," the tool-facture mentality is a hand—or manufacture mentality. Its constructed or fabricated "object"—mental or plastic—is limited to the immediate, organic physical, one might say, bodily dependence on possession of space—mental or plastic: a between-the-eye-and-the-hand possession and certainty. The solemn laying on of the hand token of the feudal principle of personal confidence during the "hommage" and fief-granting ceremonies; the personal physical relation—of combined violence and protection—between the lord and the serf or between the personified Divinity and the praying soul of the sinner; the personal physical attachment to the soil; the directness of the individual participation in wars, and the individual physical, the hand-skill in feudal crafts and arts— all this goes deeply into the dense roots of human body, or hand, awareness, the roots of what we called the manufacture, the hand-facture "mentality." The resulting "object"—mental or plastic—does not "walk by itself" but "walks with us," because of us. The same is true "when compared with our post-Baconian and post-Cartesian "walking-by-itself object" (European science and philosophy) of the scholastic European theology, of the Islamic Science of Tradition (Hadith), of the Jewish wisdom of the Talmud and their walking-because-of-us "object"- faith; and so also of the form (the what of the how form) of say, a Persian carpet—the whole of a paradise-garden possessed between-our-eye-and-hand; or the "compresence" of shape- "ornament"-and-us in Iranian pottery, metalwork, painting, or building.

The machine, on the other hand, is essentially homo faver's "success" in achieving the independence of the mind's function from the body's or the hand's function. It is the "technological" objectivation of judgment. It is—even if only temporarily or not indefinitely— "the thing which walks by itself." The idea of this independence was born (and this is part of my hypothesis), in classical Greece, although the machine as an object, as a precise technical device, was not created or applied in Greece.

The application of this principle of independence from the body, from the limitations of between-the-eye-and-the-hand, gave Europe the machine and the three-dimensionality of space—mental and plastic.

Now—and this was precisely my hypothesis—Islam, the Islamic Iran of our eye's journey, was about to create this three-dimensionality, because Iran was also about to create the machine.

(There is the feminine constant, the awareness of it, in reference to points in space. Awareness of body especially as in the points in the space of the gilims woven by Kurdish and Qashgai women or the awareness of body shown in the pottery of both the women modelers of Baluchistan who show how the craft was invented by women, as well as the male wheel-thrown forms of the millennia since until today which retain yet their feminine origins. "She" belongs to the world of touch, by which "she" participates in the world.)

The tool is usually defined, broadly, as a "continued hand." The tool, says Francois Mentre, is undoubtedly a prolongation of the hand, this universal tool, so that the ensemble of tools exhausts the analysis of all the movements executed by the human hand or by both hands associated.

Now this formula of a continued body (or hand, as an extreme result of our tactile consciousness) we saw emerging from our analysis of the visual possession of space. Only there, within the eye, this possession was automatic, self-given, while here, in the case of the tool, it is projected-fabricated, exactly as we saw fabricated a "new" art object. Yet the tool-possession is without the inner conflict-élan which is the very condition of creativeness or inventiveness in art. Thus, the tool stands exactly between the automatism of space, the automatic prolongation of the hand, and the "new," invented object of space, the art object.

How different, and yet, because of its tenacious attachment to the tool or circular motion "mentality", how near to ours, is the world of the East: a world both so incomplete in its Hellenistic "about" result or crystallization, and so more-than-complete, so prophetically ultramodern in its proximity to that total technological result to which we, "modern" (without losing our past experience), seem to be "about" to return.

Water—water mills, water clocks, manuscripts and manuscripts, and more manuscripts buried in libraries of the Orient, full of illustrated descriptions of hydrostatic automations, of water wheels, of balances, of elevations of water: that is what dominates absolutely the entire Eastern perspective of technology, as it in so many ways dominates the iconography of folk art decoration in Iran.

We were perplexed. In saying: "mobility-stability equilibrium"; in saying: "the art of the Persians was about to acquire it spatial fullness"—are we not indeed revealing the intimate mechanism of our own result-participation rather than theirs? Are we not therefore, and first of all, destroying that lovely and accessible to all, by all accepted, truth which is the simple poetical joy and ease of all Persian Art? Aren't we, with our difficult, complex and heavy "digging," destroying all this joy and ease: the simple and tangible poetry of Islamic Persia's figural, architectural, and abstract splendor; Persia's poise and playful grace; the triumph of rhythm in its imagery-crowded royal hunts, courtly mass symmetries, sky-and-flowers, trees-and-adolescence, tranquil sages and water, geometric fugues—and above all, that intimate sense of family, as life's center everywhere present there, from the cozy house-home of God to the cozy house-home of the lord, from a glistening, delicate and cozy luster piece to a cleverly-thought-out, delicate, dense and also cozy textile, a passionate sense of mother-and-father's peace, the truly intellectual ideal of the nomads, infused so constantly into Iran's life sensitiveness?

In art—our chosen concern here—this inner circle-chemistry defines the degree of our participation in our behavior toward the integral past.

First circle: we enjoy art, we enjoy its comfort. We enjoy art as belonging to the past. For art and the study of art, even if it is today's art, belongs to the past. And the past is comfortable: it is as such outside of our control, thus of our responsibility. We enjoy art, we enjoy the past, we enjoy history. The past is in the time center of the circle-aesthetics.

Second circle: ideas, rules, categories of reality. Permanence. Presence. The time center of this circle is the present. Art-comfort is rejected and with it past-comfort, history-comfort. Plato's Republic. A beautiful action is nearer perfection than a beautiful painting, or statue. People who struggle for the minimum of material aims, necessary and permanent comfort in life, hate the aesthetical comfort of the first circle-zone. They are attached to, they choose, the severe circle-perfection. The privileged—materially and mentally—are attached to the first.

Third circle: union of the other two. (Strange, yet to be expected.) The circle-past becomes here the circle-idea, the permanence and the presence. A past is now an idea-permanence and idea, any idea, any general concept is now forever a past, a certain, concrete past: terrifying thing—for our comfort—and so difficult to say!

Circle-perfectibility, Eros, where history (historicity) is the unique idea-truth and where art, which is almost-history and nothing else, become thus, almost, the unique witness of the unique Truth. And it was shown to us there, accordingly, that the time-center of this circle is the future. For the past, the history, the art of the circle-aesthetics means change—in the sense of transformation, of correspondence understood as comprehension of memory of change and motion; on the other hand, the idea, the present, the permanent in the circle—perfection means immobility, unspeakable immobility there, a timeless categorical arrest, total transfer, substitution. The union of both in the circle—Eros, past = present, past = idea, idea = past, becomes the only possible pattern of the future.

I said earlier that Iran gave birth without realizing it to a unique aesthetic form; it remains for Iran to find it again, but in full consciousness of its worth. Such a revival could have universal repercussions. It is sufficient to think what such a renaissance, which would truly continue its great past, could give anew to the artistic searchings of the modern West, searchings which are at the same time so akin to the Iranian past: the art of a Van Gogh, for example, or that, so entirely opposite, of a Picasso.

The economic and political decline of Iran in the eighteenth and nineteenth centuries, due more to the internal contradictions and chaos of a decaying system than to the violence of wars, carried along with it impoverishment of thought and of art. We can, through art, participate in a past event: can we equally influence it, correct it, change it? A complete rehabilitation of the material life of the Iranian people will surely bring about a renaissance of its creative consciousness.

I said above and long ago: "The decadence of an imperial civilization usually coincides with the renaissance of its deeply rooted popular ideology submerged under the upper levels of the huge sociological structure." For instance: the late Roman art (third–fifth century A.D.), so rude, so "decadent" (on the "what" level) yet so deeply evocative—opened of Rome's deepest, now folk, stratum: the Etruscan and proto-Etruscan worlds.

So, also, say, the Qajar court art, so brutal, so brutally imitative (thus incorrectly imitative) of Western formulae of three-dimensionality, of volume-nearness: and yet, because of this violence of imposition—as such, so creative—prophetic in its very way of deforming an import. So creative in its, Qajar's, insistence on the presence there of Iran's folk element of "mobility."

There is more. Iran is passing through a new renaissance. If all these historical deductions should be accepted as historically true in their premises, the example of that first (Sasanian) renaissance would acquire a singular value today. For it would be clear that the officially sponsored renaissance in Iran today cannot fully achieve its purposes simply by means of a well-studied imitation—no matter how intelligent and how well adapted to actual conditions of life—of a stratified court art like Safavid, but can attain its end only if the exploitation of that style is paralleled by a penetration into this art of the people which certainly exists.

I would resume thus (great-grandfatherly) to the protectors, promoters, directors of today's real (conscious) renaissance in Iran, to Her Imperial Majesty, the beautiful Empress Farah and to her collaborators (to you, the writers and editors and photographers of this volume) I would repeat:

One should vigilantly (studiously) control, promote, protect and direct on all levels of Iranian productivity, the emergence now, in full light of national, cautious awareness of Iran's most ancient aesthetic formula—apotheosis (d'ailleurs, you know all this!!!).

Only in that case will the product of the modern renaissance give to the world something absolutely new and universal and, at the same time, profoundly Iranian, profoundly national.

A SHORT HISTORY OF
THE IRANIAN HANDICRAFTS CENTER

By FARANGIS SHAHROKH (YEGANEGI)

Early in April, 1964, the then prime minister, the late Mr. Ali Mansour, informed me that the Government was anxious to form an Iranian Handicrafts Center. A number of ministries were, at the time, carrying out uncoordinated projects for the development of handicrafts, but the results were not satisfactory. Many handicrafts were facing extinction and the craftsmen themselves were experiencing considerable financial hardship. Government was therefore anxious to render maximum possible assistance by bringing all handicraft activities under one central organization. It was felt that well-planned projects would not only revive Iran's ancient arts and crafts, which were again receiving worldwide attention with the publication of the new edition of the *Survey of Persian Art,* but could also curtail the emigration of villagers from rural to urban areas during periods of seasonal unemployment. His Excellency stated that, in view of my experience and personal interest in handicrafts through my previous work in social welfare, he believed that I should head the new organization.

An important consideration was the selection of the appropriate ministry to control the newly proposed Iranian Handicrafts Center. During my various trips abroad I had observed that handicrafts had progressed well in countries in which the Ministry of Industry or Commerce was in charge, due to the fact that, apart from the arts aspect, the economic and marketing side had to be supported. As the Ministry of Economy was in charge of all similar departments in Iran at that time, I recommended that it would be the most appropriate ministry under which to place the new Handicrafts Center. The prime minister approved this suggestion, and I was instructed to report to the Minister of Economy, H. E. Dr. Ali Naghi Alikhani. The minister immediately arranged a meeting including the deputy minister, Mohammed Yeganeh, to discuss details of how best to form the new Center. It was agreed that Mr. Yeganeh would provide all advisory and financial assistance from funds allotted for the ministry's special projects. Although it was decided to commence work immediately, initially concerned with multitudes of small-scale cottage industries, it was not easy to launch a project in a ministry long attuned to dealing with large industrial units. However, this aspect was speedily rectified in view of the continued personal support of H. E. Dr. Alikhani. Just at this time the *Keyhan International* carried a full-page illustrated feature reprinted from the *English Mainichi* of Japan by Jay Gluck about an exhibition of Iranian folk arts and handicrafts he had held in Japan and the amazing reaction of the Japanese public to these simple but, as they acclaimed them, sophisticated, rural products. It was a most auspicious coincidence and gave us all a great psychological boost.

In carrying out our first and vital task to ensure proper planning, it was essential to obtain accurate data and statistics from the various ministries hitherto dealing with handicrafts. Unfortunately, none of them had any complete or accurate data available—with the notable exception of the Plan Organization which had a thorough report compiled by specialists who had surveyed the Yazd area for three months. Several meetings were held with officials from other ministries with little progress, and it became clear that we would have to go out into the country and obtain information ourselves. This required visits to different parts of the country to study closely the natural, economic and social conditions of each region, the production and distribution methods, as well as learning about problems and obstacles facing the individual craftsmen.

It then was necessary to man the new Handicrafts Center, and with personnel who were not only experienced but, above all, were genuinely interested in the work. Personnel with experience in administration, finance, marketing, etc., were available, but we had few well-qualified in arts and crafts. Fortunately, the well-known miniaturist Ali Kerimi agreed to join us, and while the constitution of the Center was being drawn up and approved by the government, we undertook a countrywide survey to compile the requisite data and statistics on the handicrafts of Iran. We visited almost every province over a period of eighteen months to collect whatever data was available as well as purchase samples of representative crafts. This was not an easy task as mere interviews with craftsmen seldom achieved satisfactory results because figures proffered by them were more often than not inaccurate and arbitrary, or they were unable to furnish any information whatsoever. Other sources—bazaars, caravanserais and even transport centers—were canvassed to gather all available information.

To illustrate just one case, we were anxious to find out whether any batik was being produced in Iran, and if so, where. I came across an item in the Tabriz bazaar which looked like batik. On my inquiring—in Persian, of course, but using the English term "batik"—Ali Kerimi replied, "But we all want to know what 'batik' is." We continued with our inquiries in the Tabriz bazaar till a customer in the local *chaikhaneh* upon overhearing our conversation volunteered some useful information, which finally led us to a nearby village called Osku. It was then that I found out that the local batik was called *kalagheh* and that it was mostly

195, 198

used as head scarves by Turkoman, Bakhtiari and Qashgai women† and as shawls by the Kurds as well as other nomadic tribes. After several abortive attempts, we finally found the house of one of the local craftsmen, but he neither welcomed us nor was he prepared to part with any information whatsoever. We requested the village head in Osku to help us, finally convincing him, and later others, that it would ultimately be in their interests to cooperate.

The village head then sent for one of his friends who was producing *kalagheh* and who agreed to let us inspect his "workshop." In a corner of his house he had set apart one room where he kept the dye pot and his other tools and equipment. Once we had convinced him that we were only out to help, the barrier was broken and he informed us that he was buying the synthetic fiber woven material from another village called Kahnamu, which he then dyed in his "workshop" by the molded batik process. Since I was already familiar with the batik industry from my visits to India and Indonesia, I suggested to our friend that I would procure material in natural silk from the Tabriz bazaar for him to print and that we would pay for all material and labor costs, with which arrangement he concurred. We returned to the Tabriz bazaar immediately and purchased three meters of pure silk material from Kahnamu, returning to Osku the next day. I suggested to our craftsman friend to work only with his golden flower design of *boteh jegheh* on a black background. He considered three meters too long and agreed to work on half of it only and to finish in two days. When we returned, the batik was ready, so we paid the craftsman and left immediately for Kahnamu village. There we made inquiries regarding pure silk handwoven cloth. We theorized that by using handwoven pure silk as opposed to the synthetic material then being used and printing as suggested by us, both groups could be guided to some degree of prosperity. Indeed, this has since come about and we now have excellent quality batik available in Iran.

I have perhaps gone into excessive detail here, but this is just one illustration of our endeavors to obtain relevant data and how, in this case at least, they were put to effective use.

The entire survey covered the following aspects: Types of handicrafts normally available in each area; number of people engaged in these; number of available workshops and production level of each; working conditions in workshops and types of equipment and tools; and the craftsmen's wages or income in each line. Raw materials, the types used and the processes, as well as their cost to the craftsmen and the total cost of products. Distribution and sales methods of products and local sale prices; salability outside the production area; and feasibility studies toward forming cooperatives. Lastly, whether a craftsman's job was permanent or seasonal and a survey of affiliated activities.

The collection of this data and writing of preliminary reports were for the most part completed even before the constitution of the Handicrafts Center itself was approved. The plans as developed were fairly comprehensive, but the date of commencement of each project had to be phased, taking into consideration the priority to be allotted to the overall requirements of regional handicraft areas. I would, at this stage, mention that the new organization was most fortunate for the special consideration shown us by H. E. Mehrdad Pahlbod, newly created Minister of Culture and Arts, who showed a strong personal interest in the basic crafts.

During the period of these activities action was being taken, in the light of experience gained, to draft the constitution of the Handicrafts Center in consultation with representatives of the Ministries of Culture and Arts, Labor, Agriculture and Economy as also the Plan and the new Tourist Organizations. The draft constitution was finally approved by the High Committee of the Plan Organization on December 26, 1964, and ratified by the Council of Ministers on January 16, 1965. The objects and functions of the Handicrafts Center's constitution as ratified are as follows:

OBJECTIVES

(1) Preservation of traditional handicrafts and improvements to existing workshops, as well as the promotion and development of new ones; (2) To raise the income and welfare of those involved in this line; (3) To assign inactive manpower to productive businesses; (4) To market the product of such industries; and (5) To adjust the handicrafts to the current requirements and tastes of buyers.

FUNCTIONS

(1) To survey and study existing handicrafts and to collect accurate industrial statistics, and to estimate the manpower available for such industries; (2) To expand the production of handicrafts; (3) To determine and meet the requirements of craftsmen in the following fields: (a) raw materials; (b) technical training in processes, handling of tools, equipment and finishing techniques; (c) assistance in improvements to designs and techniques of dyeing; (d) assistance through cooperatives for financing as well as advice and assistance in obtaining credits; (e) marketing with the establishment of showrooms, sales centers, and the training of salesmen; (f) advertising and issuing promotional publications; (4) To prepare new projects; and (5) To conduct all administration concerned with the above.

Thus the Handicrafts Center came into existence with a small nucleus of dedicated personnel imbued with determination to implement the objectives and functions of the organization. Prospects for success at first seemed somewhat remote, considering the numerous problems being encountered and the fact that the various handicraft production centers were so widely dispersed in some of the least accessible nooks and corners of our vast country. However, with the inspiring leadership, guidance and support at all times of Her Imperial Majesty Shahbanu Farah, we were able to overcome problems or obstacles that beset us from time to time. It was, therefore, most heartening for the personnel working with the organization to see their labors rewarded by remarkable achievements which helped to revive several Iranian handicrafts which were, not long ago, facing extinction. The various handicraft products were proudly displayed at the first exhibition of its kind ever held in Iran. In October, 1966, Her Imperial Majesty the Shahbanu, opened the exhibition and as always viewed each item most carefully proffering valuable advice, suggestions and guidance. Besides stimulating the home market, a flourishing export trade has been established and Iranian handicrafts have received plaudits at various fairs held in foreign countries.

The Center can fairly claim that it has taken a prominent part in reviving and developing various handicrafts. Glassmaking was facing bleak prospects, limited to rural bottles and a few items being sold as antiques at exorbitant prices. With technical and financial assistance it has made a remarkable recovery, and we now find that it is perhaps the most popular of all Iranian handicrafts in the export market.† Sale of different types of ceramics and earthenware products were earlier largely confined to the rural areas and small towns only. Baluchistan pottery, for example, was sold in the main cities as antiques.† Other than the embroideries of Isfahan, the lovely needlework found almost everywhere in Iran were hardly known.† Baluchistan needlework was sold in Tehran in the form of jackets at excessive prices, as access to the rural areas where this work was done was very difficult. The market for Baluchistan embroidery has now increased and this work is proving to be very popular due to the fact that several new products incorporating Baluchi needlework have been introduced.

Earlier, *pustin* products were confined to ill-fitting jackets and overcoats and had an unwelcome odor, which has now been eliminated and a large variety of new items of production introduced. Again, most handwoven materials were finding a poor market. This was essentially due to the fact that the craftsmen were making bad imitations of foreign machine-made materials and in doing so had lost their original characteristics and thereby the favors of a discerning public. This set in motion a vicious cycle causing the deterioration of the living conditions of the craftsmen involved due to the downward spiral in incomes. For example, some weavers were frequently compelled to barter away their finished products in exchange for the yarn and other raw materials required for the forthcoming year, with no cash income and little or no profit. The Handicrafts Center tackled this problem by offering advice and by providing a variety of designs and patterns for the handweavers of Yazd, to the workers of Osku for their batik material and pure silk products of Khurasan. The business of all these craftsmen not only improved, but at the October, 1967 Annual Exhibition their products received special attention.

Handicrafts from other places including Isfahan were also losing their clientele due to carelessness on the part of the craftsmen or use of inferior quality raw materials, just as the old records report had happened in the last century. Wooden products from Rasht frequently cracked by the time they reached Tehran. There were gilims with colors that faded or ran when even slightly wet. Apart from the advice offered by specialists, the Center took action to set up short-term training courses in different fields to improve the technical skill and knowledge of craftsmen. During our survey it was found that the tools and equipment used by most were antiquated and appeared more like relics from generations past. Any changes suggested for the better were, at first, strongly resisted. The craftsmen were gradually made to realize that many of their tools and equipment not only entailed additional work by them but resulted in considerable waste of raw materials. This was suitably demonstrated by establishing specimen workshops where improved tools, equipment and techniques were used. Conversely, there were instances when our young technocrats learned that their suggested modernizations were less efficient than some of the tried and true "antiques."

In the task of developing Iranian handicrafts, it was basically a question of facing and analyzing each of a series of problems and finding an effective solution to each on its own merit. This could not be done by individual craftsmen as it entailed variously tax exemptions, grants of credit facilities and export incentives, etc. Additionally, the craftsmen as a whole with their limited outlook lacked a sense of common interest as they were not only highly individualistic, but widely dispersed in small production units in different fields of handicraft. Unlike the more advanced and industrialized countries where most cooperatives are formed by the public with their own capital and management, it was not initially possible to do this in Iran. Government support and assistance, and coordination by one central organization such as the Handicrafts Center was necessary. Therefore, priority was given by the Center to establish cooperative companies among the craftsmen with any loans or placement of large orders made contingent upon them forming such cooperatives. The workers did form cooperative companies when they realized that urgent action was concurrently being taken to supply raw materials and tools at wholesale prices and on installments; to pay better prices to cooperatives for the craftsmen's products, whether sold through the Center's shops or by export; and to grant loans at low interest rates and without security clauses—something not possible for the individual to obtain.

Possibly the most difficult problem for the cooperatives was the supply of raw materials at wholesale prices. The Center stepped in here and, with considerable reductions, supplied their raw materials as per their annual requirement indents, which had to be supported by samples. It is encouraging to note that as of today a total of approximately thirty handicraft cooperatives are operating throughout the country.

As mentioned above, the first Handicrafts Emporium affiliated with the Center was opened in 1966—some of the items sold were located for illustration in this book. Depending upon market demand, this company places new orders to craftsmen and fixes a retail price approximately midway between the broker's and the wholesaler's price. Although at first some concern was shown by the private sector on the opening of the Emporium, it was soon realized that the policy being pursued by the Handicrafts Center was, in the final analysis, to their advantage and Iranian handicrafts have since reestablished their good name of ages past, not only in Iran but overseas as well because of improved quality and competitive price. It is gratifying to note that nearly one hundred private shops which sell handicrafts have opened in Tehran alone since the Center's Emporium started operations. In view of the success of the Emporium, the Handicrafts Center has opened several more branches in Tehran, Isfahan, Shiraz, Mashhad and a number of other towns, but with a policy only to sell products of other areas and not compete with the established local bazaars.

In order to stimulate exports of Iranian handicrafts, sales representatives have been appointed by the Center in several countries including Belgium, West Germany, France and Italy. A marketing and sales office has also been opened in New York.

On the establishment of the new Ministry of Industries and Mines in 1974, the Handicrafts Center was placed under its control and renamed "Iranian Handicrafts Organization." Upon ratification by Parliament and Senate, the constitution of the Iranian Handicrafts Organization was graciously approved by His Imperial Majesty in July, 1975. As of that date, the Iranian Handicrafts Organization has established regional offices in provincial centers in order to decentralize work and provide the required facilities and services to craftsmen.

Finally, it is well to remember that in addition to the preservation of and improvements to traditional Iranian handicrafts and the welfare and skills of its craftsmen, the Organization has fulfilled another important task of collecting, correlating and making available to interested parties and particularly to the writers of books and articles on Iranian handicrafts authentic information on this fascinating subject. It is, therefore, encouraging to note that this excellent publication which so admirably fills a long-felt void is now available to handicraft lovers all over the world.

RITUAL JAR, GREEN STONE, CARVED IN HIGH RELIEF WITH BULLS AND SNAKES
Kerman, ca. 2400 B.C.   *Slighty reduced*   Collection H.H. Prince Shahram Pahlavi

STONE

IN the tomb of Queen Shubad or Puabi of the Royal Tombs of Ur of the Sumerian Early Dynasty, 2400–2300 B.C., were found finely carved vessels of a dark green stone of unknown provenance. Similar material was excavated in Kuli of Harappa in the Indus Valley and a far-flung trade network of the early third millennium B.C. emerged.[1] At first an origin in Baluchistan was assumed for the stone and the carving was thought to have been done in Ur and Harappa, respectively.[2] In 1970 at Tepe Yahya in Kerman, the workshops of the stone carvers were unearthed, strewn with incompleted pieces and wasters. Then nearby at Shahdad

S. Piggot
Prehistoric India to 1000 BC
p. 105–117

H. Frankfort
Art and Architecture of the Ancient Orient

JAR, GREEN STONE, CARVED IN RELIEF WITH SCORPIONS AND WATER CHAINS
Kerman, ca. 2400 B.C.   *Slightly reduced*   Collection H. H. Prince Shahram Pahlavi

K. Lamberg-Karlovsky
Excavation Report, 1970
Museé Iran Bastan

**TALISMANS
CARVED STONE**
Green stone and
other chlorite
Kerman, Yazd,
Mashhad; Recent
Actual size

Preceding

Overleaf

John Shapley
Survey, pp. 3421–36
Hans Wulff
*The Traditional Crafts
of Persia,* p. 129
Iranian Handicrafts Org.
Technical Report, 1976
Shapley, *Above,* pp. 3421–36

the abandoned prehistoric mines were found. [3] Physiochemical analysis confirmed it to be the stone of the Ur and Harappa finds. A stone idol came out of the excavations at Yahya which enables a dating for the local industry to 4500 B.C. The same green stone is still mined in the area and was, until recently, worked locally. It is still shipped to Mashhad to be worked, and gives this regional craft an unbroken history of almost seven thousand years.

   The most exciting piece of Royal Tomb of Ur style carved green stone is probably the ritual bowl(?) in the collection of H. H. Prince Shahram Pahlavi, carved in relief with profiles of bulls, except that the heads are turned out to face the viewer and are in such high relief as to be sculpture in-the-round. These bovine heads suggest lug handles, and in modern stone cooking vessels, *dizi,* made in Mashhad, across the desert from Kerman, the lug handles still take the form of outlined bovine heads. These ancient stone jars, then, could have had lids and served as *dizi* for a ritual meal or offering, much as did the ritual bronze vessels in Shang China seven centuries later, and for which these may stand as prototypes.

   "Persia is stone country," [4] with rich resources of white marble (*marmar*), fine grain greenish marble (*sang-i gandomi*), grey marble as used at Persepolis (*sang-i siyah*), soft green marble of Yazd (*Yashm*), fine grained porphyry (*sang-i somaq*) [5] as well as alabaster (*sang-i ahaki*) and chlorite (*sang-i mika*). [6] Yet with this abundance, stone has played a minor role in architecture and art. Perhaps the plasticity of clay better suits the Persian aesthetic. [7]

FOUNTAINSIDE OR GARDEN SCULPTURE, FIRUZABAD, 1976.   Scale 1/2

The architectural marble industry has grown from near nothing in less than two decades with the high demand for plain building facing. Until ·fifteen years ago much of it was sent to Italy for finishing, and sometimes sold locally as imported marble. It is today exported to Europe.

Little architectural marble is sculpted, with one notable exception being the door and window surrounds of the Kakh-e Marmar, the Marble Palace of Reza Shah the Great.

Despite Islamic prohibition, there is an old folk tradition of figural sculpture for grave-stones, though rare, especially the "hero's stones" of tigers. Fountain spouts, usually of lions spitting, have been popular particularly in Fars province where a mason in Firuzabad, Habib Alizadeh working in this tradition, turns out the amusing animals shown here.†

Above

THE POTTERY SHOP
Glazed earthenware
Lalijin   L. 23 cm.

POTTERY

POTTERY first appears almost 10,000 years ago, apparently invented by women. Of the additive or constructive technologies only basketry is possibly older, for the oldest pottery known, from East Africa, was a basket base plastered with clay and fired, possibly placed accidentally too close to the hearth. Many types of pottery from Neolithic and Chalcolithic excavated sites contain chopped straw or wattle as a binder, possibly reflecting basketry origins. In living cultures subsisting today in Neolithic life styles, pottery is still made by women, with a division of labor which assigns the heavier tasks to men, undoubtedly continuing traditions of antiquity.

Women potters are found in the Valley of Mexico, among the North American Pueblo Indians, in northern Thailand, parts of East Africa, and in Iran in Baluchistan,† Kurdistan and Gilan.† Significantly north Thailand and Baluchistan are two of the three oldest true pottery producing areas—the third, Japan, is known to have been at that time matriarchal.

44, 45
51

The first pottery was purely functional, probably to store water for short periods of time— for earthenware is porous. This latter is more an advantage than not, for while liquid is lost, the motion, however slight, accelerates the settling of impurities, and evaporation of seepage on the outer surface chills the contents even in the hottest desert summer.

Art for art's sake or for ritual use had long been made in wood, bone and stone,† as we saw on the preceding pages. But the appearance of pottery and its decoration and artistry both records, as it perhaps instigated, a revolution in intellectual and technological history.

29, 30

Between 9000 and 8000 B.C. the climate in the Middle East underwent a great change, the Pleistocene Glacial era ended. This either necessitated or permitted a cultural revolution as man left his Paleolithic nomadic existence of hunting and gathering to live in fixed settlements of houses, where he domesticated animals and planted crops. It was thought that this evolution took place in the valleys of the great rivers, the Tigris-Euphrates, the Indus and/or the Nile. Arthur Upham Pope showed forty years ago that this idea does not make sense, because small groups of primitive men could not have the numbers or social organization to build dams and irrigation systems. The ideal place for such evolution would be the smaller valleys, protected from extreme weather, free from great seasonal floods, with assured regular water supply and small streams where one man might invent the idea of the dam and build one easily.

As food-producing capacity increased the possible sizes of the community they could move down river to open areas, evolving a social system which enabled the division of labor and cooperative enterprise for great dams, irrigation canal systems, temples and palaces. If the oldest city civilizations are Mesopotamia and Indus, then, he said, we must look on the Iranian Plateau for the origins. Only since the death of Pope has excavation proved these theories. It seems sheep and goats were first domesticated in north Iran, as was wheat and barley. Pigs and dogs were perhaps first domesticated in northwest Iran and Kurdistan. The oldest agricultural settlement known is at Karim Shahr in Kurdistan about 9000 B.C. The oldest villages now known are from 8000–7000 B.C., and are Iran's Sarab, Guran, Buz Hajji-Firuz of Hasanlu in the western hills while over the border in Turkey is Çatal Hüyük, and nearby in Iraqi Kurdistan is Jarmo. Near Tehran is Sagzabad, inhabited from at least 7000 B.C., if not earlier, until 500 B.C. and with thriving modern villages nearby. In southeast Iran near Kerman is perhaps the oldest true city. Here writing as old or older than Mesopotamian was found. Its copper mines and factories date to 6000 or 7000 B.C. This site was predicted by Pope twenty-five years ago, exactly midway between the great cities of Mesopotamia and the Indus, one thousand kilometers from each.

Stone sculpture, no matter how sophisticated, is a primitive art form in that the structure and composition of the material is never changed and the final work is always something less than what the artist started with. Pottery, no matter how primitive, is a creation of its own; the final form bears no obvious visual relation to the original material; texture and composition are a new creation, infinitely more than what the potter began with.

Sir Herbert Read writes, "Pottery is at once the simplest and the most difficult of all arts. It is the simplest because it is the most elementary; it is the most difficult because it is the most abstract. . . Judge the art of a country, judge the finest of its sensibilities by its pottery; it is a sure touchstone. Pottery is pure art; it is art freed from imitative intention. Sculpture, to which it is most nearly related, had from the first an imitative intention and it is to that extent less free for the expression of the will to form than pottery; pottery is plastic art in its most abstract essence."

Little wonder that Persian philosophers and poets portray God as a potter creating man as one might a pottery vessel—often a wine pot. Pottery and molding allow greater individuality, greater variety; the artist is master of the material. Carving is more limited by the material; the material is master of the artist. Carving is aesthetically linked to geometry and prose literature, associated with tightly organized cultures. Modeling, aesthetically likened to algebra and poetry, is associated with more individualistic cultures. John Shapley explores this idea in the SURVEY.*

Survey pp 3421 ff

By 6000 B.C. pottery was widespread on the Iranian Plateau and neighboring East Anatolia and northern Iraq. Techniques already include painting and burnishing. The first true pottery is basically red in color, with black discolorations caused by the reduction of oxygen: it can be pinkish in color if low fired; if the temperature goes relatively high, if there is iron in the clay, if there is plenty of oxygen while firing, the red will be clear. When this red technique was mastered, painted pottery appears: with iron-rich clay for red, iron and manganese clay for black and tin-rich clays for white. Painting often imitates basket weave patterns, but there are many abstract designs indicating that the designs had meaning and were a form of record. These designs tell us much about their thinking, for we can read some, they are so obvious, or some have come down in traditional use to recent times.

PAINTED POTTERY
Ceremonial storage jar
with serving bowl lid
Kalporegan, modern
H. (together) 33 cm.

The potter's art gives birth to the first true machine. The potter's wheel, known in Greece since 2000 B.C., in Troy from about 2600, is already in Siyalk by 3500 if not earlier. Pottery from Kerman, which may be even older, is also wheel made. About 3000, the potter's wheel was turned on its side, a frame placed on top and drawn by asses and cattle. With the potter's wheel, the making of pottery became a man's job, and with the concurrent growth of the city, the era of original women's lib ended.

43

TRADITIONAL HANDLES
Left, Kalporegan, modern *Right*, Azarbaijan, 2nd millenium B.C.

The handles, whether small rings on the lids or heavy grips on water jars, are more technically sophisticated than those found on medieval Islamic glazed wares and can be compared only with prehistoric Persian pottery.† Islamic handles are applied to the body in the same way as Far Eastern, in that the handle is formed independently and when handle and body are half-dried, they are pressed together with an adhesive of wet clay—a structurally weak arrangement. Persian Iron Age and Bronze Age and the rare handled Chalcolithic wares have a lug drawn from the body of the wet vessel which is then joined to an additional rope of clay which links again with the body either at another lug, or by inserting it in a hole punched in the body with the inside protuberance crushed like a rivet and molded into the inner surface. Or the handle is formed separately in a *Y*, arms worked around to form the lip of the jar, the trunk arched out and its base linked to the jug as above. Kalporegan handles are made in this way, with no visible joining. They are likely to be the last part of the pot to break, rather than the first as on more modern pottery.

Other shapes include the base jar for the *qalian* or water pipe. An incense burner on three or four legs with body shaped like a pomegranate,† even to its star-shaped lid imitating the leaf-topped core, is identical to incense burners from second millennium sites in northwest Iran.† There is a delightful zoo of animals—camels, wild sheep and dogs—some solid and meant as toys, others vessels mirroring the ritual libation pitchers of antiquity.†

An even more delightful menagerie is produced around Minab on the Persian Gulf coast; mounted horsemen,† cattle and wild goats of pure Chalcolithic type yellow biscuit with bold iron oxide red painted hatchwork and slashes. These again are made by the local women and sold in the markets as toys. They are fired at home in the cooking ovens, the *tanur*.

The prehistoric pottery of Gilan includes some of the most exciting, certainly the most amusing, shapes ever concocted. The quality of the local clays made many of these possible—it certainly invites experimentation. The products are light, the highly plastic clays fuse at low temperature and there is that natural glaze. Imitating the local herons are the long bird-beaked spouted ritual bronze pitchers, copied 3,000 years ago in pottery.† Expert Japanese potters claimed that such long spouts would not hold up in the kiln, but the author and his son duplicated them with heavier, less plastic Japanese clay, not by imitating the original metal straight profile of a dissected tube, but by shaping the spout in a gently tapering, curving cantilever. This second millennium B.C. local development in pottery structure could well have led by simple extension to the development of the arch, the ribbed vault and eventually the ribbed double dome. Ancient Amlash pottery are less pots and dishes than they are architecture in miniature.

Above

PAINTED POTTERY
TOY
Left, First millennium
Right,
Minab *Actual size*
VESSELS AND TOYS
Kalporegan
H. Tallest 17 cm.

49 *lower left*

49 *lower right*
Facing lower

Facing upper

50 *right*

46

54

The talismanic color of Iran is the bright turquoise blue, the best examples of which are found on the brilliant colored ceramic "donkey beads" hung on children and valuable animals to avert the "evil eye." Usually known as Egyptian faience because of numerous charms and small idols found first in Nile tombs, the oldest examples are from Sumer of the fifth millennium B.C. They are common in Persian tombs from the first millennium through Sasanian times and in Achaemenid and Parthian times small figurines and sculpted charms were known.†

Lion,
Achaemenid
Actual size *Above*

When broken open the composition of the beads is seen to be a white granular frit, harder but coarser than the body of the white ground pottery of Natanz, Nain and Meibod, which is made from a stone paste rather than an earth clay. We visited one of the two makers, on the outskirts of Qum. Hans Wulff had interviewed the other, in the Qum bazaar, for his brief article in *Traditional Handicrafts of Persia,* and again for his comprehensive study later published in the April, 1968, *Archaeology.* The beads are a monopoly of these two makers—which they protect with a curtain of secrecy embellished by false information. Every pottery shop dealer "knows the secret," each in his own version, none of which would work in a kiln.

The secret concerns getting a uniform blue glaze on a round bead, even into the hole, without having them stick together or have sand or ash imprints on their bottoms.

The body of the bead is made of ground river pebble, a good quality of quartzite—world's most common mineral, silicon dioxide—with a chlorite content. Chlorite is the stone used for the carved stoneware† discussed earlier, and the oldest examples known of the blue beads are on chlorite beads. The powdered pebbles are mixed with gum tragacanth and water into a thick dough and rolled into balls between the palms or in small molds which permit rolling several at a time. The glaze coloring is the basic copper oxide for Persian blue.

32

The glazing powder consists of a 6-6-4 mixture of "*oshnan*" or plant ash, lime and powdered quartz plus one part charcoal and a miniscule one percent of copper oxide. The *oshnan* is the key: it is the ash of the glasswort or Russian thistle. Beadmakers claim conservation laws limit its gathering now, but this seems unlikely as in America the plant is considered a useless pest. This plant ash is set in a covered bowl and a layer of beads is set in it, not touching each other, covered with ash and the process is repeated. The crockery bowl is covered and a group of them are fired in a downdraft kiln. It is this ash which enables the glaze at temperatures between 900 and 1000 degrees centigrade to bleed up and over the surface of the beads yet not stick to the ash resulting, ideally, in a glasslike surface of heavenly blue.

In pre-Islamic times finer articles were made, as also in Egypt, where superb miniature sculpture was produced in the white-bodied, blue-glazed ware. In Wulff's experiments to repeat the process in Australia, he reported a fine blue glaze inside the porcelain firing bowls. Improving the body of the beads could perhaps restore quality to the Achaemenid level.

Persian pottery is of two types, that made from clays of earth, *kuzeh,* and that made all or in large part from ground stone, the *sangineh* or *'atiq.* The blue beads are the oldest extant form of the latter and are considered by potters to be ancestral to stonewares, all glazed wares and to glass itself. The most primitive glass technology extant is the powder-glass beads of the Krobo of Ghana in Africa, which resembles the blue bead technique.

The beadmakers send their blue glaze base to other kilns where it is used to make the characteristic Persian blue stone paste wares. Refining the bead body material along the lines of the stone paste could lead to an improvement in the wares, or at least an increase in the repertoire of possible forms. The stone paste potters use little or no gum tragacanth, but mix in bentonite, a fine grain earth clay which gives the greater plasticity desired for modeling. Near Semnan we found porcelain objects being made of local material (which bears looking into further) but as the clay had virtually no plasticity it could only be formed in molds. Mixing in bentonite would probably introduce impurities and prevent the porcelain from fusing.

BLUE FRIT WARE
Glazed stone paste pottery
Made by Seyyed
Muhammad Sadatmand
Qum, modern *except*
Light blue necklace
1st century B.C.
About half scale

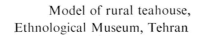
Model of rural teahouse,
Ethnological Museum, Tehran

GLAZED
EARTHENWARE
"PARTHIAN" GREEN
Lalijin, 1976
H.Taller 24 cm.

Facing

The close interrelations between potter and smith continue until recent times. Both elements are born of the soil and rock wedded with fire in the chamber of the kiln. Bronze and Iron Age pottery imitated the shapes and colors of metal objects. This was not just to economize on grave furniture, for at Hasanlu metal-like pottery was found in the kitchens as well. Waste products of the copper and bronze workers provided basic materials for glazes. Copper wastes when used in the presence of lead give the rich green preferred by the villager today for simmering his stew and pickling his *torshi*,† as it was by his Parthian ancestors of 2,000 years ago. Picked up by the Romans they spread it through their empire with such fervor that they are credited with its invention, as are also the Han Chinese who equally made it famous throughout the Orient. The porous clay water pots now coated with this magical layer of glaze, or glass, were no longer porous and could store valuable wines and oils indefinitely without loss or turning bitter.

The Chinese and the Romans carried the technique of the green lead glaze to high art— they had no other colored glaze until more exotica emerged out of Persia. In Persia it remained the commonest glaze for the commonest wares, and artists favored the more exciting colors they evolved out of this. The same copper wastes used with alkaline mixes brought forth the first turquoise blue, the color whose name in Persian, *firuz,* means victory and strength and manliness and beauty as used in popular men's and women's names. It is the talismanic color of the Persians.

Tin glazes mixed with slips of fine potter's earths led to pure white ceramics, and iron wastes to reds and browns. The ubiquitous manganese clays long used for black painting on red wares, now under alkaline influence gave forth beautiful aubergine. The yellow brown ground with blushes of greens and aubergines and occasionally blue were developed in western Iran by the seventh century B.C. on the delicate ritual frit-fired wares. Certainly by Sasanian times these colors were being applied to earthenwares, but with the low place that the silver- and gold-loving Sasanians gave to common pottery, little remains. It spread through Nishapur to Samarqand, whose golden peaches and other articles of exotica were the tradestuffs of which dreams were made in the court of T'ang China. So popular was this three-color ware— brown, green and blue, for the Chinese could not make aubergine which requires an alkaline glaze— that regardless of national origin such ware today is known worldwide by its Chinese name, *San Tsa'i*. It was popular for only a short time in China, and then seemingly only for grave furniture, until revived by the color–loving Ming Dynasty. Rare again in Persia in early Islamic times, it became popular in the ninth and tenth centuries in Nishapur, probably under influence of Samarqand, if not in open emulation of the Chinese fad.

The white-bodied glaze is also known on the seventh century B.C. frit ware, and likewise spread to China probably in late Han times. Perhaps these frit wares, a stone paste ceramic— that is made of ground up stone rather than earth, merely a purer form of silica—gave the Chinese the idea which led to the development of porcelain. This fortuitous discovery of a ground stone which will fuse completely at high temperature was denied the Persians because local impurities in their raw materials explode at the critical temperature the base materials require for fusing.

SALT GLAZED EARTHENWARE
Mashhad Exhibition 1976
Gilan   H.Taller 65 cm.

Pottery lamp, Gilan, First millennium

A predominant form of pottery in Gilan and Azarbaijan in the second millennium was a rich charcoal black, a color not painted on, but permeating the biscuit as a chemical change in the clay caused by reducing oxygen during firing. This black metallic effect is heightened by burnishing the pottery before firing, that is, when dried to a leather hardness it is rubbed vigorously with a polished stone, which tightens the granular structure reducing porosity and causing a sheen. Early Bronze Age pottery often copied metal prototypes, with structural metallic ribbing, even imitation rivets. One assumes this pottery to have been made by males. However, the earliest examples are not wheel thrown and many resemble forms still made by women in Kurdistan and Baluchistan. This black reduction firing has not been done in Persian ceramics since perhaps Achaemenid times, and while we know several possible ways of effecting it, we do not know the particular technique used by the ancient Persians.

Black wares are still produced, in our other oldest pottery traditions, in northern Thailand and among the Pueblo Indians and Mexicans—and in all cases by women. Pottery made by women is always fired in the open making reduction of oxygen seem impossible; it is difficult enough in a fully enclosed kiln. Japanese potters investigating this in Thailand found each individual piece tightly wrapped in damp straw as if packed for shipping. The flame heats the pot in its straw oven, the straw burns in a smoulder eventually dissolving to ash, but not until the deoxidized heat has worked its chemical wonder and both fused the silica clay and turned it black irretrievably. Pueblo lady potters smother the pots in dried manure, which keeps the oxygen out and itself burns with a steady intense heat.

The black burnished wares of Persia were made in areas where rice and wheat straw was plentiful and where there were barnyard animals and horses. In Baluchistan where is little of either, black wares have never been known. Significantly too, black wares ceased to appear from archaelogical excavations in correlation with the disappearance of hand-thrown wares and the predominance of wheel made; the transfer of pottery from a female trade to one for males.

I suggest that this black pottery was woman-made well into the Bronze Age. Larger storage jars, traditionally crafted by men, were not fired black.

The popular explanation of reduction firing of black ware is that the fire is choked, causing the black smoke to be injected into the red pottery, blackening it. While this is not the actual process, there are other injections into the firing which do have effects. One is the simplest method of glazing, putting salt into the flame which results in a greenish salt glaze. Along the Caspian littoral this may well have come about naturally in burning salt-encrusted drift-wood from the heavily salty Caspian Sea. The garden lanterns illustrated,† as contemporary as they are, are a continuation of a tradition known in Gilan and Azarbaijan in pre-Achaemenid times at least, that of the pierced ceramic outdoor lantern.†

Facing

Above

Left, Portrait (?) figure, clay, Kerman 3rd millennium. Archaeological Museum, Tehran. H. 50 cm.

Right, Libation vessel in human form, Marlik (?) 1000 B.C. H. 29 cm.

Idols were an important product in pre-Islamic times and appeared from excavations of some of the earliest pottery-producing cultures in Kerman. Regardless of the seriousness of their intended use, a notable characteristic has always been their whimsy and lightheartedness. A magnificent 4,600-year-old portrait figure of a man from Kerman portrays great pathos on its face,† but I feel it reflects the sadness of the artist for the loss of his friend who can also be seen as a man who in life well knew how to laugh. The less representational "idols"—actually libation vessels in human and animal form—from Luristan and Gilan (Marlik and the so-called Amlash finds) are especially lighthearted in execution.†Periodically after the coming of Islam, figurines emerge from the kilns and then devoid of any religious use are even less restricted in their gaiety.

One such period of image-making erupted in Lalijin under twenty years ago, probably in the last spasms of activity of the immediate postwar boom when the potters were working to amuse themselves just prior to the large-scale exodus of workers to the cities. Humorous caricatures out of legend and literature from wine bottle size up to immense figures the size of small children, and almost impossible to transport, emerged from the kilns and disappeared into some markets, though few have been seen since. The whimsical monkey madonna and child shown here was picked up by a passing Iranian tourist at that time.† Maison d'Iran later carried a few heroes from the *Shah Nameh*. The newly established Handicraft Center later carried a line of composite scenes of everyday life,† fascinating ethnological records, unlike anything except perhaps the little farmyard and village courtyard pottery constructions from Han Chinese tombs of two thousand years ago.

Above left

Above right

Facing right

41

GLAZED POTTERY FIGURINES

HOLY MAN, ISFAHAN
Recent   H. 26 cm.

MONKEY MOTHER and CHILD
Made by Shahban Javonmardi
Lalijin, 1960   H. 32 cm.

63

POLYCHROME UNDERGLAZE PAINTED
Upper left, Shiraz, *ca.* 1910   D. 24 cm.
Lower left, Kashan,*ca.* 1930   D. 25 cm.   *Right*, Natanz,*ca.* 1950   H. 29

74

POLYCHROME PAINTED
BOWL, FAMILLE ROSE
Hamadan, Recent(?) D. 18 cm.

75

CHINI-SAZ STONE PASTE POTTERY
CARVED AND UNDERGLAZE PAINTED
Natanz, 1976   H.Tallest 52 cm.

UNDERGLAZE POLYCHROME, MEIBOD (YAZD)
Reza Aghai Meibodi, Award for Handicrafts Excellence 1976
D. Plate 33, H. Vase 21 cm.

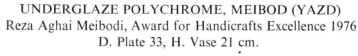

Khorshid Khanum, the Sun Maiden, is an old Yazd design, along with the pigeon and the fish, the horseman and the king. All had gone out of use due to the rise in orthodoxy, but with the revival of Persian traditions under the Pahlavis, Ms. Faranges Yeganegi Shahrokh and the late Mohammad Naraghi visiting Meibod found one single Khorshid Khanum tile remaining in an old *hamam* and reintroduced it to the potters. Meibod produces both earthenware and stone paste pottery. Reza Aghai Meibodi works only in pure stone paste.

Ethnological Museum,
Tehran

77

BIRD DESIGNS

STORAGE JAR
1976
Gonabad   H. 22 cm.

STRAINER BOWL
Ca. 1950
Yazd   D. 21 cm.

TURQUOISE GLAZE

WINE BOTTLE
Tabriz, 1976   H. 29 cm.
SMALL BOWLS
Yazd, *ca.* 1950
D. 11 cm.

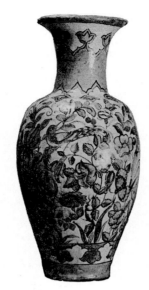

POTTERY, ENAMELED
Gonabad   D. Bowls 32 cm.
Mashhad Exhibition, 1976

UNDERGLAZE PAINTED STONE PASTE POTTERY

Overleaf
GOOSE PITCHER, NATANZ
Siyah qalam on white under clear glaze
Ca. 1960   H. 21

VASE
Morteza Musavi
(Musavizadeh)
Isfahan, H. 33

INCENSE BURNERS
Underglaze painted
Gonabad, 1976 H. *Left* 13; *Right*, 19

CARAFE; COVERED JAR
Gonabad, Mashhad Exhibit.,
1976   H. 33 cm., 10 cm.

COVERED BOWL
Underglaze painted
Estaban (Estabanat)
Ex. Shiraz Arts Fest.
1976   H. 17 cm.

Many Persian clays have the desirable quality of fusing at relatively low temperatures. Vessels fired at barely food cooking temperatures become serviceable, whereas Japanese potters claim their's or Chinese clays baked under such conditions would probably dissolve in water. In Gilan and parts of Kurdistan the women potters make highly serviceable yogurt and butter churners and other household pottery and fire it in their home *tanur* cooking ovens.†

We discussed the technical aspects of early Persian pottery with Tokuro Kato and the late Arthur Upham Pope in the latter's garden in Shiraz not long before his death. The old master a few days later carried the discussion over into one of his famous (and then secret) "seeding seminars" with a group of primary school students, including the author's sons then eight and eleven. Challenged by the old man's prompting the half dozen boys scoured the neighborhood for what they considered suitable clays. Finding some satisfactorily glutinous mud in a corner of the garden, they shaped miniature vessels in imitation of prehistoric pieces in the Pope collection, and built an open-faced, two-story kiln out of a few bricks and a cookie tin, a miniature replica of the house-size Roman type kiln the older boy had seen a few days earlier in Estabanat on a visit with Japanese potter Tokuro Kato. They fired it for a few hours with popsicle sticks, twigs, and discarded manuscripts and leaves. Much to the surprise of everyone but Pope, the toy pots were serviceable and held water with a minimal and acceptable seepage.

Sun-dried bricks become hard and serviceable without firing, however, they will dissolve under constant or heavy rains. In the villages large pottery grain storage jars are found in rooms with doors far too small to admit them—even if such immense pieces could be moved. These, it would seem, are made on the spot, and while not having been observed, the firing is described by villagers variously as accomplished by maintaining a small fire for a few days inside the jar itself—open on top, they usually have a drain hole near the bottom for taking out small quantities of grain, and this would be left open during firing to admit a draft. Others say the room itself is closed off and a small glowing fire of embers is kept going for several days. In Assalem in the wet Caspian littoral larger vessels are dried before firing to an extent that is itself almost a bisque firing, by keeping a small fire flickering inside each vessel for a day or two.

We discussed raw materials with Seyyed Morteza Musavi, a sixth-generation—"as far as I know"—potter from Isfahan whose specialty is the jewel-colored tile squares used by the mosaic tile cutters. He is one of six potter brothers, sons of Husayn, son of Abdul Rahim, son of Muhammad, son of Mehdi, son of Seyyed Muhammad the potter.

Morteza Musavi echoed the complaint of poor quality clays obvious today in the pottery itself. He said clay miners used to be particular about following only veins of fine clays, but now they will dig out almost anything. Then too the potters of fifty years ago settled their clays at least two months and as much as six.

Above

The kilns of Isfahan are fired today with kerosene, though in smaller towns they often use the cheaper and smokier heavy oil. Musavi's grandfather used logs and dried rush, especially wormwood, a fuel with ritual significance in Persia as it is used in the purifying fires of yearend, the *Chahar Shambeh Suri.*

Most of the tiles and pottery made in Isfahan still use traditional colors and glazes. Iron oxides from the smiths give yellow and coffee hues—the café au lait on the dome of the Marble Palace emulating the dome of Masjed-i Shaykh Lutfallah is said to have been developed by Reza Shah's cook who added powdered gold to the glaze and baked it in his bread oven; the story makes potters smile. Red uses *maghneh,* magnesium oxide, with gold added for different hues. Gold dissolved in aqua regia results in *parpureh,*† the rosé of fine Chinese and Persian eighteenth and nineteenth century wares treasured by Victorian collectors and London auctioneers. With *maghneh* stone added various hues of red through purple result. Blues and greens are the traditional copper oxides, usually from oxidized ore. The underglazed black is the traditional *siyah qalam* black brush, used all over the country and made of a black stone of manganese oxide formerly from Kashan but now brought from Estabanat and Sirjan.

Isfahan glazes are basically potash, silica stone and varying, but small, portions of ground waste glass. The technique of gold luster seems to be lost. A piece in the author's collection of about 50 years ago (not illustrated) is a reasonably good luster but rather reddish brown, more like medieval Spanish than twelfth century Persian. Recent attempts range from gold underglaze painting and overglaze, to the use of diluted *siyah qalam*† in Meibod a few decades ago. Ustad Abady of Natanz attempted luster for a special order from Germany for which he was sent the underglaze pigment,† but while interesting it is not even close. The Persian style luster made in Japan by Takuo Kato relies on underglaze gold low-fired rather than on the traditional reduction-fired copper, which is capable of richer gold hues.

70 lower

70 upper

Most of this confirms what Wulff discusses in greater detail, except that the fabulous dark blue cobalt glaze which has so obviously lost its ethereal qualities in the past generation has done so because the supply from Kashan has exhausted and German or French substitutes are now used. This Kashan cobalt was the treasure that Ming imperial potters bought for more than its own weight in gold, and which the great Japanese potter, Tokuro Kato, scion of a long line of blue and white makers, sought in 1969 willing to pay any price. Musavi would also love to see a lode rediscovered. He disagrees with potters outside Isfahan who use imported glazes and pigments exclusively, even *siyah qalam,* for purported economic reasons for he claims homemade glazes, besides being better colors with a meditative translucence, are also cheaper—sometimes one-twentieth the price. He says its merely a matter of availability and convenience, or in some cases downright laziness.

My own observations are that while the biscuit of Isfahan pottery today is poor, in extreme cases little better than stale bread held together by the fragile overglaze, the colors of even the simplest wares are exciting. The synthetic colors are purer chemically, but it is the local impurities that give a ware its own peculiar characteristic color and allow for what the artists call, the potter's luck—by which batches from a single firing include both rejects and common crockery as well as unreproducible treasures. It is this natural element of human imperfection that is at the core of art, especially of repetitive folk art.

VASE, CUT OUT
Under glaze painting
SHAH REZA (?)
Modern,   H. 21 cm.

HAND-BLOWN GLASS VESSELS, KASHAN
Made by Muhammad Guri
Ca. 1950   H. Tear bottle 30 cm.

GLASS VESSELS, TEHRAN
Made by Salman Durandesh
Winner of Handicraft Excellence Prize, 1975
H. Tallest 30 cm., D. Dish 17 cm.
Ca. 1964

MOLD-BLOWN VESSELS, TWELFTH CENTURY STYLE, 1976. H. Tallest 23 cm.

GLASS EWERS, SASANIAN SHOSOIN STYLE
1976 H. 25 cm.
Collection H. H. Prince Mikasa

Sasanian glass was highly valued in China, where the *lajvardi* or lapis lazuli deep blue was particularly treasured and gave both fine glass and the color its Chinese name, *luli*. Fine examples made their way into Korean pagoda reliquaries and Japanese royal tombs and that grand reliquary, the Shosoin repository of the Great Buddha of Nara. Indeed the goblet with miniature raised doughnuts—in green glass in the Korean pagoda, in *luli* in the Shosoin—was reintroduced to Iran by publication in the SURVEY and illustration in Ghirshman's *Parthians and Sasanians* and is made again by Tehran glassmakers. Its manufacture, which puzzles the finest glassmakers of Japan, Kagami Crystal, is illustrated here. Soon, button-applied designs by pioneer Mehdi Ebrahimian working in Isfahan, Salman Durandesh and others in Tehran, mushroomed, becoming the main glass attraction at the Center's opening in 1966.†

108, 109
Inset above

Photographs of the tall glass pitcher in the Shosoin,† tentatively attributed to Persia and similar to an excavated pitcher in the Iran Archaeological Museum, were shown to Ustad Takhsh. He made several copies, three highly successful. The free-form handle and the casual but efficient spout are the outstanding elements in the design. Working almost playfully to reproduce the handle, Takhsh announced that he was certain it was Persian, for only a Persian would draw the glass off that way, a Syrian artist would handle it differently.†

Facing

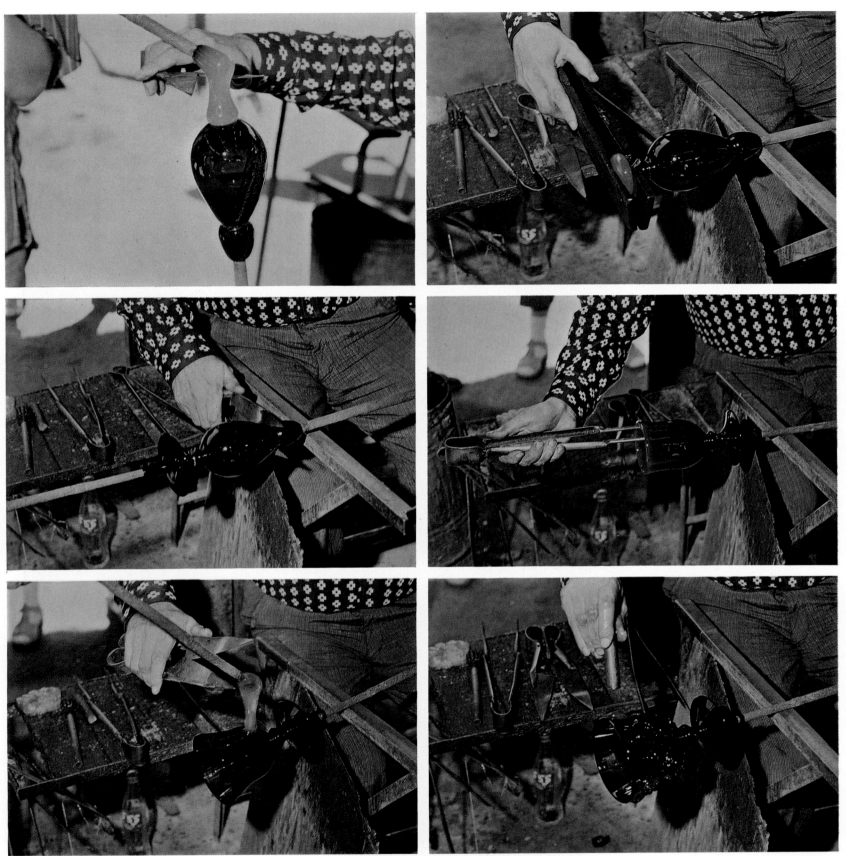

PROCESS OF MAKING CHALICES WITH SASANIAN STYLE ADDED DOUGHNUTS
Tehran, Shahin Glassworks

Above, Adding molten glass for base; Shaping base
Center, Afixing base to second rod; Cut-away end forms lip
Below, Adding buttons; Pressing button into doughnut shape.

Facing
SASANIAN DOUGHNUT MOTIF
Isfahan (Ebrahimian), Tehran makers
H. Largest 17 cm., Smallest 7.5 cm.

GLASS BLOWN INTO METAL FRETWORK

Above, Copper goblet, glass and pitcher, Tehran. Exhibited Mashhad, 1976. H. Pitcher 25 cm. *Overleaf*
Facing, Brass lanterns, Isfahan: *Left*, Ziba; *Right*, Ebrahimian, D. 28 cm. 1970. Copper glasses: Naraghi, 1970 Traditional cockshead ewer,
Glass and pitcher
Ebrahimian, 1970
H. Ewer 35 cm.

Ebrahimian perfected blowing glass into fretted brass in the style of the ancient mosque lamps.† Similar work was being done in iron wirework in Mexico—which shares many traditions in art with Iran through the "Moorish" element in Spain (who in the art field were often Persians), which entered Mexico with the conquistadores. However, the problems differ, for after ceasing heating, the glass cools and contracts faster than the iron and is not crushed by it, whereas the brass contracts faster than the glass and, unless the cooling is carefully controlled, will crush it. The advantage of the brass over the iron is especially evident in tableware, such as wine cups and pitchers,† for the choking action of the copper seals the copper against the glass, almost blending them, leaving no room for dirt or caking juices, etc. The iron shrinks less than the glass, leaving a paper-thin space between the two where dirt can accumulate and bacteria breed, and iron is at least double the weight.

Above, overleaf

The milky glass is ordinary glass which has been dipped in acid quickly, then washed off. It is an artistic effect born of faking techniques for adding patina to new glass to chemically age it. The patina of old age, or iridescence after its resemblance to the variegated coloration of the iris flower, has long been appreciated by glass afficionados and glaziers have attempted to imitate it in many ways, inventing different effects in their unsuccessful attempts.†

105 upper, 107

—JAY GLUCK and CARL J. PENTON

METALWORK

THE rapid modernization and industrialization of Iran during the last several decades has had a profound impact on all the traditional metalworking crafts of the country. In some cases they have been rendered economically and practically obsolete by the importation or manufacture of machine-made products more suitable to modern needs. This is true of lockmaking, to cite just one example. In other instances, the introduction of cheaper or lighter weight materials such as plastic and aluminum has led to the widespread abandonment of the heavier but more durable ones commonly utilized in the past. More and more, metalwork is now being made for the tourist trade, or alternatively, as expensive luxury items adapted to nontraditional tastes. Where a demand for high quality craftsmanship exists, the contemporary Iranian metalworker often displays a superb degree of mastery and skill. When this is not called for, however, there has been a marked overall decline in the quality of metalware. This is especially true when it comes to design.

Of the metal objects produced in Iran during the last century, by far the largest number are made of copper. A great many of these were meant for everyday use—pots, kettles, and plates for cooking and eating, trays for serving food or use in the public bath, and so forth—and were left undecorated, the shape of the object constituting the principal element of beauty. Copperware with a greater display value, however, usually received the additional attention of such craftsmen as the engraver, fretworker, and occasionally the embosser.

Depending on the size and shape, a copper object is normally hammered out of one piece of copper sheet or beaten out of two pieces which are joined at a toothed seam and soldered together. Such things as handles and spouts are frequently added by means of rivets. Traditionally, the finished product is covered inside and outside by a thin coat of tin to protect the metal from corrosion and to make it safe for the preparation of food. With use in time, this coat wears off and has to be replaced by a tinner or by the coppersmith himself.

In accordance with contemporary taste, dealers handling older copperware and craftsmen catering to the nontraditional buyer usually either have the tin coat removed or omit it completely† from the very beginning. With use and age tin acquires a mellowness and beauty of its own, and should be preserved whenever it enhances an object. But at the same time, the rich shades and hues of the copper itself can be as important a factor in the beauty of a piece as its shape and decoration.

139 lower

Most bazaars in Iranian towns of any size still have a section devoted to the production of copperware. This section is easily recognized by the loud noise of hammers striking metal, men and young boys working over various types of anvils and snarling irons, and smoke billowing up out of furnaces kept red hot by different types of hand bellows made from animals skins. Of the major centers of coppersmithing, such names as Isfahan, Shiraz, Kashan, Yazd, and Kerman stand out above all others.

As in painting, the copperware of the late eighteenth through early twentieth centuries is usually marked by a decorative style that is clearly distinguishable from those of earlier periods. The

TEAPOT, BRASS, AZARBAIJAN
19th century   L. 39.5 cm.
Museum of Decorative Arts, Tehran

MOSQUE WATER FONT, COPPER, ISFAHAN
Dated A.H. 1182 (A.D. 1769)   D. 39 cm.
Museum of Decorative Arts, Tehran

RHYTONS, FLUTED METALWORK
Represented in Reliefs, Apadana Stairway
Persepolis, 5th Century B.C.

major exceptions come when the classical shapes and designs of the Safavid period (1501–1722) are employed by the craftsman, as in the early Qajar bowl,† and the late Qajar teapot.†

Facing

The form of this teapot is obviously European,† for despite the long history of relations with India and China, tea drinking was only introduced into Iran less than a century ago. Prior to that the social hot drink was coffee, however infusions have been known here since at least the second millennium B.C. as teapot-like forms in pottery with a filter in the body at the base of the spout abound from Luristan and Gilan and other excavations.

Facing upper

Here the Persian craftsman has taken a newly imported utensil and adapted to it traditional concepts. The fluted body is almost as old as metallurgy, being a device to strengthen the thin sheet metal. It is found in early Islamic bronzes, illustrated in the SURVEY,† and in bronze vessels from northwestern Iran tombs of the second and first millennium B.C. A form characteristic of metal, it was imitated in the grave pottery of the second millennium B.C., especially in Azarbaijan, where pottery was being made in obvious imitation of metal.

[1327, 1328]

This bowl† is divided into two sections by a narrow band of interlaced rosettes very commonly found in nineteenth century work. The bottom half is decorated by an arabesque (*eslīmī* in Persian) design, the *eslīmī* being one of the most highly developed and characteristic forms of design in Persian art. At the top there is a lovely inscription in the delicate and distinctively Iranian *nasta'liq* script. Contained in this inscription are the names of the *Chahardah Ma'sum* (Fourteen Pure Ones): Muhammad, the Prophet of Islam, his daughter Fatimeh, and the Twelve Imams or divinely-guided spiritual leaders of the Twelver Shi'a branch of Islam which has been the official religion of the Iranian state since the beginning of the Safavid period in A.D. 1501. First of the Twelve Imams was the Prophet's cousin and son-in-law, Ali, known as the Commander of the Faithful.

Facing lower

COVERED BOWL, COPPER, YAZD (?)
Early 20th century   H. 23 cm.

RITUAL SCENE, RELIEF, PALACE OF DARIUS
Persepolis, 5th century B.C.

Reminiscent of a tomb tower or royal pavilion is the unusual covered copper bowl.† The *Facing* very finely engraved work on its eight sides consists of alternating panels of a central medallion surrounded by flowers and birds, and an allover floral pattern with interspersed birds and animals. These panels all differ from each other. The lid has two alternating designs: a cypress tree attached to what looks like a pot or vase formed by the body of a two-headed bird, and a floral design similar to those found on the body of the bowl. Seen in the medallion of the central panel is a motif very ancient in Iran: the life and death struggle of the Iranian monarch with an animal that is symbolic of the evil forces of the world. This is found in great prominence in Persepolis,† one of the three seasonal capitals of the Achaemenid rulers of *Above* the ancient Persian Empire. As will be seen later, it has enjoyed much popularity in the art of Iran during the last century.

Interlacing floral designs of a nonarabesque type encompassing a profusion of birds and animals, some of them, like the monkey and elephant, exotic to Iran, were among the most favored motifs of the Qajar engraver working on copper and brass. The birds and animals are typical of this work, while the flowers, foliage, and vines formed by, and engraved on, the fretwork of the lantern top are much more characteristic of the Qajar period than those of *121* the former.

A sight common in traditional milieus in Iran, like that of the teahouse, is water pipe or hubble-bubble smoking. Two examples of water pipe bases are illustrated here, one made of copper and tinned over, the other is made of silver. The upper part of such pipes is normally fashioned of wood, the smoke being cooled by the water held in the base and inhaled through a long wooden stem attached to the main shaft (on which the charcoal and tobacco holder rest), or inserted into a separate hole provided for it.†

Facing left

Carefully decorated bases obviously were not meant for public use. Most probably they graced the home of some well-to-do person, men and women partaking in separate quarters.

The copper base† is typical of Qajar decoration, the element of *eslimi* being somewhat greater here than in many other examples, however. Constant handling over the years has caused the engraving on the top of the neck to become largely obliterated, a sure sign that this is not a vase or decanter which were made in similar shapes.

Facing right

Silver water pipe bases are by no means a rarity. Made by a Shiraz silversmith sometime in the first decades of this century, it differs in that it is both engraved and embossed, characteristic of Shiraz silverware. This is also true of the particular scenes from nearby Persepolis.

WATER PIPE BASES, SHIRAZ, Museum of Decorative Arts

Left, early 20th century, H. 32 cm.; *Right*, dated A.H. 1258 (A.D. 1842), H. 26 cm.; *Detail*, (*facing*)

HAND LANTERN, COPPER, TINNED
Embossed and engraved, Yazd
Circa 1940   D. 17 cm.

Lanterns in a variety of sizes, shapes, and materials were used in the days before electricity to assist one through the street at night or provide a convenient light in a particular spot. The most typical kind is pictured here.† It collapses like an accordion for ease of transport and storage. A candle is placed in a holder at the bottom which, like the top, is pierced to permit the entry of air as well as the emission of light. The cloth around it holds both ends together and protects the flame from the wind as well as acting as a diffuser of the light. To inhibit it from catching fire, the cloth was always waxed.

Two lanterns illustrated here are of a size and weight to preclude convenient use by a single person. When being transported, the lantern was attached by means of its hook to a pole carried on the shoulders of two men. Much smaller ones made of copper or brass are also encountered, such as our more recent example with a finely engraved top, and dating to perhaps thirty-five years ago.†

Besides lanterns, a number of other objects have been decorated by the fretworker. These include very elaborate copper and brass lampshades, incense burners and vases. Such work is still done today† with great care and skill when sufficient incentives are involved.

Facing

139 lower

Above

Overleaf

LANTERNS, FRETWORK
19th century   D. 43 cm.

Cutting and finishing fretwork
Tabriz and Isfahan metalworkers' bazaars

Facing

WINE BOTTLE CASE
Fretwork and engraved, Tabriz
1976. Mashhad Exhibition H. 30 cm.

The intricate *eslimi* fretwork on the silver wine bottle case is as fine as lace. The branches of the vines are also engraved with a fineness befitting jewelry, that is in places barely discernible to the naked eye. The band near the bottom consists of eight panels of poetry from Khayyam, whose portrait appears in the upper right medallion adjoining the drinking scene. That of Sa'di is on the opposite face. The artisan is Amir Sami of Tabriz, who signed the work and notes that he did both the form and the engraving, two tasks often done by separate artisans.

122

Writing of the gold- and silversmiths of Persia in the early seventeenth century, Sir John Chardin said, "What they do best is the Filigreen work, they Engrave pretty well."

Zanjan, northwest of Tehran and halfway to Tabriz, continues to maintain traditions long alive in this area. Silver wire work, the ancestral form of filigree, was popular with the Parthians, as attested to by the hoard found at Dura Europos. They also developed highly the granulation technique, an equivalent process with tiny balls of metal. The Kurds have continued some of these techniques. The oldest Islamic jewelry described in the SURVEY is of the twelfth century from Rayy and includes a large portion of gold filgree. The smiths of Zanjan today work mostly in silver, only sometimes in gold. Early in the reign of Reza Shah a number of them relocated to Tehran, where they made their famous golden globes of spider-web thin filigree the most characteristic product of the Tehran gold bazaar.

In the creation of silver filigree, the silver bullion is first melted then poured off into rectangular molds with channels twenty-five centimeters long and less than one millimeter diameter. The silver rod is removed when cool and the process repeated to build up a stock of rods as needed. The bar is then reheated until malleable and is drawn out longer, thus thinner, on a wheel called the wiring wheel. Heated again, the now narrower rods are drawn again, passing them through a hole in a metal plate slightly less in diameter than the bar, which again reduces the bar to a progressively thinner filament as narrower holes are passed through in succession until the desired diameter is obtained.

Next, the wires are formed into spirals or the forms desired, building up a number of small spider-weblike elements. Then a board is set down and covered with wax smoothly. The filigree elements are assembled into a tray. If a bowl is to be made, a dome-shaped form is covered with wax and the filigree pieces set out over it until the finished shape is obtained. Then some silver filings are spread over the assembly and heated under a low flame just enough to melt the fine filings—but not distort the filigree elements—so that they bond the filigree sections together. This is the most delicate part of the operation. Acid baths and low heat remove the wax and other impurities.

This set of tea and dessert service is by Kamran Haghighi of Zanjan, one of the five winners *Facing* of the Award for Handicraft Excellence for 1976.

DESSERT SERVICE, SILVER FILIGREE, ZANJAN
1976 Handicraft Excellence Prize
D. Largest bowl, 33.5 cm.

Embossing silver, Isfahan

Of all the metalworking centers in Iran, none can approach the fame of Isfahan, the capital of Iran from 1599 to 1722. Well before and after the time when the Safavid shahs ruled from there, the copper, steel, brass, and silver objects made by its craftsmen helped to set the standards of quality for the rest of the country. This preeminent position continues into the present, and is immediately apparent to anyone who visits Isfahan's vast bazaar or walks along its principal thoroughfare, Chahar Bagh. Other once noted centers have declined in recent decades, partly due to an exodus of craftsmen from Yazd and Kerman to Isfahan, and in part to Tehran. Much of the decline in smaller cities was due to the recession after the Second World War coupled with the flood of cheaper imports. Isfahan and Tehran on the other hand were expanding markets.

Examples of the type of copperwork done two to three decades ago are seen here.† *Facing* In all, the pictorial element predominates. The motifs are Iranian and are done in Iranian style, but the total composition strongly suggests an awareness of a new type of market— one aimed primarily at the foreign tourist trade. Unlike those things formerly crafted solely for Iranians, the decorative value now becomes much more important than the functional, enabling a return to pre-Islamic canon as once known in the Sasanian metalwork.

A hunting scene is both embossed and engraved on the upper plate,† which is meant to be *Facing upper* used as a wall plaque. Scenes like this one are found on a large number of trays and bowls made since the Second World War, and are inspired by a style set by miniature painting. In recent years, much of the Isfahani engraver's effort has gone into silver rather than copper objects for obvious commercial reasons, as will be seen on the following pages.

A series of scenes from a former aristocratic way of life in Iran surrounds a finely drawn central medallion in the fluted copper tray.† Trays like this are often older than the engraving *Facing lower* on them. One of the signs of new engraving is the impression left on the back. Such work, when done in earlier times, virtually never shows through on the reverse side.

The Kerman work as on our tray,† is predominantly embossing. Here an Achaemenid and *Facing right* Sasanian motif, the animal combat, reappears set in an adaptation of a dome interior, as has since become popular with metalworkers and enamellers. The reticulated pattern harks back to at least early Iron Age metal vessels though its centrifugal movement is a hallmark of fifteenth and sixteenth century miniatures.

126

TINNED COPPER PLATES, EMBOSSED AND ENGRAVED
Above, Yazd, 20–30 years ago.   D. 27.5 cm.
Right, Kerman, 20–30 years ago.   D. 44 cm.
Below, Yazd, 20–30 years ago.   D. 47 cm.

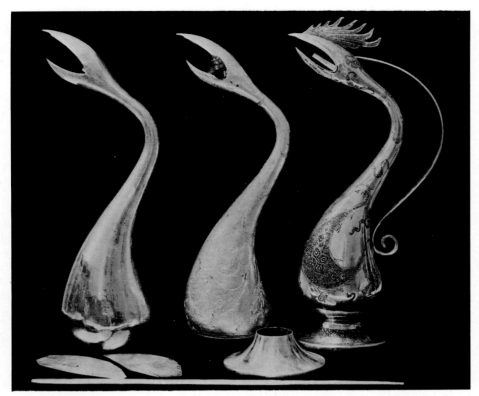

SILVER EWER, ENGRAVED, ISFAHAN
1976   H. 52 cm.

Stages in the construction of the silver ewer, facing.

Qalamzani, the use of the chisel, for engraving and embossing, is a technique as old as the working of metal itself. The exquisite bronze drinking cups from Luristan exemplify the earliest works.† The gold bowls from Kalar Dasht, Marlik and Hasanlu, both in their iconography and their peculiar characteristic of animals in relief in profile with heads turned to the beholder rising out of the relief in full sculpture in the round,† find their prototypes in the superb stone sculpted vessels of Kerman of at least fifteen hundred years earlier.† The metal workers' *qalamzani* technique would therefore seem to arise from the stonecutter's craft.

[69–72]

[1490]
29

Isfahan has long been the most important center of *qalamzani* work. An outstanding example is the door of the Madraseh Madar-i Shah in which a full seven techniques are employed: carpentry, goldsmithy, engraving, embossing, fretwork, *gablameh*, or gilding on silver, and *malaghmeh*, "fiery gold." It is signed the work of Ustad Abdul Latif Tabrizi. Today the art is enjoying a revival and a number of fine artists are working— more important perhaps, there are good apprentices rising. The most noted artist working today is Hajji Muhammad Taghi Zufan, but one would be hard put to consider inferior to him his disciple Morteza Saraian, or the elderly Husayn Ehtemam, and Hajji Abdul Husayn Parvaresh. But with such a galaxy of masters now working at Isfahan we must also mention Hajji Muhammad Ali Parvaresh, Mirza Assadullah Bolurian, Hajji Agha Reza Komeili, Husayn Alagheh-mandan, Ali Darvish and Ustad Wahab, most of whom are located along the Chahar Bagh. All work in various base metals and silver and gold, with silver today predominating due to market demand. A number of skilled craftsmen are working in gold among the Armenians in Julfa.

A characteristic Persian form is the bird-shaped ewer, a popular artifact of the Seljuq era in metal. Contemporary to these were the cock's head ewers in the finest ceramic techniques of mina'i and gold luster, which are usually thought to be pottery imitations of a metal prototype. However, a faience cock's head fragment from what must have been a small ewer is known from the seventh century B.C. Interestingly, the highly modernistic rendition of the cock's head motif by Saraian illustrated here† seems closer in spirit to this earliest example than to the more recent.

Facing

Perhaps the most popular application of *qalamzani* are the ubiquitous teacup holders. The examples shown† were made thirty years ago by the father of Ehtemam, Muhammad Reza, with a then young Husayn helping.   [LUTFULLAH HONARFAR]

Overleaf

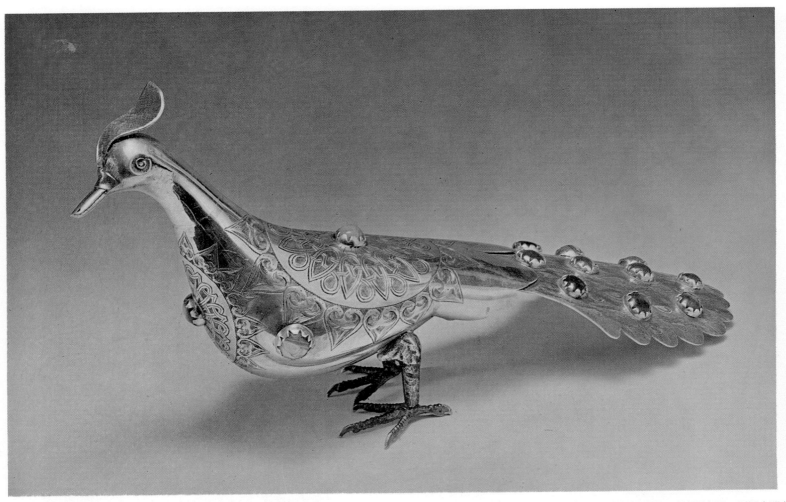

SILVER PEACOCK, TEHRAN, by Hagopian
1976 Handicraft Excellence Prize   L. 37.5 cm.

SILVER VASE, ENGRAVED, DETAIL, ISFAHAN
1976

SILVER TEACUP HOLDERS, ISFAHAN, *ca.* 1940

BRASS, ENGRAVED
Above left. Plate with 48-point star
working out from 12 points,
fantastic animals in petals.
Above right. Plate with 17 variations
on animal combat theme in a 16-
point spiral star in three inter-
twining levels.
Both Honarhaye Ziba workshop,
circa 1963. Kashan Museum
Below. Pair of carafe
embossed and engraved, Teheran
1975. Ministry of Culture and Arts
Honarhaye Ziba workshop. H. 39 cm.

CAMEL BELLS, BRASS, SAND CAST
Left, H. 27.7 cm. *Right,* H. 29 cm.
Left margin, reverse of bells

245

Above

Above left

Caravans of camels crossing the desert or entering and leaving a town were once familiar sights in Iran. Before the coming of the motor vehicle these strange and majestic animals were the desert's analogue to ships on the sea, and accordingly were treated with considerable care. On festive occasions they were decked out in various head trappings and covers† by the tribes of Iran, and to mark the end of the pilgrimage to Mecca, were often chosen to serve as the first sacrifice at the start of the Eid-i Qorban, one of the main festivals of Islam.

To prevent grazing camels from wandering off and getting lost in the desert, it was customary to tie a bell to the underside of the neck. Some bells have clappers inside, and others consist of a series of progressively smaller bells of the same shape, one placed inside the other. The two brass bells† are in fact the top pieces of such an arrangement. Both were sand cast probably sometime in the early part of this century. Seen on above, weighing over two and a half kilograms, are the ancient solar and lunar symbols of the lion and bull (see above, p. 132). Also adorning this bell are a saddled horse without a rider, a peacock with a crown inside its tail, and a large crown containing the words: "made by Hajji Muhammad Husayn." The smaller of the two is ornamented by what appears to be a deer of some sort, which is flanked by two animals resembling a dog or lion, and a large camel.

Copper worker in Kerman

HAMMERED COPPERWARE, KERMAN
Mirror in double-headed peacock frame, 1976. Scale 3/5
Tripod confection dish, 1976. H. 22 cm.

All of the examples of metalwork illustrated thus far are either representative of, or directly inspired by, the court art of the past. In the two-headed copper peacock encompassing a mirror,† we have a good example of the folk art tradition of Iran. It was made in Kerman *Facing upper* during the past year, and doubtless reflects a local tradition there. Part of the considerable charm of the piece lies in its simple yet harmonious and balanced lines which convey a feeling of unself-conscious creativity, in itself an expression of Sufi idealism supported by, or perhaps supporting, the Sufi symbolism of the combination of a peacock and a mirror. As Laleh LALEH BAKHTIAR, Bakhtiar* points out, "the peacock has played an important role in Sufi iconography: 'As *Sufi Expressions of* light was manifested and saw Self reflected in a mirror for the first time, it saw Self as a peacock *the Mystic Quest* with its tail outspread.' " Bakhtiar continues to relate how the soul of the mystic, "reaches the presence of Light, the Intellect…moves from contraction to expansion and comes to radiate from the center…from the Eye of the Heart as ornaments in the form of spiritual virtues which relate to the eyes in the tail of the peacock, brilliant centers of contraction in the midst of overall expansion." Certainly no better physical description could be written of this highly successful and cumulatively appealing piece of pure folk art.

Furthermore, unlike the preceding copperware, the surface is not highly polished in this school of copperworking. Instead, hammer marks are used to create a texture of skin that has a life in itself. Kerman is perhaps the oldest center of copper working dating back, according to archaeological finds since 1968, almost 7,000 years. The animal-footed, here bird-footed, tripod legs† are a tradition at least 2,500 years old in known Persian metal vessels, and several *Facing lower* hundred years more in pottery of the style seemingly imitative of metal prototypes.

138

Facing upper, Divination disc and
dice, brass   Scale 4/5
Facing lower, Talismans, brass,
actual size

SILVER TALISMANS
Late 19th century. D. largest, 8.7 cm.

Divining the future and determining when an act is auspicious or not have always been of
much concern to traditional Iranians. One of the ways divination is carried out is through
geomancy. At one time done on the ground with pebbles, or with dots and lines drawn at
random, the science of reading the future is now performed with a round metal plate and set
of dice, usually made of brass.† Inscribed on the brass plate starting from the outside and   *Facing upper*
going in are: (1) the names of the signs of the zodiac, (2) the names of the planets Venus,
Mars, Mercury, Saturn, and Jupiter and the sun and moon, (3) a series of lines and dots
resembling the male-female lines which made up the trigram system of Chinese geomancy,
(4) the names of the four elements: earth, air, fire, and water, and (5) in the very center, the
name of the prophet, Daniel.

There are two schools of geomancy, one attributed to the Sixth Imam, Jafar-e Sadeq and the
other to Daniel, the type shown here, the Persian for this being *raml-e ostorlāb* or "geomancy of
astrolabe." Locks *C* and *D*† resemble the dice shown here, are known as *ostorlābī* ("astrolabic").   *159 C, D*
What connections there may be between these locks and the *raml-e ostorlāb* is not clear.

Other talismans are in the shape of a hand, fish, lion. Most of these are small and may be
thrown into the tomb chamber of a saint by the pilgrim in beseeching aid. As they are popular,
the cheaper brass is normal for them.

Various types of invocations and prayers are engraved along with the owner's wishes. As
these are normally of a very personal nature, the natural tendency is to keep them as secret as
possible, something done through use of an ancient system (called *abjad*) which assigns nu-
merical values to each letter of the alphabet. Writing is thus done by means of numbers
instead of letters.†   *Above*

One additional point must be mentioned: the metals themselves are thought to have special
powers inherent in them. Most efficacious is steel, followed by silver. Given this fact, it is not
surprising that the majority of amulets and talismans found in Iran are made of one of these.

'ALAM, ISFAHAN
Pahlavi steel crown, 1972
Other parts variously to 220-years old.

'ALAM, Pl. 143 entire

Besides the lock, many talismans are round, like the three silver ones shown.† The oldest of these, *C*,† from the early nineteenth century, has a tabletlike inscription combining numbers, letters and words as well as a prayer in the outer border. Two figures, those of a man and woman, flank the tablet while a winged sun, shown here as Khorshid Khanum, the Sun Lady, looks on. In *A*,† probably late nineteenth century, the Khorshid Khanum appears in conjunction with a lion, itself an ancient symbol of the sun. The lion and sun are Iran's national emblem, and appear together in numerous art forms during the period of this survey. Much more recent is *B*,† which resembles *C* in composition, except that the winged Sun Lady is missing. Talismans such as these are worn in different ways. Many are provided with rings underside so they can be tied to the upper arm. They can also easily be attached to a garment.

Preceding C

Preceding A,

Preceding B

The tradition of steelmaking in Iran, especially during the Safavid period (1501–1722), is among the finest ever seen in the Islamic lands, or for that matter, anywhere in the world. In no other metal does one find the great variety of instruments, implements, weapons, containers, etc., that were fashioned from this metal. Chardin wrote, "The Workmen in Iron and Steel are also very well vers'd in their Trade; they Hammer both Iron and Steel cold, and succeed very well in it."

Associated with steel production in Iran in the period under discussion are places such as Isfahan, Kerend to the west of Kermanshah, and Rayen, southeast of Kerman. The latter two are little more than villages, the main income of which has traditionally come from the things their craftsmen make by hand.

With the increasing economic penetration of foreign manufactured goods into Iran in the last century, local production of iron and steel from raw materials gradually came to a halt, scrap and discarded materials from such things as machinery, pipes, and motor vehicles being reworked and utilized for local needs. Most of the more recent steel objects illustrated here are from such sources.

'ALAM PROCESSIONAL STANDARD
Ethnological Museum, Tehran
Dated A.H. 1341 (A.D. 1922) W. 167 cm.

In addition to the types of things commonly associated with this metal, various objects possessing religious significance have traditionally been made from it as well. One of the most important of these is the *'alam* or standard used during processions on Ashura (the 10th day of the month of Muharram) in honor of the slain Third Imam, Husayn, son of Ali, the Fourth Caliph and First Imam. Imam Husayn's martyrdom came about in the year A.D. 680 in the desert of Karbala, now the site of his tomb, to which thousands of Shi'ite Muslims make a pilgrimage each year.

Climaxing the extensive mourning ceremonies which start on the first of Muharram, Ashura is a day marked by long processions of men and boys flagellating themselves with chains and shouting slogans in Husayn's honor, women and girls crying and weeping, and recitation of the heroic deeds performed by the Imam and his followers. At the head of these processions is usually a *nakhl* or *'alam*,† the long cypress-shaped parts of which sway back and forth as if *Facing* doing obeissance to the holy martyr. In the case of the older standards of this kind, the base section which encompasses religious inscriptions and is protected by open-mouthed dragons, is often beautifully pierced.† *Preceding*

The one illustrated here,† made in A.H. 1341 (1922), is solid and bears the names Allah, *Facing* Muhammad, Ali, Fatimeh, Hasan, and Husayn in the center. A battle scene is etched around it. Four smaller standards are found on either side together with two peacocks, a bird, four vases, and a pair of boxlike containers. Two candle holders are attached to the rod on which the frame rests.

One of the most popular forms of contemporary metalwork is the sculptured bird and animal, examples of which are seen. The bird won the Handicraft Excellence Prize in 1976.

Inspiration for such work comes from the animal figures often found attached to the *'alam* or standard carried in the mourning processions of Muharram. Most commonly these include the deer and lion and a variety of birds, with the peacock and fantail pigeon most prominent among them. The steel bird and the silver one† could represent either of these two. In style and material the former is much closer to the sculptured figures of the *'alam* than the latter.

The bird† made in Isfahan by Mohammad Johari has the gold inlay or encrustation characteristic of the traditional steel pieces. Such work is started with a sharp short-edged knife by means of which the area to be inlayed is finely serrated in crosswise directions. Once incised, very fine gold (or silver) wire is placed on the roughened surface and hammered in with a narrowly pointed hammer. The surface is then burnished with a polished agate, which brings the gold or silver to a bright shine and eliminates any traces of roughening.

STEEL FIGURINES
Inlaid gold and silver
Above, Deer, 1960
L. 30 cm.
Facing, Bird, Isfahan,
1976 Handicraft
130 Excellence Prize
L. 25 cm.

Facing

Detail from miniature, *Jamshid Teaching the Crafts*,
showing bird-shaped snips. (SURVEY, Pl. 872)

BIRD-SHAPED STEEL UTENSILS
Above. Horsebit, bronze, Luristan
First millennium B.C. (SURVEY, Pl. 30B)
Facing upper. Snips, Safavid period
Center. Snips, contemporary
Below left. Bird-shaped horse bit
Below right. Abstract bird-shaped bit
Scale 1/2

Iranians have a long tradition of making their tools and instruments not only as utilitarian as possible, but also beautiful and humane at the same time. Decoration is never allowed to interfere with efficiency, this condition forcing the craftsman to utilize to the fullest the possibilities suggested by the metal and required shape.

An outstanding example of the simple and elegant beauty created by an Iranian toolmaker is the late Safavid steel tin snips illustrated at top.† No more subtle and pleasing a rendition of a pelican could have been achieved even if the craftsman had had the goal of sculpting this bird. Its body is formed by the two handles, the shape of which, according to Hans Wulff,* "is only now coming into use in Western countries." An eye is created by a cleverly utilized nut, and the beak, by the two blades which, when open, give the impression of the bird in the act of eating. Very fine engraving adds to the refinement of this tool.

While not in the same class, the recently produced tin snips at the bottom shares many of the qualities just described. Here the bird's beak is shorter and thicker, but the illusion of a hungry bird at work on the tin being cut would escape few Iranian artisans.

Steel horse bits with their cheeks in the shape of animals were characteristic of Persian bridlery from pre-Achaemenid times and are especially common in Luristan grave finds of the first millennium B.C. Fantastic winged beasts† gave way in Islamic times to more naturalistic birds which in turn have become more abstract, more stylized, an evolution clearly shown here. The left bit† is a pair of parrots, feathers and details engraved so as to soften the usually cold hardness of the steel. The age is uncertain, between one and two hundred years old. In the right bit† the natural features of a bird have disappeared, the body much elongated, the feathers eliminated, yet in the shape and the movement the essence of the bird remains every bit as clear as in the naturalistic bit alongside. This bit is thirty to fifty years old.

Facing upper

Hans E. Wulff,
The Traditional Crafts of Pers

Above right

Facing left

Facing right

148

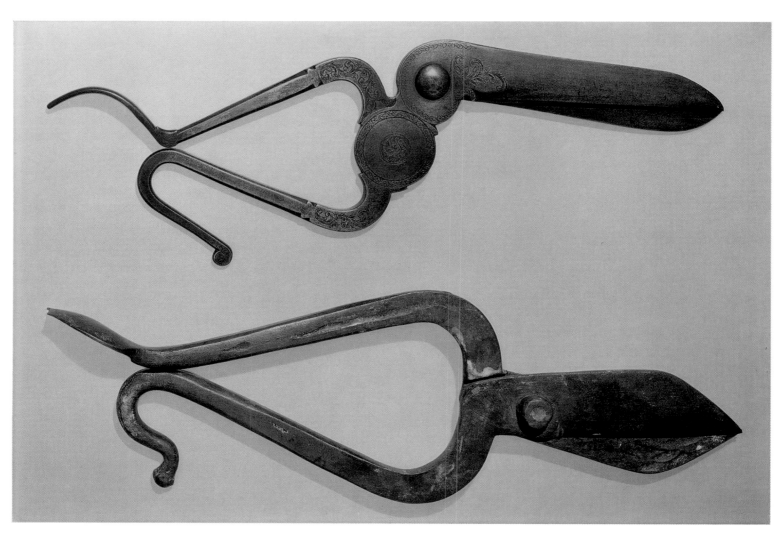

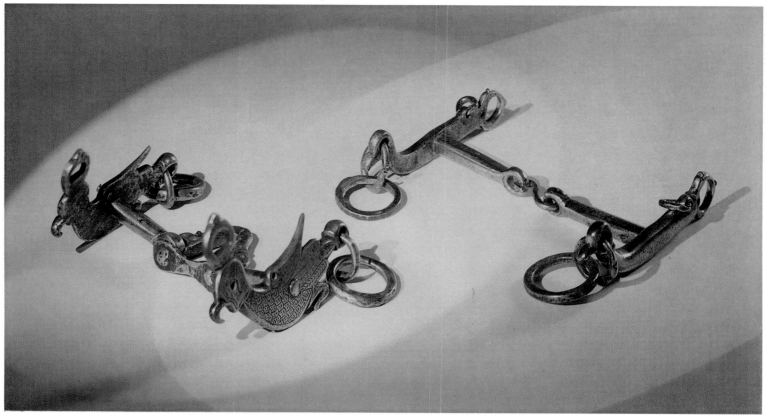

MEAT CLEAVERS, STEEL
Early 20th century. Scale 3/5
Left, reverse; *Facing*, obverse.

   Like the tinsmith, the butcher also worked with tools that were aesthetically pleasing. This is seen in the case of the two etched steel meat cleavers. One of these even shows the butcher engaged in the slaughter of an animal while someone else is out hunting.†   *Above left*

   Both have scenes from the *zūrkhāneh*, literally, "house of strength," pointing up the frequent connections of the butcher with this traditional kind of palaestra or gymnasium. The activities of the *zūrkhāneh*, an institution which still flourishes today, center around such things as body building, wrestling, and most important of all, a particular kind of ancient Iranian exercising with wooden club-weights seen in the hands of two men.†   *Facing right*

   A tacit recognition of the proper place of each member exists in the *zūrkhāneh*, the *pahlavān* or most accomplished member being given precedence and considerable respect. As these strongmen go through their exercise routines in a deep, octagonal pit following the lead of the *pahlavān* and improving their skills or competing with each other, a man who acts as a kind of spiritual guide to this fraternal association beats out rhythms on a drum and recites poetry.†   *Facing left*
Above the drummer's head is a steel bow with metal discs used in the traditional exercises.

   Large quantities of weapons and armor† in the same decorative style as these meat cleavers   143
were produced in etched steel in the first half of this century. Many were originally meant to be used in the *ta'ziyeh* or passion play performed during the first ten days of Muharram. Tourist interest also helped to keep this type of work alive for awhile.

STEEL TOOLS   A

A–D Fire steels   B

E   Candy cutter   C

F–G Charcoal Tongs   D F, G, H

Scale 3/4   E

In the days before the convenient safety matches and pocket lighters taken for granted today, starting a fire was often a laborious task. An English publication of 1832 states that "there are very few house-men, or house-maids, who can succeed in 'striking-a-light' in less than three minutes (this is the average result of many thousand experiments)." Whether in England or Iran, the problem and the means were the same. The latter normally consisted of a tinderbox, a flint, and a fire steel. To start a fire, the steel was held firmly and hit obliquely by the edge of the flint, which would knock off tiny incandescent particles of steel, which caused the tinder to smoulder and, with much huffing, and puffing, to burn.

Fire steels were needed by almost everyone. They ranged from crude and simple to highly ornamented and beautifully shaped. Some had brass bodies and a steel rim, while others were all steel. Examples of four fire steels are seen here. The first two are very old, perhaps even going back to the eleventh to twelfth centuries. The others were made within the last fifty years. A marked similarity exists between *A* and *B* on the one hand, and *C* on the other. Not content to leave his work plain, the craftsman created a bird figure by utilizing the basic shape of the piece and adding an eye with a simple punch mark. A small amount of engraving has helped to further this impression in *C* while *A* when inverted also resembles the ram decorations on pre-Achaemenid bronzes. The centers were pierced both to decorate the steels and to lighten the weight for the bearer.

Facing A, B

Facing C

A very different shape is *D*, and far more commonly seen than that of the first three. The long neck curving around from the body and down toward the front served both as a handle and an opportunity for the craftsman to ornament the piece. In the most beautiful ones this often takes the shape of a bird or dragon head. Here one finds two nesting birds.

Facing D

Included here are three steel tongs and a brass and steel candy cutter. The first and last were made in the early part of the twentieth century, while the middle pieces are new.

Tongs like these are used for opium smoking, an activity that is often at the center of an intimate gathering of friends for relaxation and conversation. Needed for this are a low charcoal brazier, a tray under it, the opium pipe or *vāfūr*, tongs, and a supply of opium. Some also applied the same ritual to smoking tobacco in the long wooden-tube pipe with a ceramic or stone bowl, keeping which going required a similar supply of coals. A pin is needed to keep the hole in the bowl open.

The tongs illustrated as *H*† have just such a pin included in it, but it is too thick for the pinhole of the opium pipe and was used to keep the hole in the base of the tobacco pipe bowl clear. The pin is attached to the small knob just below the attractive pierced work in the center. When the knob is pulled down, the tongs open and the pin comes out. The peacocks at the tip of each arm are both functional and decorative.

Facing H

Made in Kerend within the last few years, the tongs *F*† have extremely simple and elegant lines. They open the same way as *H*, but have no pin inside. The head of a fabulous creature adorns each tip.

Facing F

The center pair was made in Rayen. A pair of hands grasps the charcoal. It is levered open by pressing the bottom ends together.†

Facing G

Similar in decoration and feeling to the *raml-e ostorlāb*† and the two brass and steel locks from western Iran† is figure *E*. Quite possibly this candy cutter was made in western Iran as well.†

141

159

Facing E

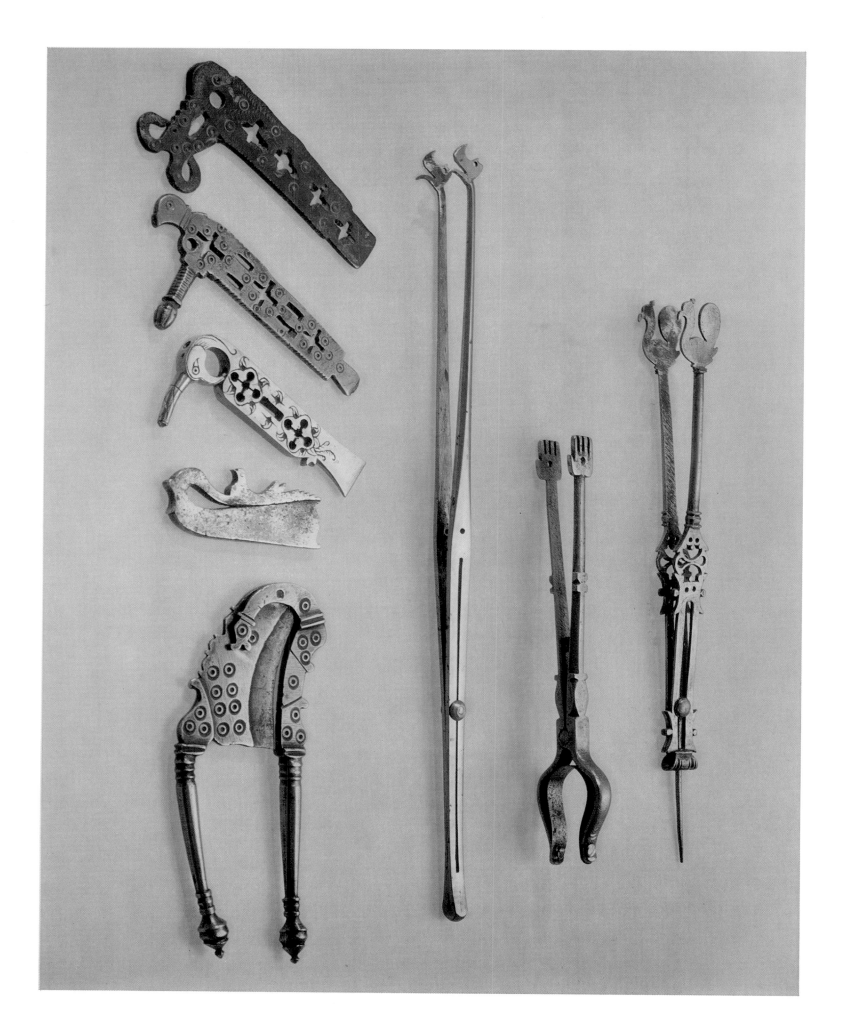

Toolmaker, hammering file teeth

STEEL TOOLS
Leather Cutter (?), steel
Early 20th century   Scale 4/5
Qandshekan, sugar choppers, steel
20th century

Exotic, strange, even amusing are terms which can best be applied to these cutting tools. Perched on top of what is believed to be a leather cutter†—though the protuberances make it difficult to grasp—is a naked man in a top hat, reading a book with a small dog beside him. The hat is obviously European and the dog, which is ritually impure in Islam, along with it can only be taken as signs of a European or of an Iranian who took on European ways. A bird emerges from between the man's legs. The meaning of this iconographic hodge-podge is a mystery, unless it is meant to portray a magician of sorts. In this case, the notorious Malkam Khan comes to mind.

Facing upper

Lined up like a steel ballet line are four sugar cone cutters,† more abstract in their suggestion of human forms. Persians use the slow dissolving beet sugar which is formed into large cones. These must then be broken, thus the hammerhead, into chunks which will then be chipped with the adze head into squares or manageable chunks which can be held in the teeth as tea is sipped through. Few opportunities to add playful amusing details were passed by the Iranian craftsmen. Handles on such tools were rarely left plain and were a good place for the smith to show his skill with the file.

Facing lower

The copper insets in the *qandshekan* on the right† are the trademark of the smiths of Rayen near Mahan. The figure is an exercise in double entendre: the arms in silhouette recall the monsters paired on Luristan bronzes, the costume details incised on his body suggest the gateway to a mosque or a great garden of delights. Rayen still produces knives, carpet tools and *qandshekan*.

Facing lower right

Placing propitiatory locks on grill of *nakhl*, shrine

NAKHL, or SHRINE
Recent   W. 180 cm.
Ethnological Museum, Tehran

Often seen hanging from the *nakhl*† or *'alam* are pieces of cloth or even padlocks. These are *Facing*
fastened by the faithful to mark vows made in the hope of divine assistance in reaching a goal
or fulfilling some special need.† The use of the padlock in Iran for spiritual and psychological *Above*
purposes is as important as the security factor.

Padlocks have been utilized by Iranians from at least the sixth century A.D., and depending
on how one interprets the evidence provided by the door of the tomb of Esther and Mordecai
in Hamadan, possibly from a time far earlier than this. Unfortunately this ancient craft
is on the verge of extinction in Iran today. The traditional locksmith can no longer compete
with modern machine-made locks, and only in a very few places are locks still being made by
hand.

One of these places is Chal Shotor, a village seven kilometers from Shahr-e Kord in central
Iran. Here some of the last Iranian locksmiths still produce beautiful steel locks like examples
J and *K*† on the page following overleaf. *Overleaf*

Locksmith of
Chal Shotor

Facing. LOCKS
Scale 4/5

A	–E–
B	F
C	H
D	
J	G
K	

Using traditional elementary tools inherited from their teachers, who in many cases were their own fathers, the Chal Shotor locksmiths† first forge the lock body (the lower part of the lock which contains the mechanism inside), then the shackle or horseshoe-shaped top part which goes through the staple or hook on a door, box, etc. Holes are made with a bow drill and details are filed before the whole piece is polished on a lathe.

These locks work on the helical-spring principle, which means that they are locked shut by means of a pin kept in place in the end of the shackle by the pressure of a spiral-shaped spring. When the key is inserted and turned, the helical spring is contracted and the pin removed. This is one of several locking mechanisms used in handmade padlocks of the last century.

Locks *G* and *H*, both steel, are heart shaped.† The former was made in the early twentieth century, while the latter, which has three mechanisms and three keys, is a product of seventeenth century Isfahan. Such locks were usually used when some kind of partnership was involved, each partner having a key and the lock being openable only when all were present at the same time. The center mechanism in both is the bent-spring type.

Among the oldest (sixteenth century) and newest (made ten years ago by Ebrahim of Kerend) dial combination locks are seen in *E* and *F*.† Only differences of shape separate these two, marked by a continuity in the lockmaking tradition from earliest times to the present.

Basically rectangular in shape with ornamentation consisting of circles and dots, *D* and *C* are typical of a type of lock made in western Iran during the last century and a half. The lock bodies of both are brass, while the shackle is steel. This is also true of *F*, while *E* is all brass.

Examples *A* and *B* represent a different kind of padlock—the figural one. From late Sasanian or early Islamic times up to the present there has been a continual tradition of figural lock-making which has drawn on numerous different animal forms, and occasionally even on human figures, for its inspiration. Two examples of this kind of miniature sculpture, the first† seventeenth century and the second made within the last few decades,† give an idea of how the lion motif was treated by the Iranian locksmith three hundred years apart. Many of the most beautiful locks ever made in Iran are figural.

Above

Facing C

Facing G, H

Facing E, F

Facing D

Facing A, B

Facing A
Facing B
Parviz Tanavoli and
John T. Wertime,
Locks from Iran

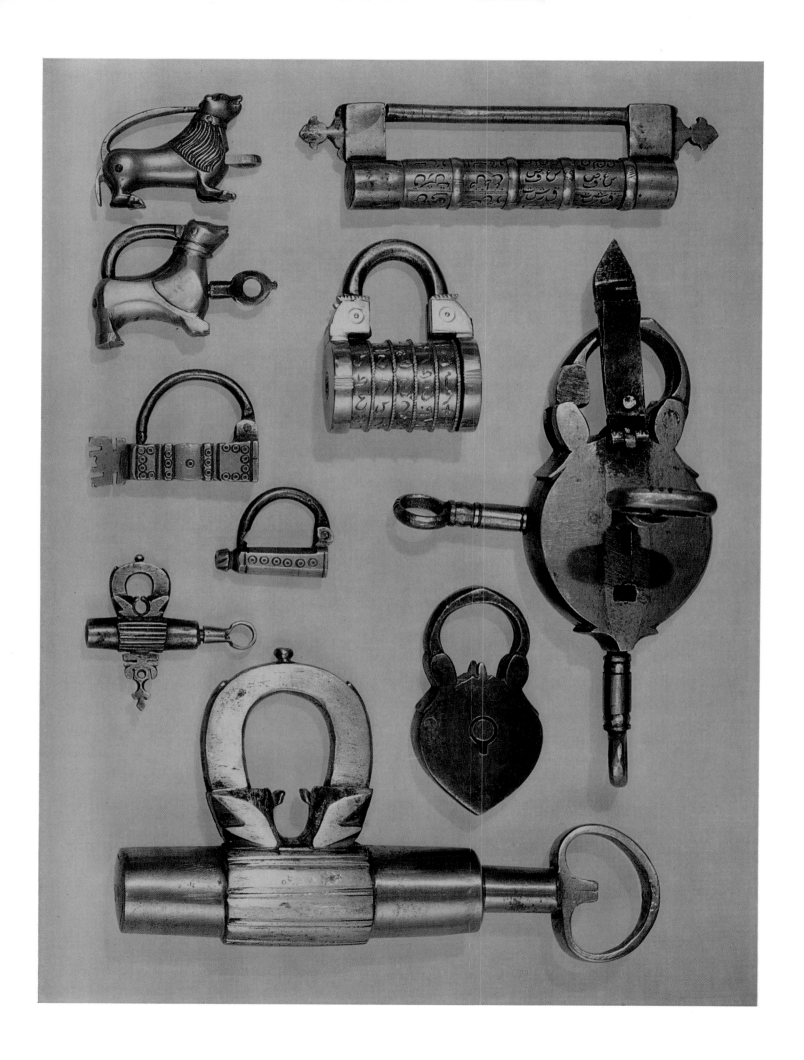

STEEL PADLOCK, MULTIPLE KEY MECHANISMS
Ardabil   Scale 1/2

The large steel padlock† from Ardabil in northwestern Iran is another example of a lock *Above*
with multiple mechanisms and keys. Before the push key (seen on the right hand side) can be
used to open the barbed-spring mechanism controlling the shackle, the helical springs located
in the two vertical pipes must first be contracted.

As indicated earlier, the padlock has not been used solely for security purposes. In the
popular culture of Iran it is considered to possess special powers to ward off evil and to assure
happiness and success. Among others, pregnant women, girls seeking husbands, and wives
trying to retain their husband's affection used the lock traditionally for its talismanic qualities.

Padlocks also figure in various rites and practices of Twelver Shi'a Islam. Pilgrims circum-
ambulating the tomb of the Eighth Imam, Reza, who is buried in Mashhad, take hold of the
lock of the grill-enclosed tomb chamber and beseech the Imam's help. Like the grill, the lock
is thought to partake of the blessing and holiness that permeates this sacred place. Those
making vows commonly fasten a lock to some sacred object to act as a reminder to their
intercessor and as symbol of their fidelity to their own promises. Favorite places for this *156*
include the grill surrounding a tomb,† the chain hanging at a mosque entrance, the grillwork
of a *saqqākhāneh* or public water fountain, and the *'alam* and *nakhl,* as mentioned earlier.

Locks employed as talismans are usually small, made of steel or silver, and covered
with numbers and/or writing. Occasionally there are human figures engraved on them, usually
a man and woman. When this is the case, the intent is to employ the lock's magical powers to
retain the goodwill or affection of the other party, or to gain it in the first place.

—JOHN W. WERTIME

Preceding
SHERBET GLASS AND TEA GLASS
CLOISONNÉ ENAMEL, *Actual Size*
Ca. 1960   Rasht

BASIN AND PLATE SET
ENAMEL ON REPOUSSÉ CHAMPLEVÉ WITH GILDED TRIM
Interior of basin patterned after interior of East Dome, Shah Mosque
by Shokrollah Saniezadeh   D. Bowl 37 cm.

ENAMEL
MINAKARI

MINAKARI, enamel, "This dazzling art of earth and fire...saturated but lucent colors"[1] thrives today in Isfahan. When *minakari* artists say they do not know when their art began here, they mean they are not sure when in the Safavid period—yet enamel on terracotta was known at Susa by 1500 B.C., on metal was fully developed in the Oxus treasure of the sixth to fourth centuries B.C. and after 500 B.C. "it was probably more elaborated in Persia than anywhere else."†[2] *Minakari* today refers only to that enamel painted flat on a metal base, usually copper, and covering it completely. It does not include champlevé nor cloisonné, enamel contained within gouged out cavities or wired borders, nor grisaille, the monochrome sculptured relief enamels. Chardin wrote that enamel was one of the arts the Isfahanis did not know how to do, yet a piece remaining from that time is described today as "one of the finest extant examples of Persian enamel,† with a pattern of birds and animals against a floriate ground, rendered in light blue and green opaque enamels and dark blue, green, yellow and red translucent enamels."[3]

As to the origins of enamel, Erwin Margulies and Léo Bronstein in the *Survey*[4] point to Iran in their brilliant and complete historical discussions. Certainly in Parthian† examples and the later Sasanian,† the art is carried to its ultimate. Its use in Early Islam is unclear before the time of Ghazan Khan (A.D. 1271–1304). The king "Acquired in a short time a knowledge of chemistry...but instead of wasting huge sums like his predecessors in the search for the philosopher's stone, etc., he rather devoted himself to the more practical part of making enamel."[5] And it is a chemist's art. "That such a material as enamel should have been evolved is a demonstration of human creative invention, for it consists of a complex synthesis in which are united, on the one hand, the humblest elements, silicum, minium, potassium and, on the other, the most sumptuous, the precious stone, to the brilliance of which enamel aspires. It is thus a wholly artificial substance which might be regarded as the epitome of human invention and industry...Enamel is a vitreous material composed of metal oxides, which under heat assume the required colors, intermixed with certain fixed fusible salts. The tone varies with the temperature and the length of exposure to heat, so that the firing has to be carefully controlled. Normally transparent, the material is often rendered opaque by the addition of oxide of tin. The composition of enamels has remained in essentials unchanged from the earliest periods down to the present."[6]

Bronstein analyzes enamel patterns in four styles. The first is decorated with naturalistic flower paintings with close parallels in textile design. The second has ogee panels enclosing animals and plants in a style in common with book covers and painted plaster.† The third is purely pictorial and dependent upon book illustration and literary scenes, in a style in which "nineteenth century degeneration is most unpleasantly apparent." The fourth type† "even more obviously degenerate...emulates the nineteenth century enfeebled continuation of late eighteenth century French style...which imports...the one aesthetic vice which the native taste, left to its own preoccupations, never suffered, prettiness."

Léo Bronstein
Survey, p. 2586

Overleaf
D. T. Rice *Survey*, p. 378
Survey, Pl. 121–2

Survey, Pl. 1426B
Hans Stocklein
Survey, p. 2577
Erwin Margulies
Survey, p. 781
Survey, Pl. 138E
Survey, Pls. 247–8
166

Rashid al-Din
in H. H. Howarth
*History of the
Mongols*, p. 493

Bronstein, *Above*
pp. 2586, 2588

1396A, 1437A-B,
Survey, Pls. 1395A-B,

Survey, Pl. 1396C-D

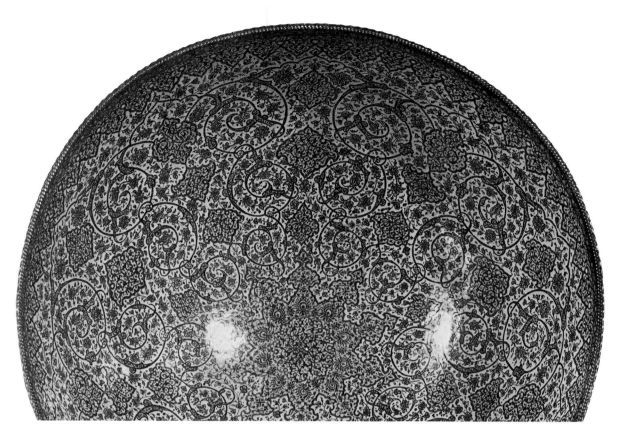

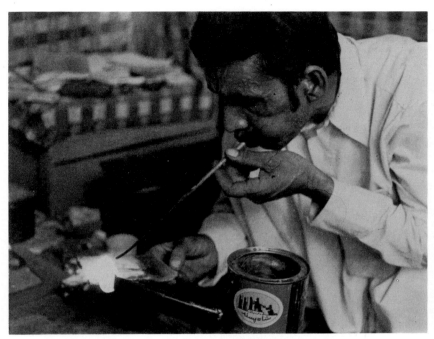
Making silver jewelry, Baluchistan

NECKLACES, BALUCHISTAN (*Half-scale*)

A. *Chamkali*, silver fish pendant, repoussé and incised with simulated coin tails, all strung on black wool cord.
B. *Farizeh*, choker or headband of flat round medallions, fringed with triangles and lozenges, punchwork, granulation and wire twistwork.
C. Necklace, plastic beads (often with matching earrings) from Khaneh Gholāmān near Khāsh.
D. *Kapak* or *Kapāku*, choker of demiglobular gold roundels with granulation, some with colored stone inset, border of plastic gold beads.
E. *Tek*, necklace of gilt metal discs in low embossing, separated by turquoise, glass and plastic beads.

Gold and silver are sold by weight, the *mesghāl* of 4.6 grams being the unit of measure. In Baluchistan, however, the *mesghāl* weighs only 2.3 grams so two *mesghāls* there are equal to one *mesghāl* in Tehran. The gram is now official and coming more into use.

Most of the jewelry discussed here is in silver, for these pieces have adhered more strongly to the traditional shapes of each region, whereas the pieces made in gold have often changed form and tend to be influenced by sophisticated city fashions and standardized countrywide.

The jewelry of Kurdistan is noted for its ornate headpieces and immensely broad belts. As exotic as they appear to urban Iranians, they are in direct descent from the oldest Persian styles. The belts, embossed in high relief from behind, evolve directly from the broad bronze cummerbands of ancient Urartu. The lovely crowns† resemble the headpiece worn by the Goddess Anahita on the Sasanian rock relief at Taq-i Bustan in Kurdistan and, though more ornate, are in the tradition of the Sasanian royal crowns. If our lovely Kurdish model resembles a Far Eastern Maitreya or Coming Buddha it is because the Buddhist crowns evolved from this Sasanian tradition.

Preceding left

Sometimes the uses of jewelry are purely ornamental. Sometimes they have their roots in the Islamic religion, as in the widespread use of the *bāzuband*, a prayer capsule worn on the forearm; or the ancient belief in amulets and prayers pinned to an infant's cap or shoulder, and the predominant use of turquoise gems or blue beads† as a protection against "the evil eye." On the other hand, some objects may also evolve from practical uses such as pinning a veil to the headdress, or as a pomander or container for scent, as the Baluch *zebadān* or *moshk-dān* enclosing a piece of cotton saturated in musk oil with tweezers, toothpicks and ear scrapers all attached to a triangular pendant, the *taytok* of the Baluch.†

Overleaf A, R

Most southern items described below were made and bought in February-March, 1973, in the picturesque little stalls of the jewelers' section in the bazaar of Zahedan (the *javahersāz*, jeweler; the *noqreh sāz*, silversmith; the *zargar*, goldsmith), and also in Khāsh, Gōsht, Dāvar-panāh and Sarāvān to the south and southeast of Zahedan, and in colorful little villages such as Varekāt, southwest of Iranshahr, and Bampur. The open market of Varekāt had an atmosphere of unabated excitement, teeming with different craftsmen at work. Their customers clamored noisily for attention or sat silently in circles patiently waiting their turn. Other pieces came from Zabol in Seistan and Bandar Abbas on the Persian Gulf coast.

Turkoman girl, see *Facing C*

HEAD PIECES, TURKOMAN, GILT ON SILVER (1/3 *scale*)
- A. Headband, fretwork and incised, set with carnelians. Yamut.
- B. Headband, with chain veil, set with carnelians, embossed appliqué. Tekke.
- C, D. Cap crowns, embossed appliqué set with colored glass. Tekke.
- E. Chin band, incised, set with carnelians. Yamut.
- F. Pendant hung vertically in pairs down back of hair. Yamut.

No tribe of Iran in recent centuries has carried the craft of jewelry making to the heights of art as have the Turkoman of the northeast. The women are bedecked in gilded silver from childhood,† embossed and pierced with designs, studded with semiprecious turquoise and carnelian and glittering colored glass emulations of gemstones, with appliqué filigree sworls and gilded studs. Gold predominates visually, but the jewelry is basically silver—and low content, two thirds or less, for the practical consideration that it must stand the wear of daily use. There are two schools of applying the gold: the Yamuts gild and emboss small rosettes and patterns of silver and solder them to the larger silver base; the Tekke gild the whole, with occasional embossing of fine fretting, then incise the gold to bring out the silver beneath.

Dating of tribal jewelry is at present almost impossible. The southwestern Iranian hollow anklets are frequently found when the shallow graves are accidentally torn open by passing herds and the silver makes its way back into the local bazaars. The Turkoman pass their treasures down as heirlooms. And as the insecurities of the national psyche until recent times have caused greater value to be placed on the antique and the foreign, Turkoman jewelry, like many northern carpets, is often attributed to our northern neighbor and to periods before the great Turkoman retreat into Iran. Yet while the northern Turkomans were superb artists, I cannot accept that they did not bring their artisans with them and that until very recently, if not yet today, fine silversmiths have worked among them turning out masterpieces undifferentiatable from those of their masters and ancestors. Certainly, until the two Pahlavi Shahanshahs restored security to the highways and ended the tribal economy of banditry, Turkoman, Qashgai, Bakhtiari and other tribal life styles had changed little from earliest times. This form of "taxation" on caravan commerce held down the development of urban crafts but enriched the tribes. Much of this wealth was lavished on the women, and often equally splendidly on the horses, which were bedecked in fabulous trappings like royal nomad burials of millennia past.

Dated Turkoman jewelry exists for the early twentieth century, and one even bears a price. A large collar button,† signed by the smith, is dated 1338 (1919–20) and inscribed in Turki is the price, eighteen tomans. Now only two and half dollars, at the time it would have had an exchange value variously estimated at between $130 and $400—a fair evaluation for such work today. The idea that handicrafts must be cheaper than machine-made mass-produced work is a recent delusion born of the inferiority complex of having fallen behind the world, common to less developed nations. For those of us who have "caught up," there is even less reason for continuing it than there was for succumbing to it.

Above, Facing C

Facing A, E, F
Facing B, C, D

Above
BUTTON MEDALLION, dated 1338 (1919–20)

174

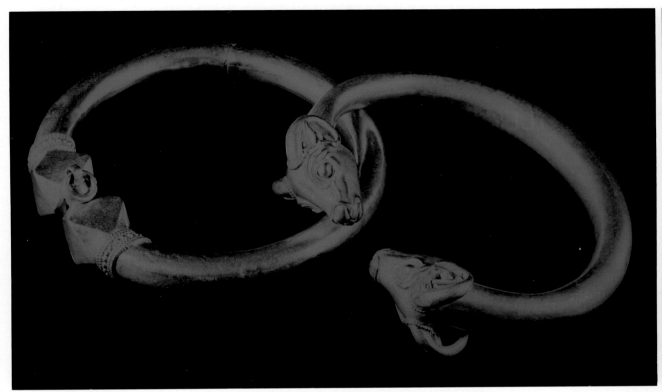

HOLLOW-CAST GOLD:
BRACELETS (*Actual size*). *Left*, with granulation, recent (?). *Right*, Achaemenid protomes, 1969.   RINGS (*Slightly enlarged*) 196?

It should also be mentioned that some pieces of jewelry found in Baluchistan, Seistan and the Coastal Province are frequently similar in motif and design, yet may have different local names. This similarity is natural considering their geographical proximity and the migrations.

Furthermore, the Bandari *siné riz* necklace and gold earrings are identical to the ones made in Lar of Fars Province, an important production center for jewelry. The *siné riz* necklace is a choker made up of twelve flat boxes often filled with pitch. The boxes are of thin gold sheet decorated with granulation and colored stones. The lower edge of the choker has streamers of delicate gold pendants with some twist wirework. The earrings are formed by two hollow cones with small clusters of pomegranates at their tapering base and mounted by a medallion with a hook at the top. They may be plain gold or filigree, *malilé-kari*, with a few pearls and turquoises strung on a wire around the center of the cone or with spiky knobs in the middle. These clusters of miniscule balls, granulation, are a characteristic Parthian technique and a tradition so closely held to even today that it is difficult to date pieces by style alone. Parthian silver coins were still in daily circulation in provincial areas less than forty years ago further reenforcing this conservatism.

Antique jewelry has always been more highly valued in the provinces, not so much in net price as in credibility: the claimed gold or silver content is more readily believed and the designs are preferred. Price by weight will differ little if at all, but the sale is easier. This has encouraged jewellers to imitate them, reenforcing thereby the traditions. The Parthian style granulated bracelets are known to make their way onto the more gullible Tehran market as antiques. And the recent stirrings of a reborn national pride in the traditional arts has even influenced the jewelry shops along Lalezar where the extraordinarily difficult Achaemenid style—if not earlier Median—hollow cast gold bracelets with animal protomes have reappeared.†

In 1969 the Handicrafts Center introduced an exquisite series of rings, with Achaemenid protomes on Sasanian spiral body with Parthian granulation and details.†

—IRAN ALA FIROUZ

172 E, B- C
172F

172 B-C

Persepolis relief
Above left

Above right

176

TEXTILES

Although Persia was always a small country numerically, its seven thousand years of achievements in the arts exercised throughout the world an influence second only to that of Greece, according to Sir John Marshall, and its textile arts remain supreme. True, they have rivals, but as a whole, the work of Persian weavers maintains its superiority: in both range and skill of weaving techniques; in sensitive exploitation of the character of the material, perfect delineation of the figures, their suitability in scale and design to the uses of the fabric (garments, curtains, cushion covers, horse furnishings, carpets and tent decoration); the sheer beauty of the patterns and their often solemn meaning which even in later, secular times may have for subject ancient myths or traditions, including moving symbols of deep-rooted national faiths. All these qualities are fused into consistent artistic wholeness.

The vocabulary of symbols thus founded persisted and expanded for nearly seven thousand years, inscribed with increasing grace, more and more supplemented with purely aesthetic elements, but sustaining the basic qualities that are inherent in profound meaning and the intensity generated by deep needs. The beauty of Persian textile arts is thus long-grounded in life-sustaining values, vividly conceived, emotionally charged. The Persians themselves consciously and also half-consciously "read" these patterns.

Eight thousand years ago (ca. 6050 B.C. according to carbon-14 dating) people living in caves —Ghar-i Kamarband or the Belt Cave, and nearby Ho-tu, from a peculiar echo—close to the town of Beshahr near the southeast shore of the Caspian Sea, were growing grain and raising goats and sheep. And what is more relevant to our immediate interests, they were shearing the sheep and, we must assume, weaving cloth and sewing it with the horned needles they left behind. At about the same time—slightly after 6000 B.C.—and some thousand kilometers west at the very edge of the Iranian Plateau at Çatal Hüyük in present-day Turkey, other excavations reveal several swatches of textiles as carbonized fossils from under the clay floor of a burned room, "reminiscent of modern light-weight woolen dress material," wool or flax.

Two or three centuries later the first concrete evidence of weaving in what is today modern Iran appears at Sialk, a large mound near Kashan in the center of Iran. The culture producing highly sophisticated painted pottery in patterns ideal for reproduction in weaving has left behind numerous ceramic spinning whorls. These objects are ubiquitous from this time on in excavations throughout Iran, in variations that indicate a considerable range in the qualities of yarn produced and hence of the cloth that was woven. At Susa, the Shushan of the Old Testament, in the land of Elam in southwest Iran from a level datable to 3500 B.C., there emerged two bronze knife blades caked in the copper salt fossilized imprints of long-lost fabrics. Spinning in both cases was fine and even, in a plain cloth resembling cheesecloth or butter muslin. Painted pottery found nearby at Tepe Musiyan shows ladies wearing skirts with an open line check pattern. Identical textiles also appear on pottery of the northwest near

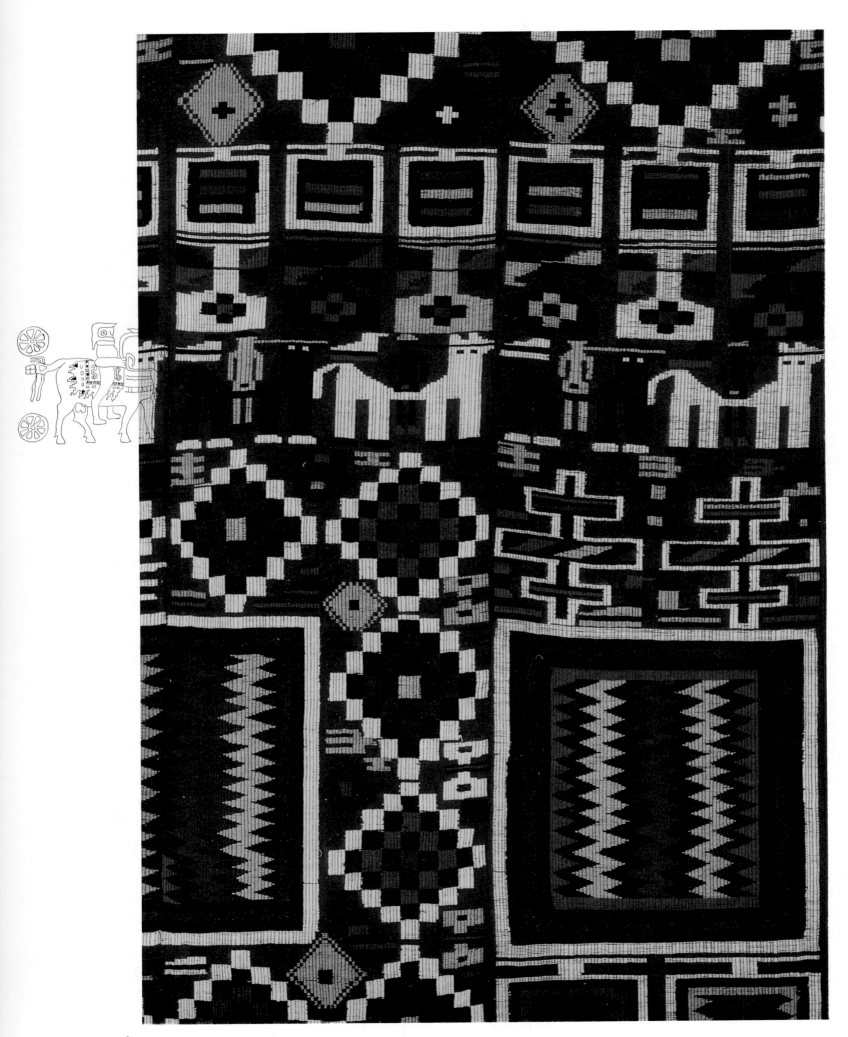

DETAIL
PERSEPOLIS RELIEF
Offering yarn, textiles

Survey, Pl. 72

Detail
Pazyryk carpet horseman
5th century B.C.

Above

Survey, Pl. 3076

DETAIL
SILK BROCADE
CHADOR SHAB
Qassemabad, 1976
W. One panel, 31 cm.

Lake Van. In weaving, such a line check would result from interpolating dark threads at regular intervals in the warp as well as at regular intervals for a few shoots of the weft.

The dignitaries in ample and elegant robes depicted on the repousse bronze situlae of Luristan†were contemporary with the Medes, famous for their sumptuous brightly colored robes. The elegance of the Medes and their clothing fashions became the style of the first great empire, the Achaemenids. We can actually see in the refined and meticulous stone reliefs at the great Achaemenid cult center of Persepolis in south Iran, the softly draped cloaks, the wide bell sleeves, and judge the fineness of the fabrics by the close, flat, even folds. In the grand procession of noble ambassadors bringing offerings of their regions' finest products, we can see rams with rich fleece, men carrying bolts of folded cloth†—some thick woolens by the breadth of its fold, and some finer cloths—balls of yarn of different thickness, followed by men carrying shallow bowls as still used by rural dyers today. Did these two bowls contain cochineal for the priceless royal purple from Sidon and the dried insect for the rich Persian *qermes,* we call carmine, which are still used today for the finest gilims and carpets.

This attention-compelling intensity, clarity and precision of these reliefs are essential factors which remain through all the great periods, in all media, and typically in textile designing, characteristic qualities of Persian art. Perhaps the crystal air contributes something to this. Literary references throughout the world fill in the unbroken rich history of Persian textiles. They were carried to medieval Europe to become treasured coronation robes for kings and popes. They were carried to China as one of the few manufactured imports respected by the dilettante emperors and to Japan where for over 1,400 years they have been treasured†and inspire native textile designers even today.

Of the universality of the craft throughout Iran we know from such references as the tribute lists of Al Ma'mun in the ninth century in which the taxes from various Persian provinces includes: from Gilan, 20 garments; from Sistan, 300 pieces of *attabi,* moire silk of different colors; Tabaristan, Ruyan and Nahavand, 600 carpets, 200 garments, 500 tunics, 300 napkins; from Gurgan, 1000 pieces of silk; and Khurasan, 2700 pieces of textile. The accounts of the Arab geographers tantalize with their richness, yet torture us with the lack of description.

The finest Persian textiles, the achievements through many centuries of a supremely gifted race, must rank high in the works of art. They abound in grace and beauty, they embody brilliant and subtle fugue-like decorative schemes, the glory of Persian art; they are rendered in techniques of fabulous skill, and at their greatest they convey opulence and splendor, dignity and reserve—subtle poetry, a moving symbolism to those who understand; and to all, charm and exhilaration.

—Arthur Upham Pope and Phyllis Ackerman

QALAMKAR BLOCK-PRINTED COTTONS

Perhaps the most popular handicraft with foreign tourists and the one which elicits most in the mind of the observer the idea of Persia, is the block-printed *qalamkar* cotton. Yet in no craft is there as much confusion as to its origins, and sometimes even the national provenance.

Printing on cloth is of two basic types: direct block as in *qalamkar* printing whereby a design is imprinted just as with a rubber stamp, and the second, resist dyed where an element is imprinted on the cloth and the cloth immersed in dye to take on color in all the areas not imprinted by the chemical which resists it. When the latter system is applied to the yarn itself, it is called ikat (p. 200); when applied to the textile it is batik, as done in Osku (p. 194). Direct printing is often used in conjunction with hand painting; thus its common Persian name *qalamkar*, which means brushwork, though the blocks themselves are called *qaleb*.

The oldest direct evidence for painted textiles comes from Egyptian tomb murals of 2100 B.C.[1] Among the outer Iranian tribes, painted textiles have been excavated from the Scythian tomb of the Seven Brothers of the fourth century B.C.,[2] and include birds much in the tradition of modern Yazd pottery, as well as Helleno-Persian vine scroll borders. While textile printing is generally accredited as being an Indian invention of the fourth century B.C.,[3] "the Greek historian Herodotus in the fifth century B.C., in his description of the peoples in the Caucasus, mentions their printed garments."[4] Mellaart believes clay stamps from the 6000 B.C. level at Çatal Hüyük were for patterning textiles.[5] The oldest extant print is from an Egyptian tomb of the fourth century A.D., "a child's tunic printed in blue star-shaped design, leaving a white grid allover pattern."[6] An actual block of the same period was also found—some five centimeters long with a printing face four centimeters in diameter. This closely resembles the stamps used both to identify and decorate Partho-Sasanian pottery, and indeed during the Sasanian period "textile printing had developed into one of the major techniques for the decoration of woolen, linen, and silk fabrics."[7] The oldest extant Persian example is an excavated fragment, sixth century, "printed in red, black and powdered gold."[8]

The oldest actual blocks known in Iran are three individual blocks carved of stone, but of the general shape and size of modern wooden *qalebs*.† These were excavated commercially in Nishapur in association with tenth–eleventh century pottery. Traces of wool padding remain in the interstices of the design, a technique used in more recent blocks for retaining the dye. Yet while stamp molds were used on eleventh to thirteenth century pottery and tile, and silks were stencil-printed in the twelfth and thirteenth centuries,[9] the Mongol introduction of woodblock printing in the late thirteenth century seems to have met no interest in Persia.[10] Block printing of textiles is a cheap system of imitating the effect of expensive brocades and embroideries. Imprinting gold gives an effect of gold brocade. In India "gold printing... seems certain that the craft was one of many which entered India via Persia in the course of the Mughal domination of India during the sixteenth or seventeenth century."[11] The heyday of the craft of hand-painted and block-printed textiles is the seventeenth to nineteenth century and here the histories of Persia and India are so intertwined as to make the provenance of individual pieces a textile collector's nightmare. In Persia, the industry was certainly well established by the seventeenth century and Rasht, Kashan, and Isfahan were all important centers, with production also at Nakhichevan, while in the early eighteenth century Yazd and Kashan, and later Burujerd, Semnan and Gonabad were said to produce the best types.[12] During the Safavid period *qalamkar-zar* or *akilili* was produced with gold or bronze powder printing, emulating *zari* metal-enriched brocades. For the color prints in red (*jiggernaut germez*) and purple (*jiggernaut banafsh*), the basic dyes were fermented for 100 days thus giving the product the name *qalamkar sadress*.

A decline soon set in for economic reasons, for India with its vast supplies of cotton invaded the market, and Chardin reports, "they make also Calico Cloth very reasonable; but they

Stefania — Eugene Holt
Painted and Printed Textiles
p. 9

Eugenia Tolmachoff
Bull., Needle and Bobbin
Vol. 26, no. 2, 1942, Pl. viii

R. J. Forbes
Studies in Ancient Technology, Vol. IV, p. 137
Holt, p. 10

James Mellaart
Catal Hüyük, p. 220

Stuart Robinson
History of Printed Textiles
p. 8

Forbes, p. 137

Robinson, p. 8

192

Phyllis Ackerman
Survey, p. 2022

Survey, p. 1732

John Irwin—Margaret Hall
Indian Printed and Painted Fabrics, p. 146

Phyllis Ackerman
Introducing Persian Textile (at press)

QALAMKAR
Painted, Block-printed
Burujerd, 114×171 cm.
Dated 1277 (A.D. 1861)

187

HAND PAINTED
BLOCK PRINTED
QALAMKAR
Mosque curtain
Isfahan, 1976

Detail of block print

Separate border
to be attached
curtain
Hand painting shown
on p.190 is this curtain

194

OSKU

SILK BATIK SCARVES
Upper, 1966

Lower, designed by
Mohammad Naraghi
90×90 cm.

195

Qalamkar or batik (?) blocks, Nishapur, 10th century　　　　　Batik blocks, Osku, modern

DANDANI—TIE-AND-DYE

Tie-and-dye is called in Persian *dandani* or *gol-i khord* and was traditionally associated with the Zoroastrian community of Yazd. It is a simple, if laborious, technique of resist dyeing, wherein the resist to the dye is provided by tightly tying up the cloth in little knots. Thus the basic design element resembles a simple flower or sunburst and may range in size from pinheads to gigantic medallions. A series of small "flowers" can outline a design, or form a ring of stars around a larger medallion. It is not done in Yazd today, but with the popularity of tie and dye in America and Europe with younger people, it might well revive.

Haft rang—seven colors, meaning full-colored—is a big square handwoven woolen head scarf with a central square medallion in brown to black encompassing a round motif in tie-and-dye in white and a warm brick color. A band of plain rich yellow gold surrounds the dark center. Two bands in red and black with a frieze of tie-and-dye flowers in circles and lines edged with a fringe complete the simple but effective composition.

Maqna-eh is a long rectangular piece of heavy silk of a dull brick color with tie-and-dye designs, measuring over three meters in length, used as a head scarf for women. The tie-and-dye form a handsome variegation of light yellow dots and slightly raised patterns, caused by scarring from the tying, of circles, *eslimi,* lines and geometric forms.

Strips of tie-and-dye material, are traditionally used as inserts† for shirts or trousering alternating with bands of embroidery or silk brocades. Typical are the two illustrated fabrics, one a sheer firm silk and the other, a coarser of tussah texture, found on panels of Zoroastrian dresses. Small pink puckered squares, created by the single knots that resisted the dye, form neat lozenge patterns on the sheer silk, while the more difficult bar-shaped motif is made by a number of small tied knots. These are joined to panels covered with tiny embroidered flowers joined together with delicately corded embroidery. Braiding finishes the hemline.

They still do tie-and-dye in Pashaki village in Gilan. Each bride spins, weaves and ties and dyes a length of silk cloth about thirty-five by one hundred fifty centimeters. On the eve of her wedding she sends it to the bridegroom who wears it at the ceremony.

193, 232

SILK BATIK
Dress Length
by Mohammad Naraghi
worn by H. I. M.
Shahbanu Farah

196

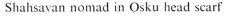

Shahsavan nomad in Osku head scarf

Batik on handwoven wool, Mashhad, 1975

KALAGHEH—THE BATIKS OF OSKU

"Peoples who lived in the area of the Caspian Sea in the sixth century B.C. had apparently employed resist dyeing methods on woollen materials,"[1] and according to the elders of the village of Osku, the art was introduced to them by immigrants from Baku on the shores of the Caspian, retreating before the expanding borders of Russia. The tribal women† of Iran have long favored the bold, colorful batik-dyed silk scarves which, in the bazaar of Shiraz hang in a forest of Qashgai-favored hues, were called Qashgai scarves, and in Turkoman Sara their bold Turkoman tints earned them the accolade of Turkoman scarves—and elsewhere as what else. Only in 1965 was the source discovered by Farangis Yeganegi and Ali Kerimi in Osku, set amid almond, apricot and walnut trees and shielded from the outside world by a thick attitude of distrust.

The old scarves had been fine silk, but the poor economy of the immediate postwar period brought the tenfold cheaper viscose fabrics into favor and the silk industry declined. Attention from the Handicrafts Center and the late designer Mohammad Naraghi† brought the silks into favor, though the cheaper viscose are still dyed for the popular market. Designer pieces† are now ordered as well, usually specifying which colors and patterns from the traditional repertoire should be used for a specific size of cloth intended for costume or specialized use. It is a rare example of intelligent encouraging and fostering of a dying traditional craft to bring it back to life.

The dyers of Osku produce for selective markets, and their designs vary according to the tastes of the various tribal clients, as now for urban and foreign buyers and the delicate taste of Her Imperial Majesty.† But taking one of the older traditional customers as an example, we will outline the process in preparing a scarf for the Turkoman tribal bazaar of Pahlavi Dej.

SILK BATIK
designed by
Mohammad Naraghi
for H. I. M.
Shahbanu Farah

DESIGNER PIECE
The last piece
made by the late
Mohammad Naraghi
92 × 300 cm.

VELVETS

Velvets are among the most luxurious, splendid products of the art of the weaver. The intricate techniques employed in the creation of elaborately patterned velvets are sophisticated and laborious. [1] Their rich and lustrous silk pile, sensuously soft and smooth, shimmering and iridescing with the movement of the wearer or the flicker of oil lamps and candles created a demand for them in the courts of East and West which encouraged the weavers to heights of technical excellence and attracted in Italy such artists as Pisanello (d. 1455) and Bellini (d. 1470) to create designs for them and in Persia helped raise Ghiyath al-Din Ali, the weaver, (fl.-1590) to acclaim as one of the greatest artists of the Safavid period.

Eugene I. Holt
Velvets East and West
p. 11

Of the origins of the rich fabric we know little. To some it is the only medieval textile to originate in Europe; Latour crediting Italy with having developed it by the twelfth century. [2] Phyllis Ackerman supports this, writing that it was then introduced into Persia in or by the fifteenth century. [3] The exhibition *Velvets East and West* supported the theory that: "almost simultaneously, yet independently, velvet weaving first developed in Persia and China in the fourteenth century, or possibly earlier. Within about one hundred years the art was superbly practiced in Venice, Florence, Genoa, Ducca and other Italian cities." [4] All that is clear is that velvet appears fully evolved almost simultaneously in Persia, Italy and China.

Latour,
Velvet, *Ciba Review*
No. 92, Feb. 1953

Phyllis Ackerman
Survey, p. 2061

Holt, *Above*, p. 13

Velvet would appear to evolve from the looped technique used in Egypt as early as 2160 B.C. Excavated material of the XIth Dynasty shows the creation of pattern by looping extra wefts and extra warps. [5] A fragment of Coptic textile in the Textile Museum, Lyons, carries extra warp threads for its pile, [6] confirming it to be a development of the looping techniques of ancient Egypt. [7]

Ackerman, *Above*, p. 2214
E. Reifstall,
Textiles in Pharonic Egypt
Ackerman, *Above*, p. 2215

From G. Vial of the
Textile Museum of Lyons

But the gap between these possible Coptic antecedents and our rich silk pile velvets is great, both in time and in evidence of evolutionary steps. A mention of what some take to be velvets appears in the Arab records of the geographer Mas'udi A.H. 332 (A.D. 943) writing of the Caliph Mutawakhil of a century earlier, that he "wore garments called *thiyab mulhama*... which in our time have come to be know as Mutawakhili. [8] The later Arabic geographer Abu-al-Qasim defines *mutawakhili dabiki*: "Towel of light embroidered with *tiraz* (identifying inscription) border, made in Egypt with two badges (*al an*) and two hands (*zunnar*) and other patterns of fine thread of perfect length and exquisite weave, with a short pile bordered with a fringe (*hushuja maskuba*). [9]

Murdj al-Dhanabby Mas'udi
A.H. 1321

In the same treatise Abu-al-Qasim mentions *kutuf Sawadiya,* a "cloth" of Sawad in Persia which later became known for its velvet hangings and curtains. The meaning of this term is in dispute, and in the SURVEY, Ackerman [10] rejects the translation of *kutuf* or *al katif* as velvet, though Jasleen Dhamija in preparing a working brief for this article [11] supports the contending school of thought that *kutuf* means velvet. Persia had long excelled in other pile techniques and had shown her predeliction for them. Weaving silk since Parthian times from unravelled imported cloth and growing raw silk since the sixth century, Persia had maintained close cultural relations with Coptic Egypt with a rich history of interrelations. It would be more than likely that the combination of these factors could have led to the development of velvet. But until archaeological evidence or clearer literary records surface, the actual history of velvet must remain unclear with scholars divided on the birthplace of the fully developed technique: Persia or Italy?

A. B. Sergeant,
Ars Islamica, Vol. IV

Ackerman, *Above*,
pp. 1996–97

Jasleen Dhamija
research manuscript

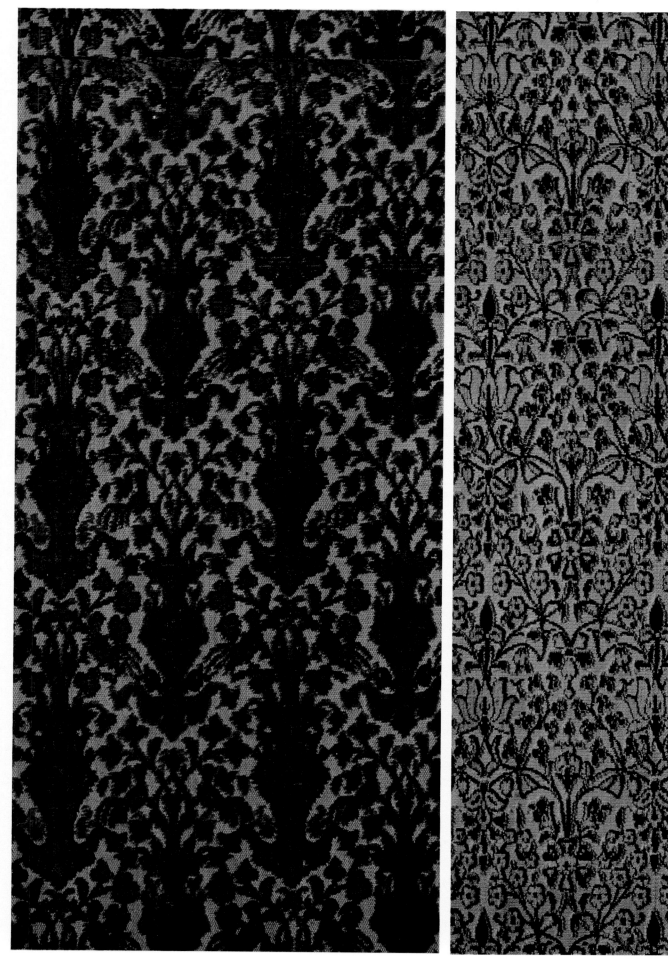

207

The earliest known Persian velvet is in the Museum of Decorative Arts in Paris, and while experts date it variously twelfth to fifteenth century, the design would fit better into the later dating. Ackerman describes the fine variety of velvets, including gold enriched, woven in Kashan and Yazd. But it is unlikely that so refined a technique should have been introduced fully developed and so late. There must be a longer history and an evolution. Other great velvet centers in Persia were Tabriz, Mashhad and Herat, and they were a major export item as early as the sixteenth century.

"All Early sumptuous, laboriously wrought velvets were costly. Some accounts and references of prices and import duties have been preserved, but it is not possible to translate ducats, scudos, shus, florins and other coinages of the Renaissance and subsequent periods in accurate relation to today's monetary equivalents. It is known, however, that only the wealthiest segments of the populace—high church dignitaries, rulers, princes—were able to afford such luxurious fabrics for the ornamentation of their palaces, churches and their own persons."[12] Holt, *Above*, p. 13
A close approximation of costs can be culled however from a sixteenth century Indian document, the *Ain-e Akbari*,[13] the Mirror of Akbar the Great (1556–1605), which lists the velvets Fazl Abl (tr. H. Blochman) *Ain-e Akbari*
on the market and their prices in mohurs. This originally Persian gold coin was quoted by travellers in the eighteenth century at one and a half to two pounds sterling. It had a gold content of 165 grains pure, so that a modern value for the mohur would approach $50, or 3,500 rials.

Brocaded velvet (*Mukmalai Zarbaft*) from Yazd, per piece	15 to 150 mohurs
Brocaded velvet from Europe, per piece	10 to 70 mohurs
Brocaded velvet from Gujarat, per piece	10 to 50 mohurs
Brocaded velvet from Kashan, per piece	10 to 40 mohurs
Brocaded velvet from Herat, per piece	10 to 40 mohurs
Brocaded velvet from Lahore, per piece	10 to 40 mohurs
Silk etc. Plain	
Velvet from Europe, per yard	1 to 4 mohurs
Velvet from Kashan, per piece	2 to 7 mohurs
Velvet from Yazd, per piece	2 to 4 mohurs
Velvet from Mashad, per piece	2 to 4 mohurs
Velvet from Herat, per piece	1-1/2 to 3 mohurs

SILK BROCADE
Yazd, M. G. Rezai
Handicraft Excellence
Prize, 1976
H. of repeat 9.5 cm.

The technique of figured cut velvet was really mastered in Persia where they developed the adding of extra colors directly onto the warp threads with the ground warp weaving. This would be introduced earlier into the basic material before pulling it up with hooks to weave the velvet pattern. The overcoming of the necessity of a repeat was well developed and was mostly used in the personage velvets. Ackerman discusses this technique in detail in the SURVEY.

Ikat was also used with velvet in Kashan and Yazd until thirty years ago.† Here the extra warp was tied and dyed in different colors and the pattern emerged as this looping warp was laid. This required an intricate intermix of the technique of tie-dyeing with that of velvet weaving so that when the pile emerged the design would not be distorted. Ikat velvet effects a soft blending outline between the different colors. Curtains and quilt covers carried a pattern of a central cypress tree with peacocks on the side,† the ground color a deep maroonish red with the patterns worked in sage green, white and yellow with a touch of black. The long *sofrehs* were made with the *hauz* or medallion pattern distributed over the surface. Others carried a border of connected medallions and the field had *boteh termeh*, the almond-shaped "paisley" then current in Kerman and Mashhad in the woolen brocades known as *termeh*.† 203 205

205

216

The curtain with the tree of life and birds† is dated A.H. 1314 (A.D. 1896), the work of Ali Akbar, Kashan, measuring 114×186 centimeters; now in the Museum of Decorative Arts in Tehran. The other with a diamond repeat pattern† with a pair of confronted birds is about the same age, with a wide border of thirty-four centimeters. 205

205

209

Perhaps the finest quality of velvet is the voided in which the design is woven in velvet pile in relief above the other sections which were left voided, that is, in simple flat weave. Until recently these velvets were woven in Kashan and Isfahan, but are now only being woven in the Honarhaye Ziba workshop of the Ministry of Culture and Art in Tehran.† This style has a close overall pattern in one or two colors similar to pieces woven in Italy in the eighteenth and nineteenth centuries. These closely woven raised patterns are known as *makhmale-barjasteh*. Here the extra warp is raised and lowered not only with the heddles but by a draw harness. The weaver, with the help of either a punched jacquard or a draw boy seated above the loom, raises the extra warp threads and introduces the pile wire. As usual, the pile wire is cut after three picks have been woven and beaten in and the raised velvet pattern emerges out of the basic fabric weave, creating a light and shadow effect. The extra warp, when not being raised to create the velvet pile design, is flat-woven into the ground fabric.

The voided section might carry gold thread twisted over silk thread, *zari,* or even wire of gold or silver, to give a rich metallic shimmer against which the raised velvet design would stand out by its lustrous pile and contrasting texture. The gold thread was woven in either twill or satin weave, or sometimes an irregular satin weave with large floats of *zari* on the fabric face so as to show almost nothing of the warp threads fastening the gold thread to the fabric. Sometimes brocaded patterns of diamonds and lozenges might be woven with the *zari* thread. This was an especially complicated form of weaving, for brocaded patterns are woven from the wrong side while velvet is woven with its face upwards. The skillful weaver had to reverse the technique of brocading to weave these patterns.

The only other velvets which continued to be woven in Iran in the beginning of this century were the plain velvets decorated with pressed designs or used for gold embroidery.†

A NOTE ON THE WEAVING OF VELVET

Velvet weaving is one of the most complicated of textile techniques. The simplest monochrome tissue, to confirm Wulff's earlier observations, is woven on a draw loom, introducing an extra warp on a separate beam below the foundation warp. As in the draw loom (*dast gahe-nakshebandi*) used for brocading, the two warps are laid one above the other with the only difference in the layout of the lower pile warp. The main warp (*chelle*) is stretched horizontally between the ware beam (*navard-e pish*) and the warp beam (*navard-e bum*) and kept tight by weights. The pile warp (*khwab*) also stretches from the ware beam but is guided upwards through a diversion pole (*samak-e pain*) at the ground level and goes up again and is suspended over warp rollers (*gargareh*) with the extra warp thread being rolled into balls and suspended with weights. Normally, the extra warp length is three times the main warp. The harness (*naqsheh*) consists of six heddles (*jujeh*), four to operate the main warp and two the pile warp, all connected to the treadles (*pah*).

The weaving is started with two or three centimeters of plain weave of the ground material, in which the main warp heddles are used. With the two heddles of the pile warp the shed is created but, instead of throwing a weft across, a long wire with a groove (*mileh*) running on the upper side is introduced. The shed is closed, three picks are woven into the main warp and beaten with the reed *shanreh*, heavily weighted so as to compact the threads tightly. Four to five pile wire are woven in this manner and then with a sharp blade each row of pile loops is cut along its wire groove and the wires removed. In this way the cut pile surface appears.

It is only in the finer quality of velvet that silk for warp and weft for the plain woven ground material has been traditionally used. For the ordinary quality the warp and the weft were cotton, *mulhama* means such mixed fabric.

The weaving of figured velvets is done by introducing additional colors. This requires a separate beam or a creel for each color. This is possible for three to four colors, but where a larger range was needed the extra warp were put on separate bobbins each of which was weighted down, thus controlling the let off. The colored warp threads were attached to a draw harness which was lifted from above by an apprentice and the shed was created through which the wire was inserted. The real skill lay in the creating of the draw harness by the workroom chief, *ustad-kar,* here called a *naksheband.*

—JASLEEN DHAMIJA

A more detailed discussion of the historical Persian velvets by Phyllis Ackerman will be found in the *Survey of Persian Art*, Vol. III/v: Textiles of the Islamic Period 2076–8, 2089–91, 1095–2098, 2102–9; Persian Weaving Techniques, (A) History, pp. 2214–21; and passim 2061, 2086, 2124, 2138, 2142, 2149, 2173, 2177, 2220, 2341, and Plate volume.

234

SILK SATIN
Honarhaye Ziba Workshop
Tehran

Left, Compound Weave
Boteh, weft patterned
1957   Scale 2/3
Right, Bazu-bandi, Ogive
in weft patterning
1960   Scale 1/2

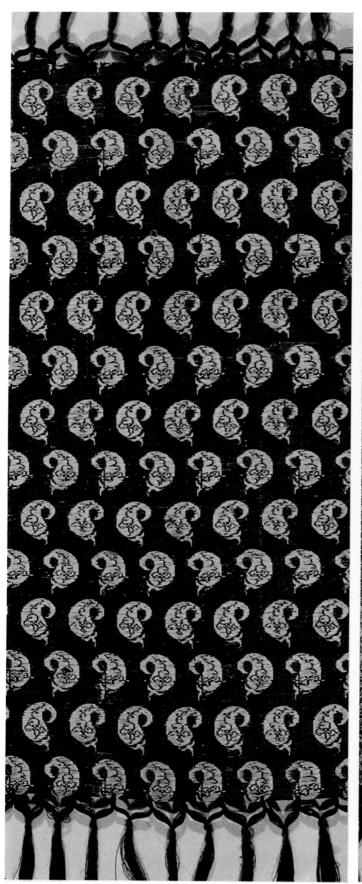

Brocade Looms
*Left,*Draw loom
*Right,*Jacquard

THE GOLDEN YARNS OF *ZARI*—BROCADE

"Brocade in the original sense means any fabric with a raised pattern. Modern English usage seems to imply a fabric with inwoven metal threads."[1] Herodotus and the *Avesta* describe what may well be brocades, but not until a Chinese annal mentions Persian gifts to the Chinese court of gold brocade do we have a specific example of what we would today consider brocade. The Chinese traveller Huan Tsang admired the Persian brocades. When Heraclius sacked the Sasanian capital of Dastajird in 628, "All the royal robes were worked with gold...one especially notable garment was woven with gold thread,"[2] what Persians even today would recognize as *zari*, brocade. And the Arab accounts of the flight and murder of the last Sasanian king, Yazdegerd III, note his fine garments of wool worked with gold and silver.

Persia was for centuries the main country producing brocades for the courts and cathedrals from London to Kyoto, whether coronation robes for Europe, or the grand *jinbaori,* the quilted vest made for the Japanese Shogun Hideyoshi in the late 1500s. The great centers in Safavid times, when the art reached its zenith, were Isfahan and Abiana, as well as Yazd which produced brocaded double cloths, and Kashan with its personage weaves famous from Sasanian times on. Brocades equal to the finest anywhere were still loomed in the last century in quantity, often indistinguishable from the finest Safavid work.

Today they are made only in two places. Mohammad Gholam Rezai (Takht Ustad) makes them in Yazd, and received the Prize for Excellence in Handicrafts in 1976.† In Tehran the workshops of the Ministry of Culture and Art have a large battery of both draw looms, and punched-card jacquards, installed in 1962 some 210 years after Jacquard developed them out of the draw loom. The product of the Honarhaye Ziba workshops are perhaps as fine as any produced in Nishijin, Japan, but the output is low. Much of it seems to go for royal use or for state gifts. The *ustad kar*, workshop master, is the scholarly Mohammad Tarighi, descendant of a four-hundred-year-long line of weavers from Kashan, whose father established the workshop and whose son in turn is following him. An avid user of the SURVEY OF PERSIAN ART in reconstructing ancient Persian weaves from Sasanian to Safavid times, he is especially proud that signed pieces by his own ancestors appear in the plate volume.

Webster's Third New International Dictionary, Unabridged

Arthur Upham Pope *Survey,* p. 2274

209

FIGURAL BROCADES
Honarhaye Ziba Workshop
Tehran   Recent
Left, H. Repeat, 12.5 cm
Right, H. Repeat, 20 cm
National Arts Museum, Tehran

Weaving brocade of sheer silk, jacquard loom. Honarhaye Ziba workshop.   *Right*, View underside

SHAL-i TERMEH —THE WOOL BROCADES

No Victorian lady would have considered her wardrobe complete without a fine shawl, usually from Kashmir but often from Persia. The word itself came from the Persian, *shal*. While referring to a fine handwoven wool brocade, it has in English come to describe the large oblong cloth thrown over one's shoulders. Persians usually attribute its origins to Kashmir—so fine were the Kashmir products and so thoroughly did they dominate the market. But Kashmir tradition has the craft introduced from Persia by a prince returning from hostage at the court of Tamerlane,[1] or by weavers brought in by the enlightened ruler Zain-ul'Abidin (A.D. 1420–1470) as recorded in the history of Kashmir as woolen textiles "of foreign origin, worthy of kings, which are now being woven by the Kashmiris."[2]

A *taq-i shal,* or length of this brocaded wool, was often considered a favored gift, especially when received by a courtier of the king. The fine wool of the *termeh* was handspun and dyed with vegetable dyes in innumerable colors. In Kashmir it was woven in small pieces and joined together by invisible mending by special craftsmen, the *rufugar*. In Iran, however, larger pieces were woven—perhaps because the wool was thicker and stronger.[3]

Some pieces were woven in true tapestry weave so that the reverse side is virtually like the face. Striped multi-colored *termeh*s were woven in wide (*shal muharamat*) or narrow bands (*haft rang*).[4] The designs in these stripes were usually floral woven with extra weft. *Termeh*s were woven with overall designs such as paisley, *boteh* or tree of life, birds and rows of spaced flowers. Later there were busier designs with a background densely covered with small flowers interlaced with *eslimis* of leaves, trees and stag horns (*shakah-i gavazn*). These *termeh* were used by men for ceremonial robes at court and by women for *chador-i kamari*, the scarf draped around the waist. The Kashmir imports in these were usually in larger patterns, while the Kerman product had smaller more numerous repeats. In time the more somber colors came to prevail, and in recent decades only dark overall effects have been produced as the recent generation has associated them with use in mourning. This is being overcome again with its use in ladies' suiting, bringing back even the metal-enriched brocades.   —IRAN ALA FIROUZ—SUMI GLUCK

TERMEH
Brocaded Silk
Yazd   1976
H. Repeat, 11 cm.

Ahmad Beshir
in conversation, Delhi
Jasleen Dhamija
Cat., *Exhib. of Royal
Iranian & Kashmir Termeh*

Rahim—George Anavian
*Royal Persian and
Kashmir Brocades*

Dhamija, *Above*

Overleaf
SHAL-I TERMEH
Wool Brocade
Left, Paisley
Kerman   Modern
H. Repeat, 8 cm.

Right, Overall *boteh*
Kerman   19th century
H. Repeat, 19 cm.

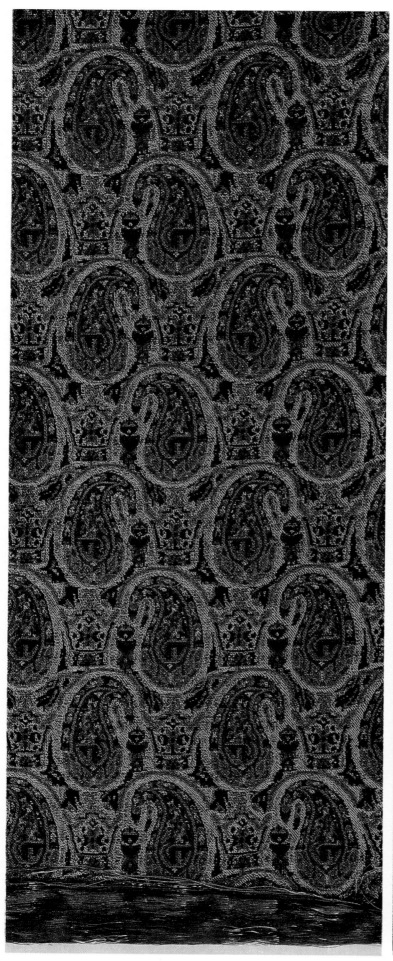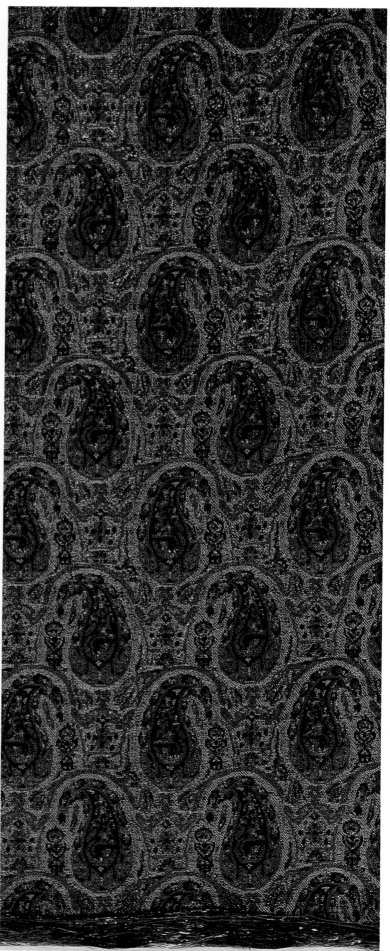

216

Detail, ornately worked garments
Rock reliefs, Taq-i Bustan

NEEDLEWORK

EMBROIDERY in some form must be one of the oldest techniques for embellishing a garment. As textile is fragile, no actual examples support this assumption. Chinese believe they did embroidery as early as 3000 B.C.[1] To the immediate west of modern Iran, fragments of more complicated soumak weave have been excavated from Çatal Hüyük datable to 6000 B.C.[2] Egyptian tomb murals show embroidery. The costumes on the nobles on the stone bas reliefs at Persepolis suggest embroidery, and Alexander "was amazed at the splendor of the embroideries he found there. To show his countrymen...he sent home the embroidered tent of Darius."[3] Fortunately, excellent examples of this period have been recovered from the frozen barrows of Pazyryk. A saddle cloth from Barrow 5 has delicate floral spray, flowers and birds on coarsely woven tussah silk clearly worked in chain stitch in colored silks.†[4]

Gold embroidery, third century B.C., was found in excavations in Southern Russia in the mid-1800s. Finely twisted gold thread is worked onto woolen cloth in scrolling vine garlands and ivy leaves. Another fragment was ornamented with bands of woven or braided gold yarn.[5]

The historian Florus recorded how in 53 B.C. in the final great battle of Carrhae, Marcus Licinius Crassus's exhausted Roman troops gave up when the troops of the Parthian king Orodes, "unfurled their brilliantly colored, gold-embroidered banners in the afternoon sun."[6]

Chinese dynastic histories record the first Chinese embassy was sent in 105 B.C. to An-shi, Arsacid Parthia.[7] Silks and embroideries must have been included in the exchange of gifts, for it was a custom of Chinese rulers to pacify neighboring nomadic chieftains with such gifts. In 174 B.C. the Chinese Emperor notes that he sent "an embroidered garment, worn by myself, unwadded, lined with silk and woven with flowers; a long tunic, embroidered and unwadded ... ten pieces of embroidered silk...."[8] Excavations at the turn of the century in Central Asia at Lou Lan, and followed up by Sir Aurel Stein with his outstanding find at Noin-Ula in northern Mongolia, uncovered quantities of textiles. Excavations in 1965 at Tunhuang in Kansu Province unearthed a panel of silk embroidery, datable 487 A.D., similar to wall paintings uncovered by Stein, le Coq and others, depicting five figures in garments "quite un-Chinese and resembles Toba Turkish dress.... T'ang pieces show Sasanian influence."[9]

The Japanese Emperor Shomu's personal belongings were cataloged and stored in the year 752 in the Shosoin Imperial Repository in Nara, Japan. Many excellent embroideries show Central Asian influence if not origin. Most reached Japan as gifts or tribute via the T'ang capital where there was such Central Asian influence that even the Chinese court ladies dressed after fashions from the West. A century previous, Yazdegerd III's survivors had taken refuge in China from the Arab invasion. The beautifully ornamented garments in the rock carvings at Taq-i Bustan† remind that when "Dastajird was captured and sacked by Heraclius in 628 A.D., among the precious objects in the booty were various carpets...while some were embroidered with the needle...heavy with precious metal and elaborated with jewels."[10]

In the following centuries neighboring "Byzantine embroideries copied the ornate designs of Persia in rich colors, often enhanced with gold and silver threads and pearls...for many centuries they were considered superior."[11] With the Mongol invasion definite Chinese ele-

Verla Birrell,
The Textile Arts
p. 344

James Mellaart,
Catal Hüyük,

Birrell, *Above,* p. 344

Sergei I. Rudenko,
Frozen Tombs of Siberia
pp. 175–78, pl. 178

Eugenia Tolmachoff,
Bull., Needle and Bobbin
Vol. 26, no. 2, p. 53

L. Boulnois,
The Silk Road
p. 8

Ibid, p. 39

Alfred Salmony,
Bull., Needle and Bobbin
Vol. 26, no. 2, p. 5

Michael Sullivan,
Chinese Art: Recent Discoveries
pp. 24, 54; pls. 40-41

Above

Arthur Upham Pope,
Survey, p. 2274

Birrell, *Above,* p. 345

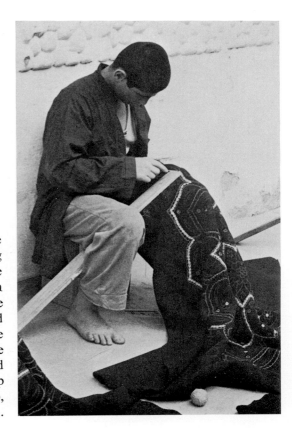

A full-scale design paper traced with pinholes is spread atop cloth. Powdered chalk is rubbed through the perforations, the paper pattern lifted off, and the lines connected with a white paint of chalk and water. (The same process employing either chalk or charcoal, is used in a variety of Iranian crafts.)

The embroiderer holds the cloth in place by pressing a long wood under one knee—the lower knee becoming the bottom part of the "vise" that holds the cloth. A wooden handled metal crochet hook pierces the cloth from above, pulling up the first loop. The next downward thrust within the first loop brings up the second loop, producing the chain stitch.

ments entered and although no Persian pieces of this period survive, Phyllis Ackerman has drawn upon the miniatures to give a good picture of the embroideries of that period.[12] Marco Polo in the thirteenth century visited Kerman and wrote of the embroidery.

Chardin, in his copious work on Safavid Iran, admires the fineness of the Persian embroidery which "exceeds" Europe's as well as that of the Turks "we so much admire," and all kinds of embroidery was found, especially gold and silver threads on textile and leather.

Phyllis Ackerman,
Survey, p. 2157

Sir John Chardin's
Travels in Persia,
p. 275

Phyllis Ackerman[13] carefully analyzes embroidery to have three distinct conceptions—one in which the foundation material is completely covered with stitches and seemingly "imitates" weaving cloth, creating a new background color and design. This is rarely seen in the cities, but characterizes Kurdish, Baluchi and Sangsari work today. Another is "like brocade" in that the foundation material lives and acts as a partner for whatever picture or design is worked onto it—it is the characteristic form of Persian embroidery and the one we begin with here. The third is "embroidery in its purest essence, the development to the utmost potentialities of fancy sewing," including drawn thread and cutwork, a European style done today in Isfahan.

Phyllis Ackerman,
Embroidery in Persia,
p. 1

Golab-duzi, the chain stitch, was employed in overall embroidery. Superbly done in Rasht, which supplied the Safavid court at Ardebil, this work came to be known as *Rashti-duzi*. It is characterized by its use of the foundation material (*mahout*) flannel wool, felted to appear like a fine grade of felt, embroidered in firmly twisted silk thread. The predominant background color is a red, almost scarlet. In older pieces, patchwork in bands of different colored materials frame the central motif;† appliqué work (*tikeh-duzi*) constituted various elements of the designs, i.e., different colors for petals of flowers, feathers of birds. The designs are elaborate and rich—*boteh*s in rows, beautiful floral sprays with birds in scrolling branches. Some older pieces have busts of women and men in medallions. This chain stitch is on velvet or leather saddle cloths, cushion covers, table covers, wall hangings, bed covers and garments. This has traditionally been men's work and still is.

RASHTI-DUZI
WALL HANGING
19th century
140×215 cm.
Detail, scale 1/6

Facing

There is a revival of this work in Rasht. The red table cover illustrated here shows the central medallion richly worked.† It was made for the Handicraft Organization's exhibition in 1975. The beige cushion cover was shown at the opening of the Center's salesroom in 1966.†

Overleaf lower
Overleaf upper

"The women and young persons work with the needle, in embroideries of silk and gold, in a variety of colors and patterns, representing birds and beasts, with other ornamental devices. These are designed for the curtains, coverlets and cushions of the sleeping places of the rich; and the work is executed with so much taste and skill as to be an object of admiration." —*Marco Polo*

PATEH-DUZI CURTAIN
Kerman, early 20th century
Gracefully interwining
Tree of Life

Above, 93 × 272 cm.
Facing, Detail
W. Inner panel 54 cm.

Preceding

Pateh-duzi or *selseleh-duzi* of Kerman is quite distinctive. The embroidery is done on both fine and coarse handwoven fabrics. The thread is usually of fine wool, with which silk is sometimes combined. The finer embroideries were used for *korsi* covers, coverlets, women's veils (*chador*), borders on men's robes (*aba*), small table covers, etc. The stitches used are mainly stem stitch, darning stitch and the running stitch which forms the trademark of this embroidery—a row of small squares or boxes outlining the motifs. The patterns consist generally of a central medallion and a special design such as the *boteh* in each of the four corners. The piece is framed with bands of designs, the outer border being completely filled with stitches—flowers or infinite variations of small *boteh*s.† In some pieces flowers, leaves and *boteh*s are scattered over the background. There is flow and motion bounded by an organized pattern. The effect of the overall color scheme is usually very warm. Sometimes the smaller covers are quilted (*pambeh-duzi*) in a simple running stitch in spaced rows and have a four-to-five centimeter edging or a bias-cut handwoven, striped wool *termeh* border on the back that slightly overlaps onto the front edge, a typical feature of lined or quilted pieces.

The coarser work was used for curtains, usually made in pairs or multiples measuring 93 centimeters wide and 272 centimeters long.† The background is wool in twill weave with embroidery in woolen yarn. The sparkling bright blue highlights this typical curtain.

In recent years, there has been a revival of this work in Kerman and there are about six or seven cooperatives. The embroidered table cover (1.5 × 1.5 m.) in white twill weave was exhibited at the Handicraft Exhibition held in Mashhad, July, 1976, and made by Battool Iranmanesh, who belongs to a cooperative with about 150 members. The peacock blue embroidered cushion cover was exhibited at the inaugural opening of the Handicraft Center in September, 1966. At that time there were also many *pateh-duzi* embroidered panels for dresses and jackets.

A special type of work used for dervish caps should be mentioned here. Made in Māhan, Kerman, center of a dervish community, it is a quilted piece of work (*pambeh-duzi*) and stitched with fine parallel lines creating raised, *barjesteh,* patterns. This work is called *ajideh.*†

Facing

Ajideh

222

223

Bokhara work, reminiscent of Pazyryk motifs

Old *naksh* made up into handbag

Isfahan in the sixteenth century under Shah Tahmasp (1526–76, A.H. 930–84) reached a period of great refinement in the decorative arts, followed by a long period of opulence under Shah Abbas (1587–1628). References to the clothing and furnishings of that period reflect richness and elegance. At this time, different types of overall embroidery now not done— *musaif, naksh,* and *landareh-duzi*—were popular.[14] *Musaif,* characterized by pastel tones, employed a darning stitch in overall geometric patterns usually outlined in black stem stitch. Similar work is found in the Caucasus type to the northwest with the characteristic geometric designs of their carpets in bold colors, while the "Bokhara" to the northeast had its large abstracted floral motifs worked in long float, diagonally couched in predominant colors of wine red and dark, almost black indigo, recalling Pazyryk patterns.† All of these had variations in which certain small areas of the foundation material were exposed, giving relief to the heavy pattern. The *naksh* or *zileh,†* used for women's trousering through the nineteenth century, were embroidered in diagonal parallel bands, using tent stitch, a short slanting stitch with each stitch crossing diagonally an interesection of the foundation. Fine work used silk threads on a cotton foundation, occasionally wool. Besides the main centers of Isfahan and Yazd, this was made in Shiraz and Kashan. Colors were mainly green on beige background, soft blues and oranges.

During the Safavid period it was not uncommon to find pieces fully covered with *golab-duzi,* the chain stitch previously discussed under *Rashti-duzi.* In the older Isfahan patchwork, *landareh-duzi,* pieces of cloth of various shapes and colors are joined together in a patchwork mosaic, not appliqué like *Rashti-duzi.* Chardin keenly observes that the "patchwork" sewing was done so neatly that the figures appeared to be painted not sewn.

Golab-duzi is effectively and skillfully used to bring out a third dimension in the animals and people in the door hanging illustrating the story of Joseph.† Three inscriptions describe three of the twelve main episodes in his life. "*Farzandan-i Ya'aqub*" (Sons of Jacob) shows the ten older brothers beating Joseph while the younger looks on. The second "*Yusef va Zoleikha*" (Joseph and Zoleika) is an episode not in the Judaeo-Christian version in which the master's wife Zoleika, to prove to the other women the beauty of Joseph, calls him into the harem where several of the women peeling apples lose control of themselves and cut their fingers. This is the most popular art motif from the story of Joseph and will be found again on page 189 where nine episodes of the twelve are illustrated. It is often seen in tiles. The bottom inscription "*Forukhtan Yusef*" (Selling to Yusef) shows Joseph selling food during the famine to his brothers in exchange for his younger brother.

Today most of this work is done by housewives in their homes. The ever-popular camel, people in old costumes,† cats and flowers† are worked onto cotton, linen or a linenlike synthetic fabric. A revival of embroidery on shirts and blouses† in inexpensive coarse muslin—floral and pictorial for women, geometric and pictorial for men—has brought about a profusion of colorful, freely executed designs.

Victoria and Albert Museum, *Guide to Persian Embroideries*

Above

Above

Preceding

GOLAB-DUZI, 1976
Upper, Linen mat, 40×50 c
Left, Shirt, unbleached mus
synthetic yarn
Right, Linen mat, 45×47 c

Facing

Facing

226

SOKMEH-DUZI, LAMPSHADE, COTTON, ISFAHAN, 1976   H. Motif, 20 cm., Overall 40 ×140 cm.

In contrast to the carefree work of the blouses, the drawn work (*sokmeh-duzi*) is patiently and painstakingly worked in fine linen tablecloths, napkins, lampshades and doilies.

Sokmeh-duzi or drawn work involves drawing out certain weft and/or warp threads in a given area. After drawing the required number of threads, embroidery stitches are taken to fill the open spaces thus created with lacy-looking embroidery which at the same time binds the loosened warps and wefts into a definite pattern. The junction where the threads are cut is carefully "held" by various stitches—in those illustrated here, by rows of closely worked fine chain stitching. Supplementary interlacing embroidery brings out the star pattern in the cut-out area. The upper panels in linenlike fabric are for lampshades,† while the lower is a table mat.†   *Facing*

Golab-duzi is done on frame with *golab* hook. The thread, held underneath the frame, is pulled up to form the chain stitch.

228

SOKMEH-DUZI
Above, LAMPSHADE, COTTON, ISFAHAN
    1976   H. Motif, 20 cm. Overall 40×140 cm.
Below, TABLE MAT, COTTON, ISFAHAN
    1976   D. 46 cm.

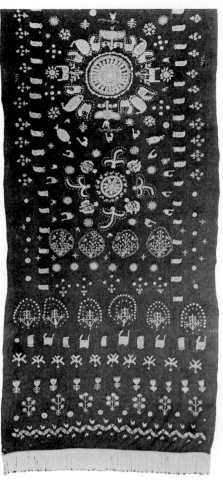

Family in traditional costume, photo taken forty-odd years ago.
In the surrounding villages, these garments are still seen; while for
big weddings, treasured garments are brought out for the bride.

MAQNA-EH,
BRIDAL SHAWL
19th century, 94×329
Above, General
Facing, Detail, H. 54

Overleaf
ZOROASTRIAN
WORK
Late 19th century
DETAIL:
Upper, Tie-dye,
embroidery on shirt
Lower, Trouser panels,
shiluneh stitch, right

Tehran Women's Assn.
Negar-e Zan

Facing

Overleaf

232

Yazd and the area around it has been the center of the surviving Zoroastrian community since its general demise elsewhere in the early centuries of Islam. Secure in the comfort of its traditions, it has held out against waves of foreign invasions. From archaeology and such friezes as Taq-i Bustan which obviously included embroideries, we know of the great love the Zoroastrian Sasanian dynasty had for fine textiles, how they influenced the court weaves from Europe to China and Japan. On the popular level, the ordinary folk have continued this love of fine fabrics and a major element in a Zoroastrian girl's dowry has been her skill with the needle. As with most isolated ethnic groups, they are conservative and have kept their traditional costume. Even today, for weddings, the brides will be dressed in traditional finery. Formerly, "soon after the birth of a daughter, the child's wedding dress was started. It required years of patient, painstaking work to complete the intricate embroidery that made the wedding dress a work of art.... Over the head, a small triangle of woven cloth called a *lachak* was worn. Over this was draped the *maqna-eh,* a long shawl, about a meter wide and three meters in length."[15] Pictured here is a detail of the center motif of one in fine black wool with the embroidery in silk.†

Much work went into the embroidered panels that were combined with silk brocades and tie-and-dye panels in the dresses and shirts†—panels beautifully joined with finely couched cord. Motifs include stylized trees, animals, birds, peacocks, flowers and geometric designs in stem stitch, overcast stitch and the characteristic fine cross and interlacing stitch, *shiluneh.*†

The bottom portion (about 50 to 60 cm.) of the trousers† is composed of narrow strips of different colored fabrics—sometimes all silk with delicate embroidered floral patterns, so fine that a magnifying glass is required to see the stitches, alternating with different colored silks or with gaily colored floral prints imported from Russia. Each trouser leg panel, measuring about 130 centimeters long and backed with coarse cotton at times woodblock printed, is tightly gathered at the ankle giving a balloon effect.

QASHGAI DRAWSTRING BAG
Recent   D. 32 cm.

BAKHTIARI TALISMANS
Recent   D. Large, 20 cm.

238

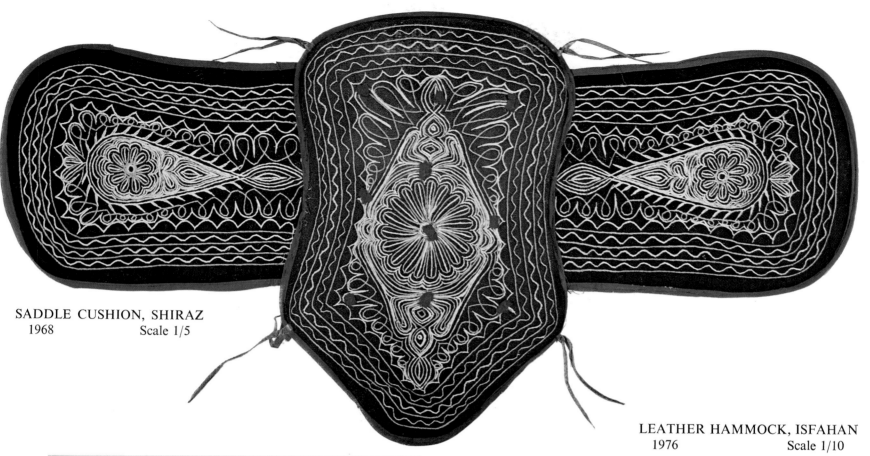

SADDLE CUSHION, SHIRAZ
1968   Scale 1/5

LEATHER HAMMOCK, ISFAHAN
1976   Scale 1/10

239

KURDISH EMBROIDERY, MAMAQAN

Preceding
PUTTEES, Scale 1/2

Above right
WALL HANGING
1967   H. 41.5 cm.
Above left
TABLE MAT
1966   H. 60 cm.

The Kurds are a partially settled, partially seminomadic people of Iranian stock speaking an Iranian language related to Persian but linguistically an older form, less evolved. This, along with their notable inbred cohesiveness, would indicate that they are the direct descendants of some of the earliest Iranian migrations onto the plateau. They have the world's oldest tradition of family names going back to the time of the first Achaemenid kings 2,500 years ago. This is unlike most Iranians for whom an inherited family name—as opposed to a personal name as individual title, like Omar the Tentmaker (Khayyam)—is a recent innovation. Kurdistan as a linguistic-cultural sphere overlaps into Iraq and Turkey and there are Kurds in Russia. Within Iran there are scattered settlements established by various shahs to stabilize the country or the Kurds. The Kurdish cohesiveness has as its root a fierce and unbreakable loyalty, which they have transferred to the various shahs who have treated them with dignity. Thus there are Kurds, retaining their individuality, in areas which have at one time or another been the outposts against invasion: in Azarbaijan, in Khurasan and the gates to seething Central Asia. Their mixed history is evident in their religion—most are Sunni Muslims, like the Muslims bordering Iran on all sides. But some are Jewish (as are some Lurs). They have been horsemen and craftsmen from time immemorial. Perhaps more than most nomads, they have given outlet to personal individuality in their arts and crafts. The *golab-duzi* embroidery covering in the centerfold† is in overall chain stitch in fine wool in traditional Kurdi coloration of russet brown, on a soft Kurdish herringbone weave wool ground. The border elements identify it as Kurd. But the people and animals are virtually taken from paleolithic petrogylphs.

Facing
MAMAQAN HATS
PLACEMATS,
BELTS
1976

Overleaf

241   Puttees† worn by Kurdish men (16×75 cm.) have one end embroidered in a miniature carpet design in stem, darning, chain and couching stitches in bright yellow, purple, wine, green, and black silk threads. Material is cotton grosgrain weave, fine old ones in silk. Illustrated: one 80-years old (upper left), 40–50 years old (upper right) and two recent ones. Now being used on handbags and other accessories.

The brightly colored hats worn under the turbans were the sole article made in Mamaqan, Azarbaijan, in this technique until nine years ago. Inverting the hats to adapt them as purses brought new wider popularity and many new adaptations from wall hangings to costume appliqué. The making of full jackets and skirts followed. Colorful embroidery with sprays of flowers and leaves framed by *boteh*s, sunbursts, circles and geometrics cover the wall hangings. The embroidery is usually worked on a layer of black cotton backed with old cotton prints, sometimes starched for stiffness, mostly in darning, couching and closed fishbone stitches, stem stitch and edged with a close black buttonhole stitch. Colors are distinctive, bright warm reds, oranges, yellows, green, white, and purple with black detailing in shiny loosely twisted silk or rayon threads.

The large cities in Iran, as all the world, inevitably tend toward uniformity. In provincial areas, traditions die harder and a certain demand for traditional crafts still encourages supply. The craftsman can still find his identity, for his creations are steeped in traditions with tremendous potential for further development. But he hesitates and wonders if he can or should continue—threatened by machines that make work easier, the costliness of raw materials (cotton, silks, etc.) and the availability of cheap synthetics. The lure of city life invades his environment with the prospect of better paid jobs and marvelous opportunities for his children to go to school and aspire to a more sophisticated existence.

244

**KURDISH
EMBROIDERY**

FLOOR COVERING?
Overall chain stitch
Wool on wool,
Recent?   161×256 cm.

245

Sangsar is a lush green village in hills covered with juniper forests north of Semnan. The Sangsaris are a pastoral people. They travel widely seeking pasture, to Bandar Shah, Bomishan, Gurgan, Gonbad-i Qabus where settlements of Sangsaris produce fine gilims and woolen covers. One of the finest of their handicrafts is the head scarf, *mekoneh,* of their women. It is made of handwoven raw silk, plum or red colored, in long rectangles three meters long with embroidery motifs influenced by gilims.† Rows of chevrons of small squares cover large panels, interrupted by bands of stylized flowers and leaves and geometric forms, finished off by a narrow embroidered band. The only stitch used is a fine cross stitch done with white, black, green, orange, blue, purple, and dull yellow silks. Dating: twenty-plus years ago.

Facing

This head scarf is worn with a silver ornament call *changak,* a belt made up of fine chains with medallions of silver filigree, hooked to the scarf at each side of the head, passing under the chin.

The Kāzakh or Bilish live in small communities around Gurgan (60 families), Gombad Qabus (40), Bandar Shah (250), and Pahlavi Dej (10). They came from Kazakhstan between 1918 to 1923. The women embroider the cuffs of their trousers and sleeves, the neck and front opening of the bodice,† the hem of the skirt and scattered designs on the dress. All are now often embroidered with the sewing machine. However, the big square head scarves† are hand embroidered in solid blocks at the corners, with a central motif in a large satin stitch in predominantly plum-colored cotton thread punctuated with green, orange, yellow, red and blue details. In the geometric motifs, a form of meander seems most popular, solidly embroidered. The fabric is heavy white cotton. Recently, the author took a twenty-year-old red silk shirt† with fine embroidery neckline for further ornamentation at cuffs and side slits, and exactly the same embroidery was executed, hardly distinguishable from the original work.

Overleaf
Overleaf

Overleaf

The Turkomans cover eastern Mazanderan and northern Khurasan in Iran and straddle the borders into the Turkmenistan S.S.R. and northwestern Afghanistan. The Turkoman woman or girl, like her sisters in other regions of Iran, has a magnificent costume, painstakingly and lovingly embroidered. Nowadays, these priceless embroideries are worn mostly on weddings and religious feast days, for time should be more profitably used making marketable carpets. However, the Turkoman woman still takes pride in using her creative skills to enrich her life.

The embroidery,[16] extremely rich and intricate, has a tremendous impact. All the tribes embroider the lower portion of the trouser legs, although more simply than in the past.

Mugul and Peter Andrews,
Turkoman Needlework

249

The robe† with false sleeves, worn with the left armhole draped over the headdress, has traditionally been the main recipient of the finest embroidery and was once totally covered. Today the Tekke tribe still continues this traditional embroidery, if in a simpler form, with each young girl preparing a red and black robe for her trousseau. Now only wide panels of embroidery adorn the neck, front openings, side slits, hem and sleeves of the robe. Geometric repeat patterns and motifs reminiscent of flowers and leaves radiate from the side slits. The shape of the token sleeve has changed too, and now is a sleeve, though still never worn as such.

During the summer of 1975, in the village of Dashtak, in the plain of Jolgeh Ma'neh, a Turkoman woman sat embroidering her robe with but few guidelines. Since the embroidery is done in organized compartments, the embroideress only bastes a few rows of the lines to confine the various motifs, and then without so much as a pattern, commences building up her embroidery in intricate designs memorized at her mother's knee.

SHAWL,
CROSS STITCH
SANGSAR
On plum silk, two panels
1955   50×326 cm. (full)

The embroidery of the trouser cuffs and robes is stitched through a double thickness of silk lined with cotton fabric in a single or double plaited stitch to form ridges, a chain stitch, a sort of closed feather stitch and a stem stitch. Colored silk threads are used, with red, black, green, white, and orange for the trousering. The robes are embroidered in repeat geometric patterns in red, black, yellow and white with a kind of open herringbone stitch at the seams.

247

Baluchistan embroidery on garments of Piip (*left*) and Gosht (*right*) on orange background with red, black, white and green

The main stitches are: *sarāfl,* a large double back stitch;
    zarif-duzi, a double braid stitch forming ridges, an eyelet hole stitch, a running stitch, a geometric satin stitch at time forming a chevron design;
    perivār-duzi,† a fine interlacing stitch used often for trouser cuffs and head veils;
    Baluchi-duzi, small blocks of satin stitch forming a geometric shape; *Joak stitch.*

    The patterns are compartmentalized and are mostly geometric. The colors are gay: bright orange and red predominate with details in green, maroon, blue, white and black. Some mirror work is used held down by a buttonhole stitch in the village of Piip† and Davarpanah. The bodice opening and neck have a special finishing touch usually done with cotton thread.

    Other items embroidered are Qur'an covers, kohl containers, the ends of cotton belts for men's trousers. These latter are decorated with colorful couched cord joined to form a net or fillet and edged with pompoms.† Such net made up as pouches is also used to hold dishes as a charming decoration for the walls.

    Sekeh-duzi should also be mentioned here. Although not embroidery it does involve sewing. These are long rectangular pieces (about 3 meters) concealing the stacks of bedding in the corner of the room. They are made up of different colored fabrics joined and decorated with mirror work and a multitude of white shirt buttons. These pieces are edged with six-tiered wool pompoms with lots of shells sewn on and are lined with felt. The same decorations are used for the trappings of camels,† and newly designed bags.†

    The fans† of Bampur are of stiff crochet lace, edged with colored fabric scraps and decorated with plastic beads of gold and turquoise. The handle, a long hollow cane filled with grains, acts as a musical rattle while waving the flies off baby, is decorated with bits of colored fabric.

    Baluchistan is the southeastern corner of Iran and there is naturally an affinity in the culture of this area with that of the neighboring region of Baluchistan in Pakistan.

256

Above

255

BALUCHI WORK
Embroidered panels for
blouse back, sleeve and
left bodice

254
255

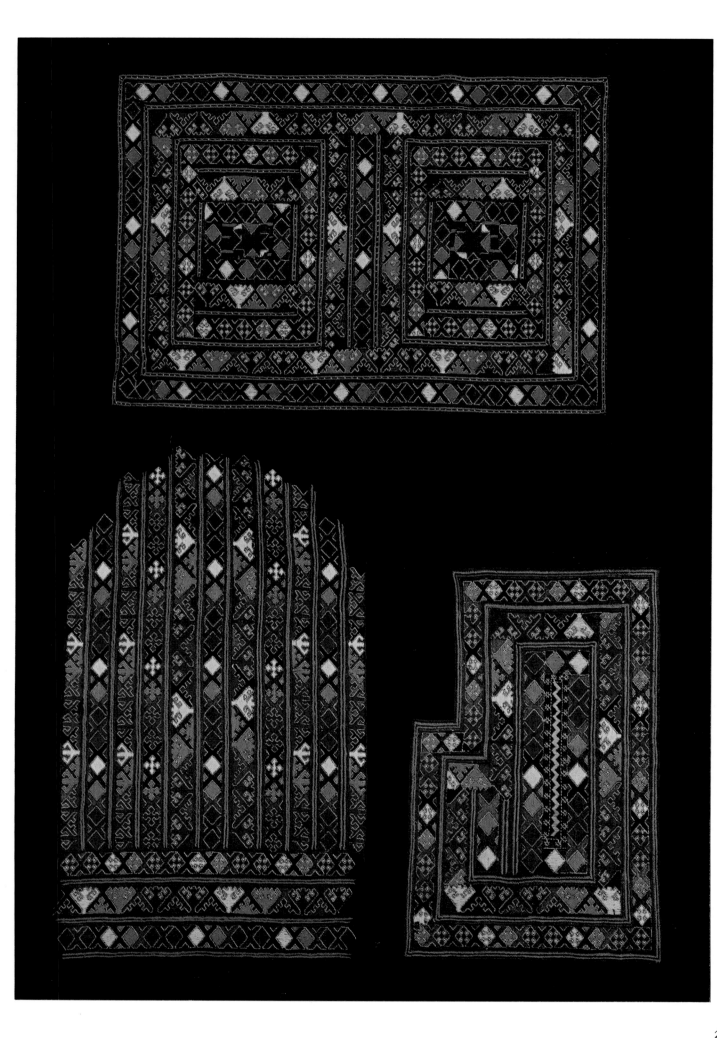

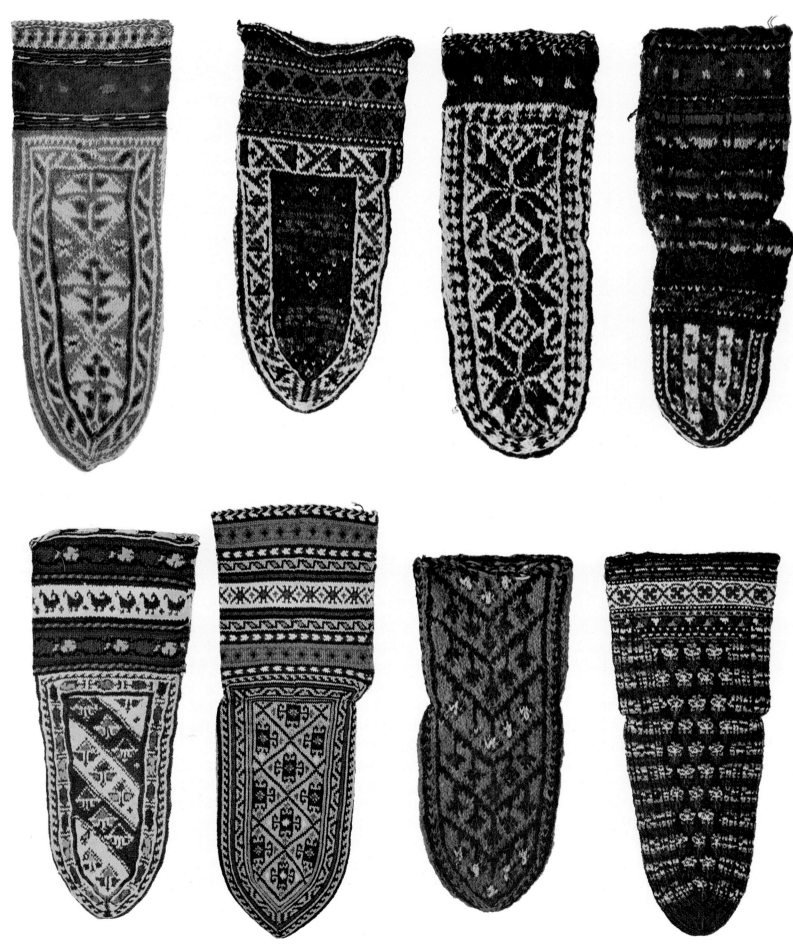

HAND KNIT SOX, wool and silk yarn

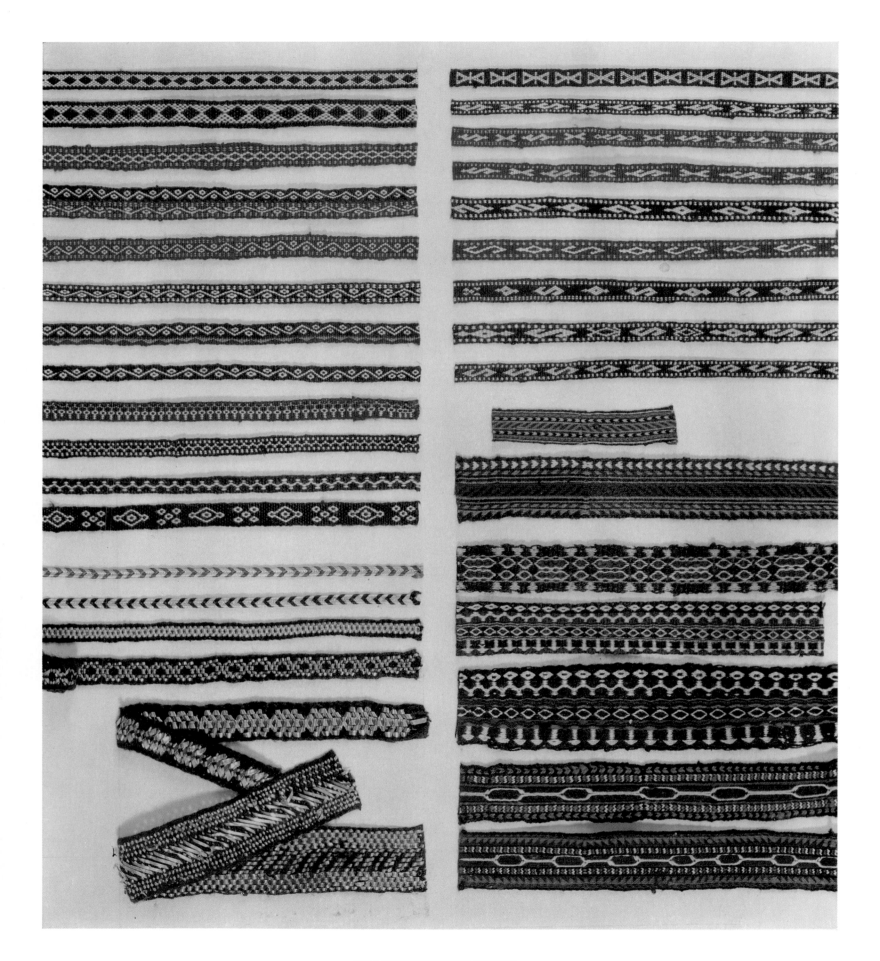

HANDWOVEN EDGINGS

Top of both columns, Qoleh Zoh and Zovin. *Lower left*, Metallic braids from Bandar Abbas; *Right*, Ferdows and Guchan.

WALL PANEL EMBROIDERY, TEHRAN, 1960   *Above,* Entire panel in satin stitch, 72 × 200 cm.
Left (detail), Reverse presents impressionistic work. *Right* (detail), Charming angel in modern garb.

These embroideries constitute part of the foundation of handicrafts upon which we must base our efforts to sustain our cultural heritage. This heritage must be preserved and respected to consolidate our future. First let us try to renew the pride and respect of the craftsman for his profession and encourage him to continue using his innate good taste, his sense of harmony and his sense of colors—for he is a true artist.

We must only offer guidelines and create better opportunities for marketing genuine handicrafts oriented to modern life yet having continuity with the past. Any change must be natural and within the context of the craftsman's tradition.   —IRAN ALA FIROUZ

Reed boat at foot of Kuh-i Kwaja, Seistan

Hut, cane basket construction
roofed and floored with reed mat
Baluchistan

BASKETRY

BASKETRY is probably man's first handicraft, universally made by all peoples in all climes no matter how primitive their technological level and known archaeologically from imprints of woven reed mats from Çatal Hüyük in Anatolia and Jarmo in Iraq in the sixth millennium and in Iran itself from the imprint of such a *hasir* found at Shahdad† datable to the early third millennium. Actual carbonized basket remains are known from sites of more primitive societies in the Americas, dated to 7000 B.C., and even today some of the most technically advanced and beautiful work is done by people at the lowest technological levels. And as no satisfactory basket-weaving machinery has been perfected, it remains solely a handicraft.

270

Baskets are made in two ways, by plaiting or by coiling. Plaiting is the crossing of two or more elements and resembles weaving, except that neither warp nor wefts are held rigid in any way. Weaving nomenclature is used because of this resemblance, but where the elements are indistinguishable by direction or rigidity, both are called weft. Coiling is building a basket with a single element only, from a center in coils, the layers of which are sewn together. Both types are widespread in Iran, where the materials include reeds, bamboo, rushes, canes, grasses, kanaf, date palm fronds and the stalks of rice, wheat and maize and, for such as strainers, even leather strips.

BASKETRY, RASHT BAZAAR

HASIR MAT, twisted kanaf on cotton warp, W. 65 cm. COVERED BASKET, twilled, D. 40 cm.

BASKET TRAY
Wheat straw
Lazy squaw coiled
Kazerun, Fars D. 47 cm.
Kurashiki Folk Art Mus.
Preceding
Preceding

Overleaf
COVERED BASKET
Swamp rush
Simple coil H. 39 cm.
Minab
Preceding

Above, 269
BASKETRY, MINAB
Hasir W. 75 cm.
HANDLED TRAY
Swamp rush
Simple coil
W. 27 cm.
ROUND TRAY
Reed skins twilled twos
D. 46 cm.

All sorts of carryalls and storage containers are made. The reed boats† of Seistan and the cane- and mat-covered huts† of Baluchistan are in effect basketry.

The *hasir* is a reed weft on a cotton thread warp. The simple loom in Iran today is identical to that shown on the murals of Beni Hasan, Egypt, of 2000 B.C. We may assume the looms of Shahdad, Jarmo and Çatal Hüyük were no different.

The *hasir* mats are used all over Iran—in architecture as a roofing material over the log structure to hold the mud roofs, as flooring in poorer homes or under carpets, and as wall and roof in temporary architecture such as the huts of Baluch nomads.† They are made in many places in Iran, but Mazanderan produces notably thick and pliable kanaf *hasir* with raised patterns,† and Minab on the Persian Gulf offers *hasir* made of rush with colored stripes.† The industry of Seistan-Baluchistan is on record as exporting fine *hasir* since medieval times, some of the material for which they imported from Mesopotamia.

The plaited basketry of various areas usually has a discernible characteristic, usually dictated by the material. The baskets of the Caspian littoral use hemp (kanaf) and similar grasses and are distinguished by their pliability, almost like burlap. In Tehran a basket tradition continues in busy urban Tajrish where attractive baskets, both plaited and coiled, add color to the bazaar.

268

Nomads working a horizontal or ground loom. Photo Pope, 1926

RUSTIC FLOOR COVERING

THE craft of fabric weaving for floor coverings must have begun at an early date and probably in many places at the same time, but how, where, and when must, perhaps always, be a matter for speculation. The need was urgent, nor was it only for floor coverings. Heavy fabrics were required for bedding and in general to give warmth and ease in many situations for which bare matting did not suffice. The fleece and pelts of animals would have provided models, but the supply of these, in the earliest periods a by-product of the hunt, was of necessity precarious, and the hides improperly cured must soon have disintegrated. Thus there was a pressing motive for inventing artificial substitutes. The first logical step would be to replace the perishable pelt and for this the matting would serve. Such mats with bits of bright wool interwoven are to be found even to this day among the Qirghiz tribes. Also apparently a pelt substitute is the Uzbek *dschulchit* or "bear skin," the most archaic form of pile carpet woven. It uses a variant of the Turkish knot, knotting only the upper warp thread while the lower one is woven into the weft: thus the pattern does not appear on the back. The long pile threads are cut with a knife. The carpet is woven in narrow strips then joined together.

The conditions of nomadic life especially favored the development of carpet weaving. For to the wandering tribes of Central and Hither Asia, the rug or carpet was a utility of prime importance, simultaneously serving a great variety of indispensable uses. It was door curtain or floor covering for the tent, bed and blanket at once, saddle, saddlecloth, and bag, and general carryall. It was unbreakable and durable and easily packed for transportation. It was in many ways economical: the materials for making ready at hand, the skill indigenous. It was in itself a ready depository of primitive wealth and could be sold, bartered, or exchanged almost anywhere in the nomads' world; and finally, it was one of the few objects of beauty the nomad might hope to possess.

On the making of rugs, the nomads have, these many centuries, as they still do, concentrated what they had of artistic capacity, and it was not inconsiderable. Their life, simple, intense, effective, disciplined by the most rigorous necessities, favored sound and practical work. Although historical details are wanting, it is certain that nomadic peoples made important contributions to rug weaving technique, if they did not in fact invent the art. Moreover, the individual motifs, and the patterns and color schemes frequently attained a degree of merit that has been insufficiently appreciated. In the nature of the case the development of knotted rug weaving among the primitive nomads must have been very gradual, and their contribution to the art as practised by settled and urban peoples must have been just as gradual, but certain and fundamental despite our lack of knowledge as to when and how it occurred.

We assume that the woven reeds are the oldest form of woven floor covering.† The oldest examples are from Çatal Hüyük, 6000 B.C. In Iran a hardened earth imprint, a fossil, of a *hasir* was recently excavated at Shahdad in Kerman datable to about 2700 B.C.† Nearby Sirjand was still famous throughout Persia in the Middle Ages for its *hasir*. Of woolen weaving, old examples exist on the borders of modern Iran. At Çatal Hüyük in eastern Anatolia on the high plateau, archeologists have revealed on the 6000 B.C. level a wrapped twine soumak "of excellent quality displaying a complete and confident command of the necessary textile crafts." The same soumak weave is still the characteristic product of neighboring Iranian Azarbaijan. Also at the 6000 B.C. level are wall paintings showing geometric patterns common to the simplest gilims. At the 5700 B.C. level, remains of actual gilims emerge. By 1500 B.C. the basic slit tapestry technique is fully developed in Egypt. The first pictorial representation of a carpet—we cannot tell if the original was gilim or tufted—is carved on Assyrian threshold stones. The best example, from Khorsabad, now in the Louvre, has a pattern of repeating quatrefoils in center, guard stripes and a lotus border similar to modern Kurdish rugs.

266, 269

270

297

Both Athenaeus and Xenophon refer to a special kind of carpet, *psilotapis*, for the Persian king's exclusive use, "spread under the couch so that the floor should not offer hard resistance that the carpet might yield." Experts disagree whether this was pile or namad.

Arrian described the tomb of Cyrus the Great as seen by Alexander to have had, "carpets underneath of the finest wrought purple." About this time in Siberia, beyond the marches of the Achaemenid Empire, one of the outer Iranian tribes, the Scyths, were herding and marauding in a free style of life still seen among the Turkomans and Lurs until order was restored by Reza Shah in the late 1920s, one which Aurel Stein experienced among the Qashgai in Fars just prior to World War II. The Scyths accumulated and created great wealth, which they tried to take with them in their great tombs. Fortunately for us the great burial grounds had been permanently frozen for thousands of years and excavators have brought back to the pleasures of this world a magnificent pile carpet with a design that could have come straight off the reliefs of Persepolis. There were also many rich felts. The carpet from Pazyryk also reminds us of the account of Ptolemy II "Philadelphus," (285–246 B.C.) who "had the floor spread with Persian carpets ornamented with animals." As we know from today's nomadic weavings, the pile and gilim were not restricted to floor coverings, but among the common people of the tribes and villages are used even more plentifully for saddle furniture and bags of all sorts, from pocket purses to immense double sack camel bags. In antiquity it was no different, and we have numerous representations of saddle cloth in Persia from tomb figurines of horses from the early first millennium B.C.† A sarcophagus from Sidon shows a Persian hunter's saddlecloth in red and worked with confronted lion griffons.

312

Greek sources tell us of sumptuously gold-threaded carpets among the Persians and the Avesta refers to floor coverings enriched with gold. At Noin-ula a box of carpet scraps in a "fine lustrous wool principally dark blue…very thick and dense, the knot loops having been compacted as firmly as in the best modern rugs," was found with a date equivalent to A.D. 3 on it. Gilims were also found here. In Outer Iran, in an area of the U.S.S.R. where Persian is still spoken, gilims of the Parthian period were found in the Tarim Basin by Aurel Stein and many Coptic textiles of fourth century Egypt are gilim weave in Partho-Sasanian motif.

GILIM, TURKOMAN
Sanduq Ortman, Yamut
Cotton warp, wool weft
116×229 cm.

The throne pavillion of Khosrau II, the Takht-i Taqdis, is described as having thirty different carpets, one for each day of the month. These were probably enriched and embroidered gilims. When Dastajird was sacked by Heraclius in 628 the booty records many "soft" and "fleecy" carpets and the Byzantine Greek word for their own rug weaver is derived from the Iranian. Perhaps the greatest carpet ever was in the audience hall of Ctesiphon, the great Winter Carpet, almost 26 meters wide. This was enriched with jewels much in the style of a bejeweled silk pile saddle cover which was an appurtenance to the Iranian throne in the nineteenth century. The great carpet represented a beautiful pleasure garden with running brooks and adorned with trees and spring flowers. The wide border represented planted flower beds in many bold colors. The description in general, excepting the opulence of its detail, could apply to many weaves of today, such as the Khamseh soumak† or the Qashgai pile illustrated.† The "interlacing plants" are repeated today in the checkerboard Bakhtiari garden carpet.† An eighth-century Sasanian silver plate shows Bahram Gur enthroned upon what may be a section of this carpet.†

297, 309

325

326

Survey, Pl. 208A

The first Arab invaders in the eighth century treated such luxury with disdain, but almost immediately they took to this symbol of luxury with the same fervor that summer vacationing Arab sheikhs from the Persian Gulf states show in the carpet bazaar of Shiraz today. In the Qur'an true believers who reach heaven, "Will delight themselves lying on green cushions and beautiful carpets." For the next few hundred years we have only literary archaeology from Arab and Chinese sources to indicate the state of art. The Persian word for pile carpet, *qali* is said to derive from the Armenian carpet-making town, Qaliqala, where carpets were made. But Persia was already developing a large industry in almost every province, and the early Arab geographers have left a good deal of information concerning the places of manufacture and the general trade, even if they are tantalizingly silent or brief concerning the character of the carpets themselves.

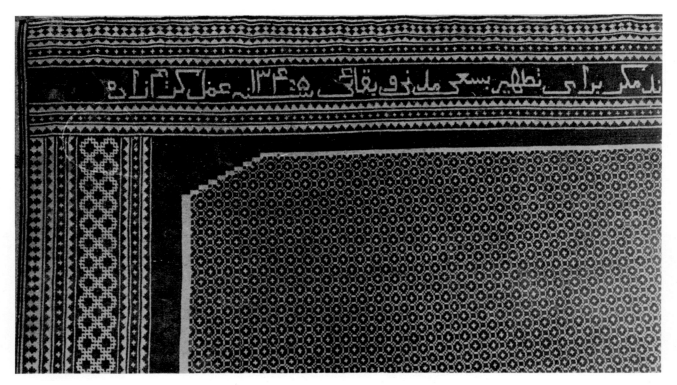

Zilu, flat-woven
Mosque carpet
Masjed-i Jami'
Nain

Above

By the tenth century there was evidently a large production in Azarbaijan, and the industry may have been connected with that of Armenia, for one of the towns that produced both *zilu* and prayer carpets was called Vartan, an Armenian name. *Zilu* carpets were also produced in large quantities in Khoy, Bargri, Arjij, Akhlat, Nakhichevan, and Bidlis. The term '*zilu*' is used today to describe a flat-stitch carpet made principally for the·mosques.†
The contemporary examples are usually blue and white and have Kufic inscriptions in the border. Muqan on the Caspian shore produced madder dye and *palas* rugs in great numbers. 'Palas' means a coarse woolen fabric. Fine rugs have come from Muqan down to the present day and the commonest border design of these modern Muqan rugs is the ancient Achaemenid-style rosette.

Finally from the late fifteenth century there remains a rich store of actual carpets, mostly pile. These have been discussed and illustrated in numerous books, not the least being the SURVEY, Vol. VI text and its companion volume of 168 plates, a fourth of which are in color. These are the great high school carpets made by the best weavers for palace and mosque clientele. These are not handicraft or folk art. The poorer pieces must rank as some of the finest industrial art, and finer ones are certainly amongst the greatest art ever produced by the heart and hand of man.

Certainly the nomads and villagers through all of this time were producing pile carpets and gilim for their own personal use. For the nomads the carpet is the ultimate portable prefabricated floor, and for the villager a necessary insulation on the hard packed earthen floor. Many ancient travelers recount how at festival times carpets were hung in homes and in gardens and in public places, a custom which persists today in villages and nomad camps.

The Persian wool is ideally suited because of its hardness and shine for carpet weaving. The gilim weave in these wools is amazingly hard wearing and the soumak and pile even more so, so that the purely utilitarian articles such as saddle bags will be made in gilim or soumak and the edges and corners which receive the most wear are often enforced in a lush almost everlasting pile.

The designs continue the same ideas expressed in the carpet of Pazyryk and the representations of Khorsabad of 2,500 years ago: Abstract renditions of paradise gardens to sit on in one's main room amid the brown earth of desert encampment or khaki mud village.

[*with additions]

—ARTHUR UPHAM POPE*

276

Laying design outline strips

NAMAD
FELT MATS

According to a folktale of the namad makers of Semnan and Mazanderan, the son of Hazrat Suleiman (King Solomon) was a shepherd who had long attempted to use his sheep's wool to make a fabric. After repeated failures he gave up, and beating the wool in frustration wept bitter tears—which ran into the pile of floss and felted it together. He realized that wetting the wool and rubbing it had formed a fabric. Thus the first namad was created and his memory lives on today as the patron saint of namad makers in northern Iran.

Such a creation myth supports the thesis that felt making is the oldest cloth making process. Chinese records of 2300 B.C. refer to mats, armor and shields of felt.[1] Sir Aurel Stein excavated at Lou Lan a tablet listing items of trade between India and other countries and one entry is "*namadis.*" The kurgans excavated at Pazyryk in Central Asia revealed in their artifacts frozen in the ground since Achaemenid times the wide usage of felts as wall hangings, rugs, horse blankets and with beautifully sculptured decorative felts of flying geese of remarkable technique.[2] The richly colored appliqué felts of lion heads and other designs, as well as the knotted carpets showing traditional Persian designs (which continue today on artifacts illustrated elsewhere in this volume) indicate that these felts were of Iranian origin.[3] Namads are made by most of the nomadic peoples as far east as Mongolia and the Korean border. The oldest extant namad rugs are in the Shosoin Imperial Repository in Nara, Japan, antedating 752 A.D. They were imported trade-cum-tribute goods. Pope cites Ibn-Hawqal on the fine quality of felt rugs of the tenth to twelfth centuries from the Fars towns of Jahram, Qurqub and Basinna and that excellent ones were made in Kerman.[4]

As we see from the creation tale, a namad requires no loom or machine for its production. It relies upon two properties of wool, crimp and scaliness, to hold its fibers together. In the presence of moist heat wool will crimp, its fibers interlace and its scales prevent its fibers from slipping. The result is warm, durable, relatively inexpensive, practical, often attractive and, if so treated at the beginning, waterproof. Tribal hats,† including the different and distinctive ones worn by the Qashgai and Bakhtiari, shepherds' cloaks and outer and inner linings for tents are among the practical namad items, but its most widespread use is as a floor covering, and "namad," which means felt, commonly signifies "felt floor covering." These namads are used in both houses and tents, particularly by those who cannot afford all-knotted carpets or woven gilims. For, although the wool in a namad may weigh as much or

Hans E. Wulff, *Traditional Handicrafts of Iran*, p. 222

Sergei I. Rudenko
Frozen Tombs of Siberia, passim
R. D. Barnett
Survey, p. 3507

Arthur Upham Pope
Survey, p. 2279

280

Left, The face of the design in outline strips on a *hasir.*

Right, Setting the strips.

more than that in a woven rug, the labor involved in a good-sized namad—usually little more than two men for one day—is far less and the dyeing and mechanical expenses are also smaller so that a namad costs much less than any woven rug of equal size.

Traditionally, namads have also been used under pile carpets; this use has declined in the Occident replaced by synthetic felts. Now chiefly items of local or regional trade, the attractiveness of many designs could make them more marketable in the cities and as an export. Overseas little or nothing is known of them as published material is limited to a few brief entries in the SURVEY,[5] a single column in Wulff,[6] and short observations by traveler-writers.

Their production in Iran today is closely associated with the nomadic tribes. Most felt makers are sedentary and located along the route of the tribal migrations, supplying their needs as they pass. In Fars, Shiraz, Marvdasht and Firuzabad have long had a flourishing namad trade. The Qashgai tribe moving towards summer quarters sheer sheep and supply wool to the namad makers. The namads are ready when the tribes return towards winter pasture. Behbahan in Boyer Ahmad country has namad makers who receive orders for pieces by weight, from four to six kilograms normally. The nomad client gives double the weight as is to be made up. The wool profit goes into namads sold to local townsmen for cash.

The handcrafting process of namads, unchanged since earliest times,[7] shows some variations locally, though the basic steps roughly agree. The agents added to the wool differ somewhat, notably in the use of pure water as in Mazanderan versus soapy in Fars and Kermanshah, or the fuller's earth reported by Wulff,[8] but unlocalized. Such variations probably account for certain different characteristics such as the lighter texture of the Mazanderan namads dictated by the climate and their usability in damp climes as opposed to the dry coarseness of those of Fars with their quality of absorbing almost their own weight in water in conditions of sustained high humidity. A namad maker in Fars† said the humidity is no problem there, but the heavy, thick namads are preferred by his clients as they insulate better against the hard rocky ground prevalent. Namad making involves hard labor and is usually done by men, though there are areas, as among the Turkomans or in parts of Fars where this work, like most of the heavy labor among the tribes, is done by women.

Ibid.
Wulff, *Above,* p. 224

NAMAD, LIGHT-
WEIGHT WOOL
Abadeh design
Shiraz Bazaar
1976   L. 254

Irene Emery
*The Primary Structures
of Fabrics*
p. 22

Wulff, *Above,* p. 224

Facing, above

279

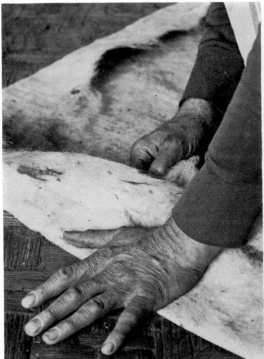

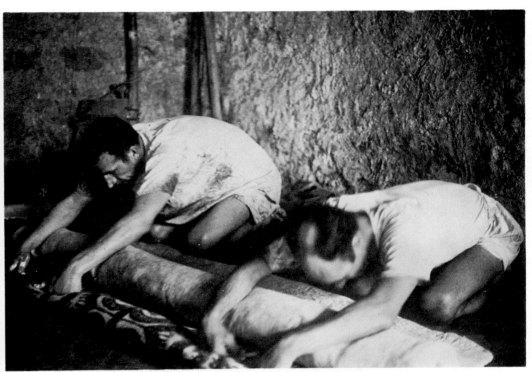

Doubling and rounding the edges   The final rolling of namad of Pl. 279, Shiraz

among the Turkomans may be the *marpich* or twisted snakes,† *bazuband* or armlet or the *haft-hasht* sevens and eights. The central pattern is then set, in one case in Ramsar three large diamonds, their corners similarly held in place with stones. The wool yarn is moistened as it is laid down, corners spit on to secure them, and pieces for small details are bitten off with the teeth to simultaneously cut and moisten.

284 left

The design detailing and filling, *vajeh,* now starts, and in some places others join the master pair, even children. When the design is complete, the bowed natural wool is heaped atop the pattern,† some three centimeters, covering the most attractive stage of the design for later the process will cause it to shift and wiggle and lose some of the power of its naivety, and the crispness of the fresh color which will not be seen again until the design has worn in with some years of service. The background bowed wool is raked over, for the laying of the design is finished, and the building up of the main body stage begins. Quality wool is used now for it will see the most wear and be seen the most. The fork, *panje,* rakes the knee-deep pile evenly.

Preceding left

In some areas a second layer of poorer wool is added now, but in the Ramsar area the next step is to sprinkle the whole namad lightly with plain water, *ab pash-i kardan,* then roll it up in the canvas around which rope is tied. Now begins the hard work for the two (or more) fullers who stand on it and roll it for over an hour from wall to wall, sometimes stopping against one wall and pressing their hands against it while going through a series of complex foot movements to compact the namad into a relatively thin and stable piece. Usually a rhythmical vocal times the process to the cadenced breathing of calling upon the name of Ali, inhale "*A,*" exhale the "*-li.*"

NAMADS

SHIRAZ
Dated '44—1965
L. 220 cm.
DYED GROUND
SHIRAZ BAZAAR
1970   L. 160 cm.

The craftsmen put their feet on the roll, hands on knees, then roll the tied namad forward with heels pressed down firmly, lift their feet and hit it firmly, exhaling loudly and pulling the roll backward under their toes, rolling it forward again by the heels. The rhythm is simple, forward one-two-three-*four,* back one-two-three-*four*; emphasis on the four is similar to the rhythm of the *tonbak* drum used by the folk musicians when they start playing.

NAMADS "WITH FEATHERS", GILAN   1972   L. 177 cm.   Coll. Ura Senke Foundation, Kyoto.

283

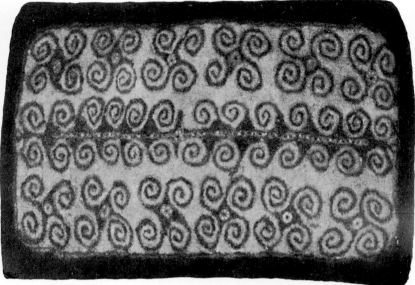

TURKOMAN TWO-FACED NAMAD

After working it for an hour the namad is opened and it emerges carrying the impression of the woven mat, the design embedded in the wool. The craftsmen hold it on both sides and pull at it to stretch and correct its shape.

Soap mixed in hot water—in Ramsar only hot pure water—is sprinkled over the edges, rubbed in; the edges are turned over to the back of the namad and the corners are rounded so that the edges are straight and of the same thickness as the rest of the namad. The edge is firmly rubbed in to bind it together.† *282 left*

286 left
With a small brush made from the root of a bush, the mixture of soap and water†—or again just water—is sprinkled over the entire surface. The namad is rolled and now they work on the rolling of the felt with hands. The namad is unrolled, is sprinkled on the wrong side, and rolled again. Now, the hard work begins. After this a cake of soap may be rubbed over the entire surface and the namad rerolled. The rhythm of felting now becomes more intense. Forearms rub it hard, turning the namad over as they cry out "Ya Ali." This movement is now followed by a still harder rolling, which is followed by continuous hitting of the namad with knees and hands.

Most difficult is the final stage when two people with arms crossed, lift the namad in unison, turn it over and slap it down with their hands, pushing with full weight as they raise themselves on their toes. This completes the actual making process. The namad makers carry out these processes stripped to the waist and are bathed in sweat when the finished piece emerges. It is then laid out to dry for a period of three to four days, depending on the time of the year. After that it is washed and brushed so that the surplus wool is removed and the pattern in subdued colors shows through the wool. *282 right*

An interesting technique of decoration in some namads is when additional "flaps" of felt are added to the design.† This is done by adding wool wherever this added scalloped edge is wanted. The inner edge of wool is rubbed into the namad to make it adhere to the namad while a paper is inserted between the other edge of the newly attached wool and the namad. This is now rolled. The paper prevents the open side from becoming attached to the background namad. After the namad is finished the paper is removed and the open or loose side of the newly attached border is cut with a scalloped edging. This is called *namad-i parakdar* *Preceding upper*

NAMAD, TURKOMAN   Ohara Gallery of Art, Kobe

that is, namad with feathers. Sometimes this extra fringe is in a different color and stands out in contrast. This technique is found in Semnan, Varamin, Khuzistan, where it is done especially on saddle covers, and throughout the Caspian area.

Facing

The namad-making technique is practically the same all over the country. In the Turkoman area and in Estabanat in Fars they make double-faced namads with different patterns on each side, sometimes in contrasting colors.† The doubled-sided pattern is prepared by working out the design on the second after the second stage of the namad making, applying the design directly onto the namad.

288 center
288 left

Manufacturing caps worn by different tribes is well described in Wulff. The only information to be added is that caps made for the Bakhtiari tribe are only rounded and made with black wool. To intensify the natural black color,† the wool is immersed in dye made from the nut of *shah balutt,* the wild horse chestnut. The caps of the Qashgai are quite different, being made in beige wool and shaped like a crown with the edges turned up and cut from the sides.†

Besides floor coverings and caps, one of the most important articles made with namad are shepherds cloaks called *kapanek* with long narrow sleeves, which are closed and are used as pockets by the shepherd for carrying his belongings as he moves with his sheep. The surface of the coat is often treated with oil to make it waterproof. These coats are made all over Iran of the same shape with only a slight variation in the slope of the shoulder.

Overleaf

Other products are saddle mats placed beneath the leather saddles, and *jol-i asb,* the horse blankets. In the Turkoman areas the horse blankets are enormous and cover the horses completely, used especially after the Turkoman races.† Felt is also made as the covering for the yurts used by the Turkomans and the Shahsavans.

Final soaping of namad of Pl. 279, Shiraz   Blocking a felt hat, Shiraz

Each area of Iran has distinctive designs and coloring which distinguish it. In southwestern Iran the finest namads produced today are from Estabanat in Fars where fine quality of wool is used and a light namad with delicately worked patterns is prepared. The Shiraz bazaar also has good quality namads with brilliant glowing colors and bold designs. Both Shiraz and Estabanat often dye even the wool of the background. Marvdasht and the villages around who only supply to the migrating tribal people have simpler designs with an allover pattern of "hauz" or pool, a repeat medallion or squares, with peacocks and stylized shrubs at the edge of the namad.

Dezful and Khorramshahr produce a much simpler pattern similar to Marvdasht since these are also purchased by the migrating Luri tribesmen. Behbahan however has more elaborate patterns with the use of four to five colors. The effect is quite bold and striking.

Some of the most attractive namads with bold patterns worked in black and white on a deep red background are prepared by the Turkomans.† Designs used are the whirling swirl signifying the Sun, or circles enclosing the sun and stars. These namads are prepared by the women and not by men as is the general practice all over Iran, except in Baluchistan.

In the past few years the manufacture of namads in Baluchistan in the southeast has been greatly reduced because of lack of wool. In 1972 while touring Baluchistan only one namad was seen in the village of Kalegan near the Pakistan border and approached from Khash. The namad carried an allover pattern and was prepared by the local women, as normal for the black-tented Baluchi tribe.

To the northeast of Baluchistan in Bujnurd the namad makers prepare namads for the Kurds and the Turkomans and there is a marked difference in the designs. Those for the Turkomans are either on a deep red ground or off-white and carry motifs reminiscent of those prepared by the Turkomans in Gonbad-i Qavus, while the ones prepared for the Kurds are on a black background with an allover pattern worked in lozenges.

Khurasan has other centers also. In Nishapur fine quality namads with large circular patterns and even stylized hawks are reminiscent of Turkoman carpet designs. In Kerman a large number of workshops for namad making are at Rahbur, a town in the Baft district. These are namads made for the Afshar tribes who migrate here.

Preceding

NAMADS
TURKOMAN
JOL-i ASB
Horse Blankets
1970   L. 246 cm.

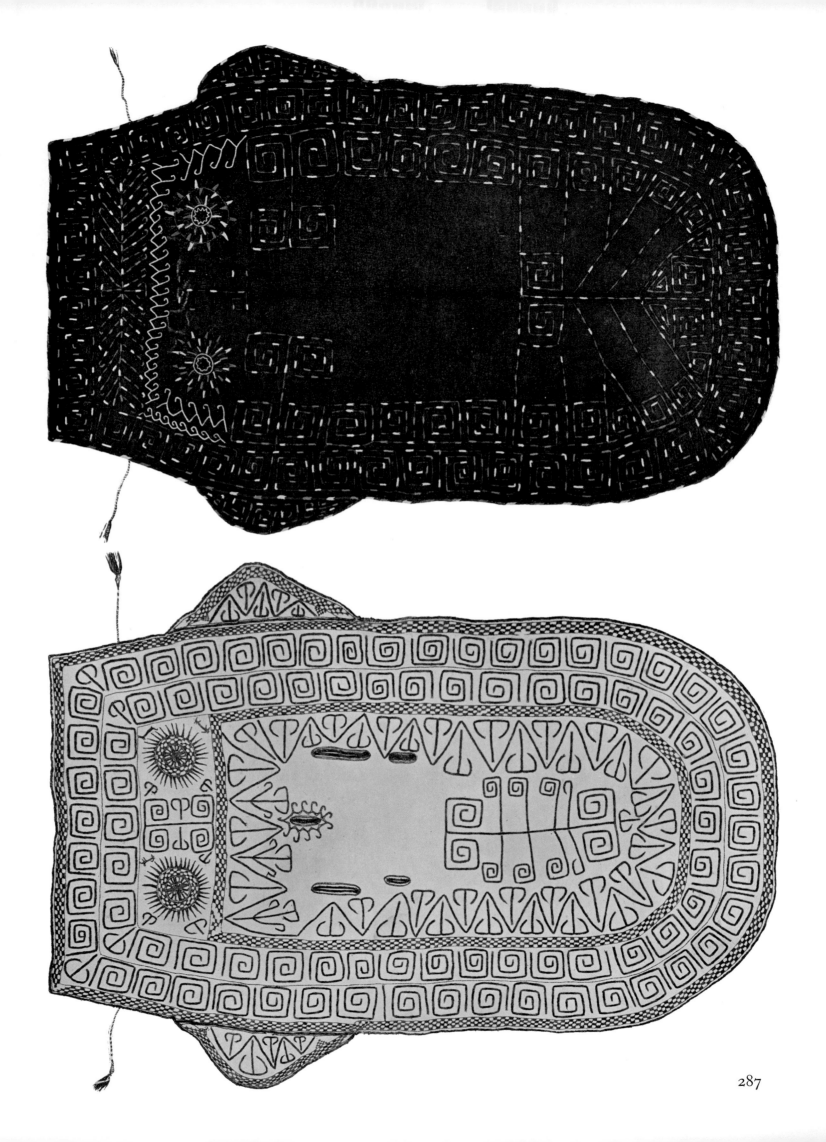

FELT HATS—QASHGAI NATURAL, BAKHTIARI BLACK AND GENERAL VILLAGE

The Caspian area has a number of centers. There are a large number of namad makers in Amul, in and around Chalus, Ramsar, and also in Qassembad-i Aulia. Fine namads are produced and used locally. The room which receives guests is first covered with woven rush mats over which are laid the namads. Most of the namads are with added "feather borders" *parakdar*; colors are natural undyed white, off-white, brown and black with designs delicately worked in deep red, white, black and sometimes, green.† *283 upper*

Here there is another tradition. The namad maker is invited to other villages for making namads. During the season he travels on his donkey, carrying his bow, his canvas cloth, the rake, and brush along with the specially made soap. The young son will probably accompany him to assist him in his work. They would be the honored guests of the village, bringing news from the town and would return to the workshop after completing their work.

The changing pattern of life, lack of capital among the craftsmen and no assistance in marketing the namad through other outlets and inroads of synthetic fibrous mats are fast lowering the standards of craftsmanship. Yet the patterns of namads are often harmonious and striking, not only in their basic design, but also in methods used to give a multilayered look and other special effects. The felt making craft is still very much alive and shows continued creative design abilities by craftspeople with no formal training, working within a medium that imposed far more limitations than many other textile crafts. Though if largely shunned by the well-to-do and by foreign buyers, namads still meet both practical and aesthetic needs for many Iranian at prices they can afford.

The Japanese flower arrangement grand master Houn Ohara has a large black and red Turkoman namad† in his palatial home in Kobe, set under an exclusive design living room set *285* of glass table and steel and leather French chairs. He smilingly recounted how much they all cost, then added the comment, "and thanks to the fifty dollars I spent on this namad to set them off, they look their price."

—JASLEEN DHAMIJA, NIKKI KEDDIE and KHOSROW PIR.

FLAT WEAVES

EUROPEAN painters recorded for posterity the value attributed to pile carpets in their portraits of European lords and merchants, and author-travelers of the eighteenth and nineteenth centuries investigated their manufacture and real costs in Iran in great detail. The merchants of past centuries actively encouraged scholarly study of the pile carpets of Persia and the Near Orient, but the flat weaves were generally ignored. Flat weaves, the gilims, *jajims*, and *zilus*, were for the peasant. Except for the Kurdish Senneh and Bijar gilims and some of the fine silk gilims of the Qashgai, flat weaves were not produced commercially for export and rarely came on the domestic art market except locally as surplus barter goods between producing nomad and consuming villager. The *zilu* has been so denigrated that to say a man had only a *zilu* and make no mention of his owning a carpet is still an insult of the first order. As recently as 1963 the editor was denied export permission of a few personal *zilu* on the grounds of carpet quality control. In 1966 even gilims were difficult to argue or coax past proud Persian customs officers.

The flat weaves of Persia can be categorized by tribal people and area, or by technique. Within each tribe all techniques are used, with only marginal variation in the way threads are spun or in their preference for certain techniques over others. Each tribe retains long-standing traditions of design, but there is as much interchange in patterns between them as of technique, so that by identifying the subtleties of design and dominance of certain techniques the provenance of an individual woven object found on the open market can often—but not too often—be established. Even in identifying the woven goods illustrated here, different provenances were suggested by different experts, including rural bazaar merchants or big city commercial experts from whom the editors and cooperating experts obtained some of the goods. The basic techniques should first be described, as defined in the SURVEY OF PERSIAN ART*

Survey, pp. 2177–84

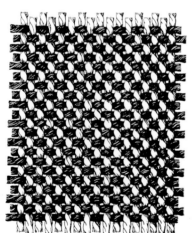 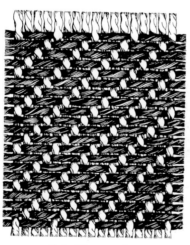 

Plain cloth weaving; Twill weaves: weft twill over three warps, warp twill over two wefts

Simplest is the plain weave with the interlacing weft and fixed long warp (in our illustration white) and woven cross weft (here black) threads achieving a balanced plain weave.† There are two variants, the warp-faced plain weave and weft-faced plain weave. Twill weaves vary in their proportion of warps over wefts or vice versa.†

Above left
Above right

The warp-faced plain weave is accomplished by increasing the number of warp threads proportionate to the number of weft threads so that in our illustration the white would predominate numerically and when the weaving is tightly compacted by hammering with a comb, the black weft would be hidden.

The weft-faced plain weave reverses the proportions, with black weft outnumbering white warps and thus dominating the effect seen. As the warp is invisible, a lower grade of unattractive wool or goat hair is commonly used.

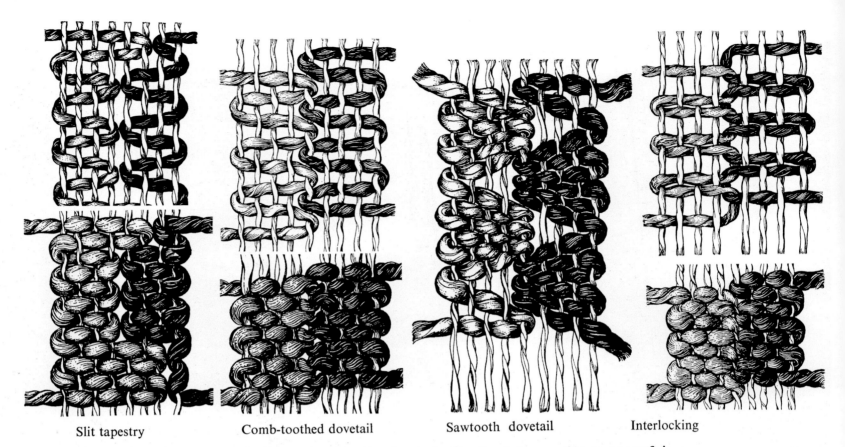

| Slit tapestry | Comb-toothed dovetail | Sawtooth dovetail | Interlocking |

Tapestry has each color of weft inserted only within the area required by the design, so that no one weft is carried the full width of the loom, unless by rare chance the pattern should necessitate it. This means that where the margin between two colors coincides with the straight line between two warps, there is an open slit. Designs in this technique are geometric, and oblique lines and curves must be built up by a series of steps. Long vertical lines must be avoided.

This open slit between warps can be eliminated by looping adjacent colors alternately over the common warp. If a single weft of each color alternates, the result is a comb-toothed dovetailing;† if several of one alternate with several of the other color, there results a saw-toothed or serrated dovetailing† most characteristic of the early Middle Eastern tapestry. Dovetailing should be kept distinct from interlocking,† typical of eighteenth century Gobelins, which solves the slit problem by looping together at the point of contact the wefts of each of the two adjacent colors in each line of the weave.

Innumerable decorative devices are used within the tapestry weaves.[2] Some of the common ones are: [J.D.]

Outlining the pattern by introducing an extra weft thread which is wrapped over two warp threads and back under one, continuously. Often mistaken for embroidery. Found mainly in the gilims of Khalkhal, East Azarbaijan.

Also, inserting extra wefts between two weft threads creates a variation in color and texture. Beaten in closely, the larger areas of weft threads adjust themselves around these inserts, though they are thrown slightly out of alignment. Seen in gilims of Sanandaj† and Qazvin.

Compound weaves with more than one set of either warp or weft threads, or both woven together to produce a woven patterned fabric, are found all over Iran. The easiest way of preparing a pattern is with extra weft threads.

Extra weft patterning with a continuous thread running across the warp is of two types. With limited areas of patterning on the face of the fabric, the remaining weft is left as a float on the back side, as in Turkoman gilims and Khurasan *palas*. This patterning created on both sides of the fabric is characteristic of the ends of Qashgai gilims and some horse blankets.

Patterns woven with discontinuous extra wefts which do not have any floats are compound weave. In some cases the whole surface is woven by weft wrappings, that is, by twining the weft thread over two warp threads on the face of the fabric and bringing it out on the reverse side between warp threads, so that there is no trace of the warp on the face. Areas are wrapped with different colors and the threads, in the case of the Shahsavans of Azarbaijan, are left free at the back to form a pad.† This technique has come to be known as soumak, from Shemaka, a town in the Russian Caucasus where it was done. With slight variations, weft wrapping is practiced by all the tribes.

Compound weave with extra warp threads are more complicated and are synonymous with the *jajim* weave.† The linkage of the warp threads to the beams on both ends, which form the basic frame for the fabric to be woven, restricts the flexibility of extra warp patterning, for no warps can be added once weaving has begun (though in some techniques extra warps can be added, as is discussed under velvets). The simplest form of patterning is where two layers of warp threads are laid over the same beam and are lowered or raised as the fabric is woven, thus creating a double-sided pattern. This is done by the Qashgai in their small bags, *chanteh*, and horse trappings.

Above
Above
Above

Irene Emery
*The Primary Structures
of Fabrics*

301, 303

GILIM, QASHGAI
Natural dyes
175×306 (fringes 13+13)
Detail   Scale *ca.* 2/5
Coll. H.H. Prince Shahram Pahlavi

299

317

BEDDING BAGS

MAFRASH, QASHGAI
Tenri Museum   L. 130

UNSEWN BAG, SHAHSAVAN
Kurashiki Folk Art Museum 126×166

JOL-i ASB, TURKOMAN
Ethnological Museum Tehran
142×159 (+10)

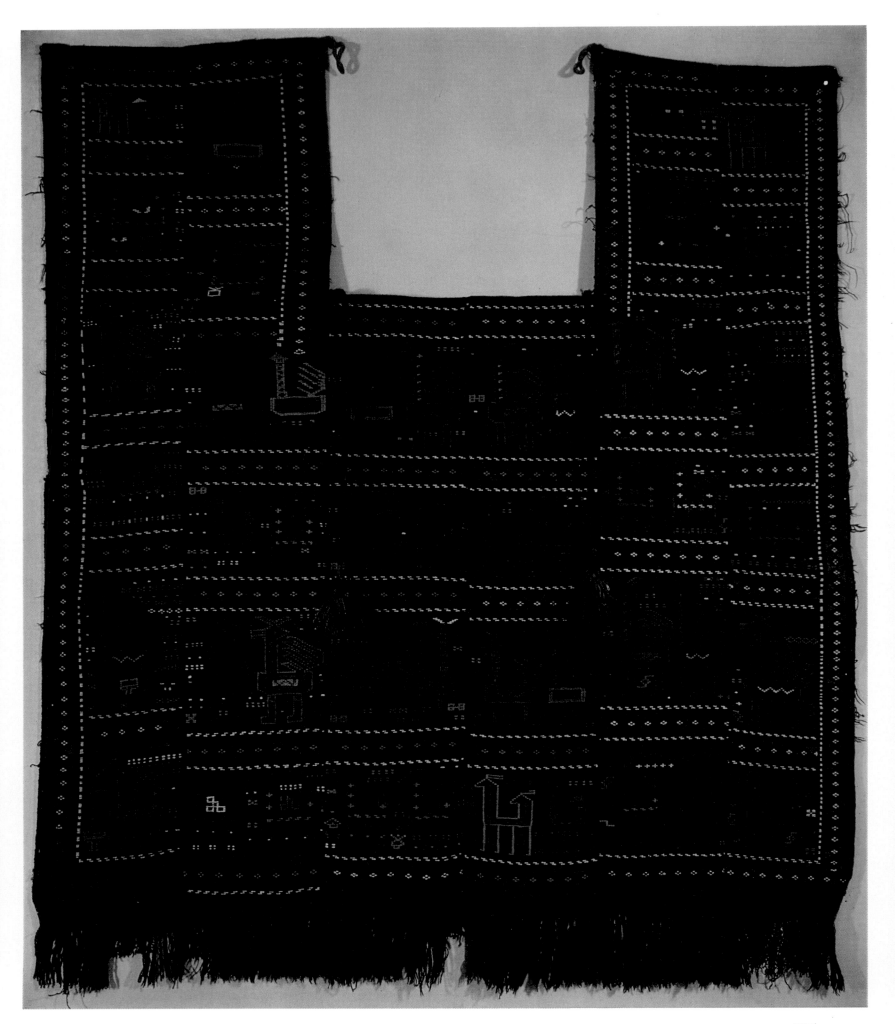

Camel bags of Shahsavan on road to Astara

Shahsavan camel fully loaded

young girls—who thereby become more valuable prospective brides in being able to add this important wealth-creating skill to the total value of their dowry. At the time of our visit the two elderly master weavers were nearing completion of a sixteen-meter-long gilim in deep, vibrant, natural dye colors: the same gilim can be seen in the catalog, *The Qashgai of Iran*, Pl. 14B, showing the same two teachers just as they commenced weaving it over a year earlier.

Where in most tribal areas the ancient natural dyes have given way to imported German synthetics, in Fars two important projects have been promoting successfully the renaissance of the richer, more long-lived natural vegetable dyes. Here at the Qashgai carpet weaving school tribal dyeing experts teach the young prospective brides the age-old secrets of gathering the proper plants and preparing them. These dyes will not lose their colors for centuries nor contribute to the decay of the fibers they infuse. Also in Firuzabad, several hours' drive to the south on the lower plateau in what is generally a winter habitation area for the Qashgai, the former section for Rural Cooperatives nonagricultural activities, has also been promoting the development of natural dyes and marketing them through their own outlets and that of the Handicrafts Organization. Both projects have been reasonably commercially successful and could be more so.

The Qashgai weavers put their greatest efforts and show their highest skills in producing the *jol-i asb*, or horse covers, for the horse is the great love of the nomad man and the main status symbol of the nomad family. Then there is a great variety of luggage ranging from the double horse bags or *khorjin*s;† and the big bags for clothing and bedding reenforced with leather, the *mafrash*;† down to the smaller bags for carrying flour and grain, the *jawal*; and the little cooking spoon holders, the *chanteh*.† Decorating the black goat-hair tents are numerous woven bands and retaining lines in pile, gilim, and brocading, and frequently mixed weaves.†

307

294

335

337

SHAHSAVAN

The Shahsavans inhabit northeastern Azarbaijan as a confederation of nearly fifty different tribes from Anatolia and Turkestan. They were settled in the area by Shah Abbas to stem the encroachments of the Ottoman Empire and given their present comprehensive name. Shahsavans are also in the U.S.S.R.

The most important Shahsavan weaves are the finely brocaded rugs known as soumak, and locally known as *varni bafi*—though in some locales this term encompasses many types of flat weave. They weave the intricate patterns on the horizontal loom in a wide variety of designs, usually on long and narrow rugs of some three meters length. The surface is fully brocaded with intricate designs.

Facing

SOUMAKS, SHAHSAVAI
104×260   111×29
Right, Coll. H.H. Prince Shahram Pahla

296

297

QASHGAI *MAFRASH*
Woven to shape, before sewing
Kurashiki Folk Art Museum

PAINTED POTTERY
Azarbaijan,*ca.* 1500 B.C.
Coll. H.H. Prince Shahram Pahlavi

DETAILS: SHAHSAVAN SOUMAK
Upper, Mafrash, W. 90; *Lower,* W.105 (L. 270)

A common pattern is the *kayak-i Noah*, Noah's Ark—usually three lozenges shaped like a boat with a tree in the center flanked by different pairs of birds, animals and crawling things.† Noah's Ark is described as having three stories with a tree in the center and was to be filled with seven of each clean animal and bird and pairs of all unclean beasts and crawling things.

Another important weave, the hearth rugs, are similar to the *jajim*s of other areas in being woven on a narrow loom, five or six pieces sewn together to make a single rug. Most *jajim*s are woven with extra warp designs, but these are woven with extra weft brocaded or compound weaves. The end pieces on each side have a border design running the length of one side and both ends of each of the pieces also carry an end border so that when all strips are stitched together the finished cloth carries a four-sided border. The most distinctive element of the hearth rugs is the stylized dragon shaped like an '*S*' with two ears and a tail, so abstract that it is difficult to associate it with an animal.

Shahsavan horse covers are some of the finest to be found in Persia in their bold stylization of animal and bird figures and rich use of colors.† Horse covers are usually woven in one piece, or two joined together. Only among the Shahsavan are horse blankets woven in six pieces, frequently with alternate ground colors and an unevenness in the lengths because of the different colored warps from having been woven on different looms, perhaps in different tents.

The large box-shaped woven bags, tied on the sides of the camels† for bed clothes and household goods on the migration from winter quarters in Dashte Moghan to summer quarters in the Savalan mountains, carry designs worked with brocaded technique or combining slit tapestry with brocading. They include design elements and treatment of animals carried over from the prehistoric pottery of the district.† The particular treatment of the great stags, the totemic animal of the Scythians, perhaps recalls descent from those earlier nomads who built the Pazyryk tomb mounds.

Preceding
Facing lower

295

Facing upper, 296

Above

299

GILIM, AFSHAR
150×246

GILIM, KURD SENNE
134×20
Mashhad Exhibition, 197

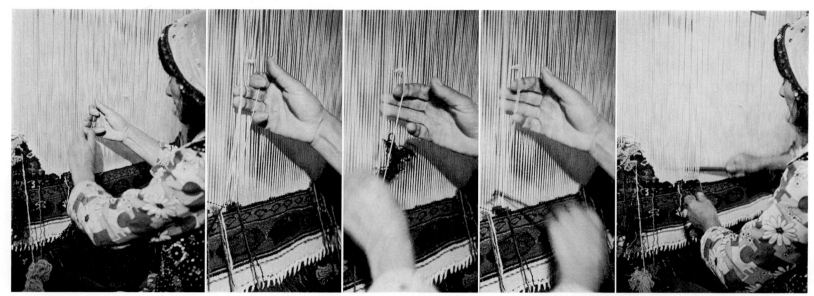

Commencing weaving gilim (pair) facing, July 14, 1976 Sanandaj

KURDS

The Kurds have two important centers for gilims in Bijar and Sanandaj. Bijar and Senneh carpets have long been export in classical patterns. These in turn influenced the gilims.

The finest Senneh gilim—especially the noted coverall known as *sajjadeh,* woven in split tapestry—has a central medallion with the background color in white with finely woven *boteh* in the medallion. The ground has a stylized version of the *mahi darham* a central flower with curving fishes flanking.† The weaving is fine and the limitations of the technique have been so mastered that the motifs are curvilinear. Another popular *sajjadeh* pattern of Bijar is of roses.†

In rural areas the gilims are bolder and of a different style: a composite pattern of large areas of different colors with linear separations combined with bird motifs.

Around Bijar, they weave horse blankets with matching *khorjins.* Patterns are worked with continuous extra weft threads in a rich geometrical pattern. Borders are large raised circular flowers woven in a special knotting.

Another style in rural Kurdistan is a brocaded pattern on horse blankets, either in stylized animal motifs or geometrical patterns quite distinct from either the Luri Bakhtiari patterns or the Shahsavans of east Azarbaijan. One possibility suggested was that this is the work of the Shahsavans who had settled in the areas around Bijar. It is, however, likely that this may be the work of the local Kurdi population. This is borne out by the fact that Kurds settled in Khurasan weave brocaded patterns.

The *jajims* are woven in the towns for the use of the peasants and are called *rakte khab pich.* Spun wool is given by the villagers to the weavers who dye it and weave checked patterns with borders and fine patterns of lozenges in the diamond twill weave called *cheshme bulbul,* nightin-gale eyes. They also weave patterns with discontinuous extra wefts in plain weave. A popular motif is *shamshir,* the sword, while a checkered black and white pattern is called *tagar,* hail-storm, and a zigzag pattern is lightning. Alongside these motifs are others related to the dervishes—the begging bowl, *kashkul,* sign of the wandering dervish and also the crossed axe, *tabarzin,* signifying the path of truth—reflecting that other aspect of the Kurds.

GILIM KURD
Rose pattern
Cotton warp, wool weft
Made by Fatimeh Kassem
115 × 168 cm.

Preceding
Facing

302

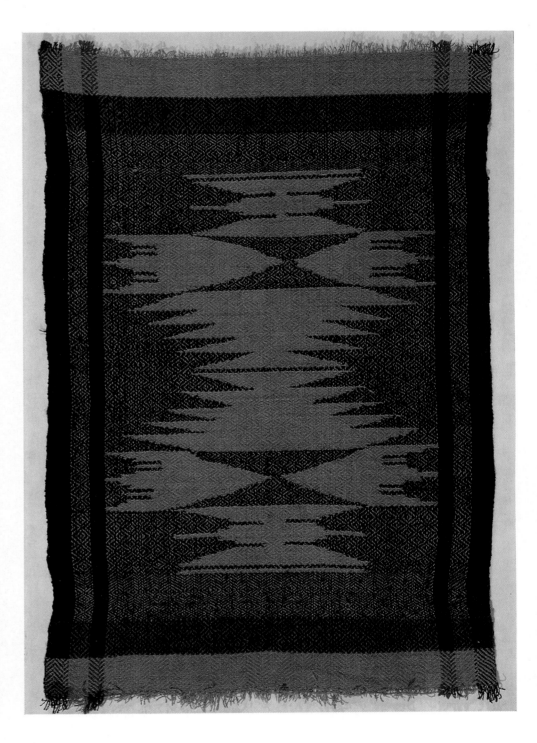

MOJ-i KURD
Left, MOJ-i KUH (mountain) W. 44 cm.
Right, MOJ-i SHAHR (town) , Sanandaj
Woven by Mohammad Ali Ramai,
Winner local prize 1976, W. 55 cm.
Cheshm-i bulbul, nightingale eyes, pattern

GILIM, VARAMIN
Slit tapestry, Wool warp
Detail, "Scorpion" pattern
W. 160 (L. 380)

305

TALIS STORAGE BAG, LUR
with pile reenforcing W. 104 (L. 137)
Below, detail of reverse

GILIMS, DETAILS

SAVEH, Slit tapestry, cotton warp   W. 98 (L. 300)

VARAMIN, KURD (?) W. 130 (L. 317)
Slit tapestry, cotton warp

Similar designs, Azarbaijan and Qassemabad

Tokyo National Museum

LURS

The Lurs are in Luristan, Isfahan, Fars, Khuzistan, Ilam, Kerman and Hamadan and inhabit the Zagros mountain chain through which they migrate. The Bakhtiaris, distinctive, yet one of the Luri tribes, migrate from the Char Mahal and Faridan districts down to the plains of Khuzistan around Dezful, Shustar and Masjed-i Suleiman. Shahr Kurd is an important summer headquarters of the Bakhtiari. They weave fine quality gilim in slit tapestry as well as in double interlocked tapestry. Long narrow somber gilims of black, maroon, blue and green with a touch of white are typical of the Bakhtiari of Char Mahal and are not to be found anywhere else. With multiple borders, a large skirt border on both ends of the carpet and *boteh*s in the middle, the dominant motif is worked in a red and white continuous linked swastika pattern. This appears elsewhere in Persian art only in the prehistoric pottery of Siyalk and Sagzabad.† In certain gilims a cruciform design appears which is interpreted by some to be a Christian cross, possibly due to influences of Armenians in the area, or to the fact that some Bakhtiari are Christian—some also are Jewish as are some Kurds. The cross, however, is more likely the *chahar bagh,* four corners of the universe, as Phyllis Ackerman points* out.

The finest weaving is in the *talis,* large bags in which household goods are kept.† The corners and bottom edge are woven in pile for strength. When the *talis* are placed one atop another the visible end is pile, which at a cursory glance appears to be a stack of carpets, showing off the prosperity of the tent. Not only is the face of the bag woven in brocade the back also carries exquisitely woven patterns—but only on one section.† Here the weaver displays her pride in making even the backside of the bag, which would perhaps never be seen, almost as intricately worked as the front.

KHAMSEH

The Khamseh, Arabic for "five," are a federation of five ethnically unrelated tribes centered around Shiraz. Two tribes are Arabic speaking, two speak Turki of which one is an ethnic Qashgai, and the fifth, the Basseri, speaks Farsi. In order to balance the power of their Qashgai neighbors, they were combined in 1865 under the control of the Qavams of Shiraz, who ruled them from the Narenjestan, the "Orange Garden" palace.†

Their wares appear in the Shiraz bazaar, where the soumak weaves shown here† are called Deh Bid after the town on the edge of their domain through which the weaves enter the market, and are often attributed to the neighboring Afshars. The commonest pattern for rugs and covers is a star-crossed field on natural or dark dyed ground, with floral stars arrayed obliquely in alternating color rows to form interlocking lozenges. Patterns like this field of *boteh*s† are rare and probably adapted from pile carpets, as woven by the neighboring Qashgai. The garden motif is also common in Qashgai† and other pile carpets, but exceptionally rare in flat weaves. These pieces are estimated to be about thirty-five years old and to have been woven by the Khamseh Sheibani. [Parviz Tanavoli identified this rare weave].

Pieces with the star-field pattern are frequently woven narrow in half widths and sewn together. Newer pieces are sometimes on a white cotton ground. In many the loose soumak wefts form a heavy pilelike cushion underside. A few pieces are not soumak, but brocaded.

Above

Phyllis Ackerman,
Survey, pp. 2914–29
307

307 lower right

GARDEN CARPET
SOUMAK WEAVE
KHAMSEH SHEIBANI
Fars   160×198

Preceding
Facing

Preceding
325, 326, 327

Ohara Gallery of Art, Kobe

JOL-i ASB, TURKOMAN
Woven in five panels
and two sideflaps
135×155 (total)
Left, on horse
Above, Libation vessel
in horse form,
Gilan, First millennium
317

TURKOMANS

In the northern part of Iran extending from the eastern shore of the Caspian along the borders of U.S.S.R., in the Gurgan area and across Khurasan live the Turkoman tribe. They extend across the borders into Afghanistan and the U.S.S.R. The women weave carpets and flat weaves to decorate their mobile felt yurts. The woven *palas* of the Turkoman is generally worked on a narrow background with patterns in black or blue-black, a light red and touches of white.†

The weaving is of extra weft with multiple weft threads that are continuous in some cases and discontinuous in others. The pattern is by either plain weft-faced weave in finer quality pieces, or weft threads floated across the face of the fabric to cover a fairly large surface without being tied down to the warp. The sides carry a number of smaller borders in geometric patterns. The central field always has a related allover geometric pattern covering the entire surface.

Bags for camels and horses are all woven with similar motifs. In the finer quality, smaller stripes with finely woven geometrical patterns in weft-faced float weaving are combined with plain weaving.

Finest, however, are the long narrow woven strips which decorate the inner circumference of the yurt. These are in black and the favored dark Turkoman red, usually with intricate geometric designs (in extra wefts), but sometimes figural and, on rare occasions, with the design raised in pile carpet weave.† They are almost always 17 meters long, the circumference of the standard yurt.

337

The area around Quchan in Khurasan has a number of tribes which carry on their distinctive† styles of weaving. These isolated tribal peoples have preserved many older traditions which have been lost in the areas of their origins. Local Kurds continue fine brocaded soumak weaving. Among the Turkoman can also be found the extra warp *jajims* with fine patterns. The local people of Khurasan, absorbing these traditions, make fine striped *jajims* carrying extra warp patterns which they also work here in wool.

315

Kalat-i Naderi area, with the influences of Baluch, Kurd, and Turkoman settlers, has experienced an intermingling of traditions and the development of a distinctive style.† Gilims and *khorjins* are similar in style and color to the local silk textiles.† On the dark background brilliant red, yellow and green flowers are worked into an overall pattern. The technique is of weft-faced plain weave with extra weft floats at the back. The bags woven here carry the same technique on the face and a variation at the back of slit tapestry technique combined with the outlining of the pattern with an extra weft thread.

317
181

313

BALUCH

"When God was making the world He made everywhere all the different countries for the people to inhabit. After He had nearly finished, God realized He had forgotten to make Baluchistan. So He put together all the darkness, the dust, the leftovers and slapped them into shape with the very little water He had left and thus we got our Baluchistan."

In constant battle with the harsh nature, the Baluchi express their longing for water and for pasture land in their poetry and in the stylized motifs they weave. Baluchi poetry is full of such imagery as pools filled to overflowing in which water trembles like the leaves of the wild pistachio trees and the waves bend like the jointed sugar cane. One sits in the mud hut of the Baluchi as the wild whirlwind they call *sheitun,* the devil, rages outside while the Baluchi entertain you with one of these songs, waiting for the duststorm to abate.

These pastoral people reside in *ghedan* tents made of the usual nomadic coarse woven black goat-hair cloth, but here stretched over a frame of wickerwork formed from the branches of the tamarisk bush. An assemblage of *ghedan*s constitutes a *tumum* or village. In the *ghedan* the floor is spread with gilim [woven with continuous weft threads which leave floats across the back, with multiple threads used to introduce different colors]. The edges are trimmed with large cowrie shells, which in ancient times were used as coins; the four corners are finished with tassels. Cushions in carpet weave often carry a flowerlike design sometimes called the crest of the Baluchi, a stylized cock's comb. The word Baluch derives from *baloc,* which in Old Persian means cock's comb or crest. Sides of the pillow and the back are in gilim.

On the side of the tent are large salt bags, which here are not woven in the usual rectangle with a smaller rectangle on the top for the opening,† but formed so that once filled with salt or sugar one looks like a pot.

308

One of the most distinctive woven articles is the square *sofreh,* which is known amongst the Baluchi as *jahizi.* This has a four-sided border in either pile work or brocade. The field is woven with natural camel wool and often carries a medallion in the center in pile combined with gilim.

Baluchi carpets† have been greatly influenced by the designs of their neighbors, frequently mistaken for Turkoman.† Their flat weaves, however, are distinctive. The gilims carry patterns woven in stripes over the entire surface, often each stripe has a different geometrical design, varied not only in motif but also in color. The colors are dark but relieved by chrome yellow, clear red or green. Ground colors used are natural camel wool, as well as dyed brown, rust, maroon, a dark red (nearing brown) and blue.†

331 left, 333
331 right

314

The account of Charles Masson, a deserter from the British Army who traveled Baluchistan from 1826 to 1840, gives an interesting description of their weaving. "Wool is beaten with a stick...made into threads and woven into carpets." Concerning dyeing of threads he also mentions that the wool is "coloured with madder, indigo and turmeric.... The leaves of the apple tree at their fall in autumn are preserved for their yellow dye, which is, I believe, a novel application of them. The hair of camel is often used by the Baluchis.... The dwellings of Baluchis...one side are piled their bags of grain which are concealed from view by a carpet spread over them, while above them are piled their stock of carpets and felts neatly folded. They place their cakes of bread in carpet bags also for their flour and salt."

Left, 114×210   *Right*, tufted border, 110×235

GILIMS, MAZANDERAN, KURD (?) Sangdeh near Sari, Rural Cooperatives project for promoting natural dyes

328

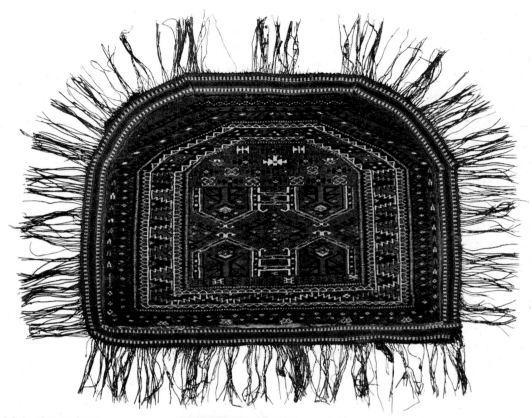

GARDEN CARPET, INDIGO GROUND
Bunat near Persepolis. Wool warp, wool weft
120×170

TURKOMAN SADDLE RUGS
Wool warp, wool weft
Above, 41×56
Below, 110×112.

EAST PERSIAN *GUL* DESIGN
Wool warp, wool weft
Left, Baluch, 110×212
Right, Turkoman sampler, 27×87
The Turkoman with approx. 9×9.5 knots per square cm.
(23×24-1/2 per sq. in.) is of such fineness that its total
knots approximately equal those of the larger Baluch.

The warp is usually thicker and more tightly spun than the weft. The looser spun weft must be beaten in around the base of the knot, the more firmly it is beaten, the more tightly packed around the base of the knot, the sturdier and stronger the finished piece will be; the photo shows Qashgai women using a beater to pack the weft firmly in around the base of the knot. Most nomadic carpets have several wefts, while urban pieces usually have only one resulting in a higher knot density in urban carpets but not necessarily a more tightly packed carpet. The backside of the carpet, saddle bag, tent bag or other type weaving will indicate how many wefts are used; in many Qashgai carpets the wefts are dyed red or blue, though this is not the case with most Turkoman, Kurd or Baluch weaving.

Above

Selvages, that is the overcast or woven sides of carpets and bags, are often quite intricate in village and nomadic weaving, while in urban pieces they are quite simple. Qashgai and Khamseh tribes often use two colors for selvages, red and yellow, red and green or red and blue, with short tufts of colored wool attached at various intervals along the selvage. Baluch selvages are often wide and woven of lustrous goat hair which is particularly attractive.† Again, unlike the refined urban product the village and nomadic carpet has paid attention to the fringe, that is the warp extending from each end of the woven piece. Often these are woven into tassels or tied off in various other ingenious ways. Such details make the village and nomadic pieces expressive and individual as well as gay, lighthearted and decorative.

Facing left

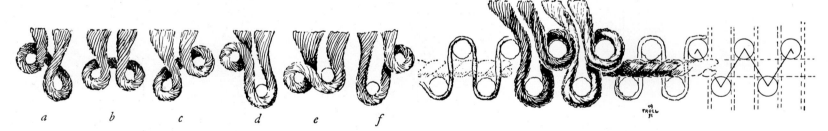

Typical knots: *a–c*, Ghiordes; *d–f*, Sehna.   Horizontal section shows Sehna tied on warps on two levels

Knotting is of two types, either the Persian or Sehna knot, or the Turkish or Ghiordes knot. The Sehna knot† is most common among Yamut Turkoman weavers around the Caspian Sea and Pahlavi Dej and Gurgan areas; Baluch weavers marketing their goods in Mashhad use the Sehna knot, and Qashgai, Afshar and other southern Persian weavers use both the Sehna and Ghiordes knots.†

Above   d–f

Today's loom has a heritage of several thousand years: it is horizontal among all nomadic† people, while both horizontal and vertical looms are found in villages.† The horizontal or ground loom can be strapped to a camel and be moved along with all the other household effects to the new home where weaving can continue as before.

Above a–c
305
321

331

337

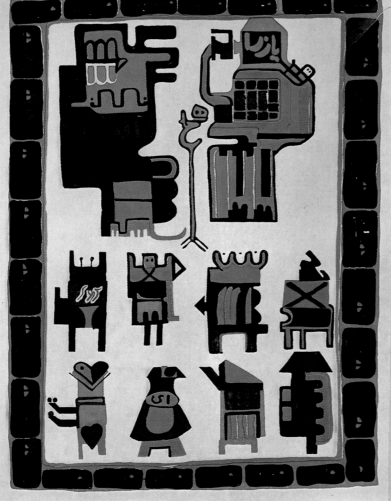

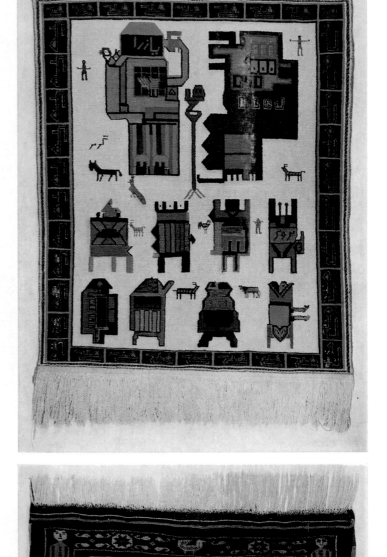

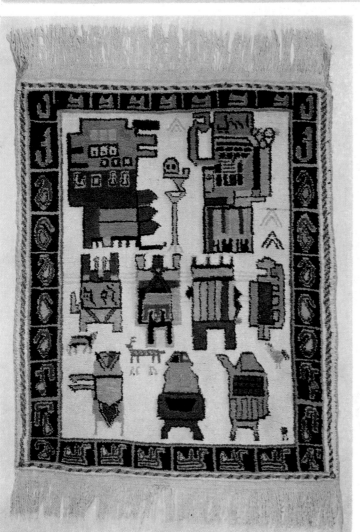

Preceding
PITCHER and LADLE
CARVED FROM SOLID BLOCKS
ALASHT VILLAGE, ALBORZ
1970   H. Pitcher 31 cm.

Persepolis
Apadana relief
Median courtier
carrying
wooden chair
5th century B.C.

WOODWORK

SANANDAJ, nestled in the midst of vast forests of walnut (*gerdu*), pear (*golabi*) and maple (*kaiko*), has long been famous for its woodwork. The swirling, sworling, cloudlike patterns of the grain in the tortured old walnut knots invite artistic interpretation, challenge the artist to find the bowl or board or inlay they were created to become, and thus assign them their place in posterity. The finest wood artist is Majid Nematian,† who learned the trade from his father, Nematollah, and who at over seventy recently won the Award for Excellence in Handicraft for his salad bowl and plate and fork and spoon.† Carved from a solid block of walnut, not turned on a lathe, and as thin as the finest Japanese lacquer on wood or even papier maché, its total simplicity and testimony to a lifelong mastery of a humble craft project an intensity unexpected in so common an object and so base a material. There is a full ten days of solid work in carving one set. It is made in the tradition of a fine penbox (*qalamdan*) made by his father.†

 <!-- margin refs -->

Marquetry is an old craft in the area and the Nematians are masters of it in a town where the ordinary is excellent. The contrasting colors of walnut and the almost golden pearwood are an ideal combination, often seen at its best on game boards, *takht-i nard*,† for chess and backgammon, built like a box which can hold the game pieces when closed, or open out to a chess and checkerboard on the outside or a walled backgammon board inside. There are many producers of fine game boards in Sanandaj, and the average board takes a week to ten days full time to produce. Nematian father and son, Abdol Hamid,† take an average of six weeks per board and have a long waiting list. Even the iron hinge they make themselves, though it cannot be seen as they set it in deep and cover it with wood.

The marquetry details on the boards are the traditional vocabulary of the Persian carpenter and will be found in the doors of fine buildings like the Narenjestan of Shiraz.

Wood is certainly the first material worked by man into artifacts and much of Iran a millennium ago was covered with thick forests. The annals of Alexander's invasion describe great forests in Fars where now there is only open space except for the reforestation and park projects of the past decade beginning to spread their green carpets across the brown desert. The great pillars of Persepolis were roofed with wooden beams, which fueled the great firs, and Darius' inscription at Susa tells us, "The *yaka* timber I brought from Gandhara and Karmania." The *yaka* is the *jag* or sissoo tree, which grows today in the sub-Himalayan region of India and Pakistan, Gandhara, and in Baluchistan and the Makran of Iran, Karmania of old. The throne of Darius† in the Persepolis relief was wood and obviously turned on a lathe—they served as models for a series of Isfahan-made furnishings first turned out for the Shah Abbas Hotel a decade ago by Ebrahimian and Chaichi.

350

351

361 upper left

353

352

SHERBET SPOONS
ABADEH
19th century to recent
L. Longest 44 cm.

Above

346

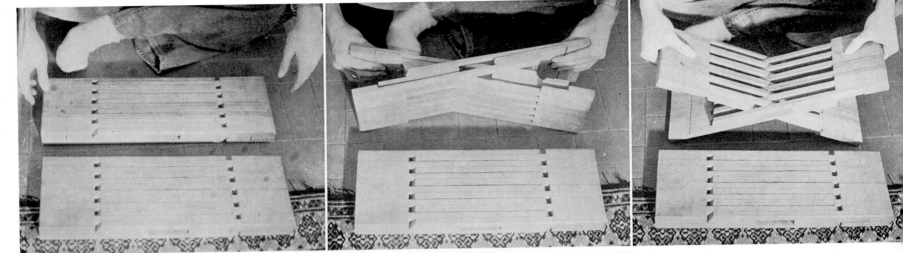

Setting up the
Qu'ran stand

COLLAPSIBLE
QU'RAN STAND
Golidaghi Turkoman
North Iran, Recent
L. Folded 47 cm.

TURKOMAN CHEST
Golidaghi
North Iran, Recent
96 × 125 × 53 cm.

TENT ROPE, QASHGAI
With wooden fixtures

The influence of the Holy Qur'an on all aspects of Persian arts and crafts is ubiquitous and in a land where the furniture of a house is limited virtually to the finest craft of the people, the carpet, there is little domestic outlet for the woodworker beyond architecture. Two exceptions to this are stands for the Holy Qur'an, to leave the book out, covered in fine cloth, where it is readily available and on which it can be readily referred to. Finer homes would have fine marquetry or *khatamkar* stands.† Simple homes would have such as the intricately carved stand shown.† This has been cut from a single block of wood and cannot be separated, though it is now four separate but intertwined boards. Of a pair, one is shown open, the other closed in stow position.

The Chinese owe the origins of most of their furniture to the nomadic peoples to the west of them, thus most early Chinese and much later classical Chinese furniture is modular and can be easily dismantled and reassembled. In Persia, though most nomads use the large carpet bags for storage, the searoving people of the Persian Gulf make beautiful sea chests, legless, embellished with designs in brass nailheads aboard ships to pass the time on long voyages. These are shared with most of the littoral peoples of the Arabian states and east Africa. The Turkoman nomads of the northeast also use chests.† The odd arrangement of the door, not flush at bottom with the floor of the box, nor opening full in front, is also characteristic of Korean furniture, equally inspired by the furniture of the central Asian nomads who carried many other artistic elements in common between east and west Asia.

361 lower
Facing upper

Facing lower

354

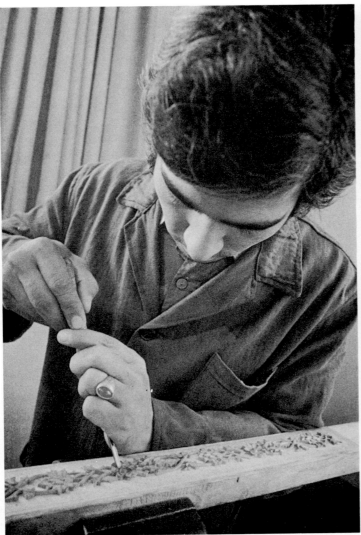

MARQUETRY
HONARHAYE ZIBA
GAMING BOARD–BOX
Upper, Inside Backgammon
Lower, Outside Chessboard
National Arts Museum
Recent   55 × 66 cm.

PICTORIAL PANEL
National Arts Museum
Recent   H. 160 cm.

Sculpting fretwork

Sculpted fretwork for table edge

Marquetry† has been a craft long appreciated by royalty and patronized. But when for the court the inlays have not been limited to the regional fine woods, and imported exotic darkwoods and ivory and even base and precious metals have been added to the vocabulary of the artisan.

Facing -359

When Reza Shah instigated his crafts renaissance, he paid particular attention to marquetry. The art workshops set up on the grounds of the old home of Persia's greatest artist of the day, Kemal al-Mulk, now the workshops of the Ministry of Culture and Art, have trained craftsmen and produce fine furnishings for the court and for use as state gifts for decades. They have served to set a standard of excellence for commercial craftsmen of the marqetry and *khatamkar* workshops not far away.

Here a chessboard and backgammon combination box,† inset with ivory and exotic woods, was made for Reza Shah and is now in the Museé Honar-i Melli, Museum of National Arts.

Facing

Pictorial panels† attaining a polychrome effect by the use of numerous woods are a particular craft of Persia. The oldest known, but of unknown provenance, are in Japan in the Shosoin Repository in Nara and date prior to 752 A.D. Their motifs are Central Asian, if not west Asian, of laden camels and sheep and men in nomad garb, but the game played on them is the Chinese *go*, which takes a different board arrangement than chess, being a simple line grill. New adhesives and finer fretsaws developed in recent years have enabled the attaining of fine results not hitherto possible.

Facing

356

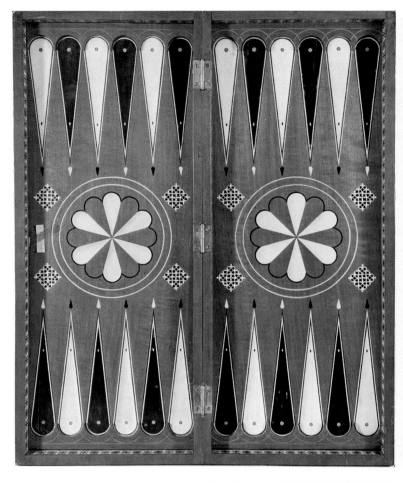

Above, Sawing, filing and inserting light wood design in dark wood ground. Honarhaye Ziba, Tehran.

Right, Detail of *Minbar*, facing.

358

MINBAR, PULPIT
MARQUETRY
Honarhaye Ziba
...onal Arts Museum
H. 410 cm.

CARVING QALEB—PRINTING BLOCK FOR *QALAMKAR*, ISFAHAN

A. Drawing design directly on block of pearwood.

B. Detail, drawing directly on block.

C. Transferring design from perforated tracing from an old block to a new block.

D. To make larger block, to balance stress of shrinkage, piece together two adjoining slabs from same log.

E. Carving the block.

F. The carver's tools.

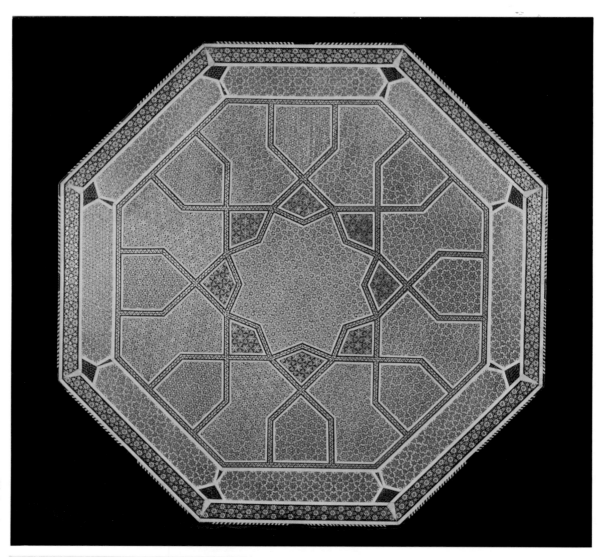

KHATAM-KAR
TABLE TOP
By Golriz, Isfahan
1976   D. 50 cm.

COLLAPSIBLE
QU'RAN STAND
Shiraz   19th century
Decorative Arts Museum
L. 47 cm.

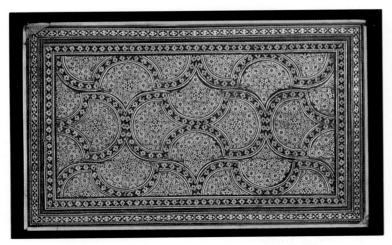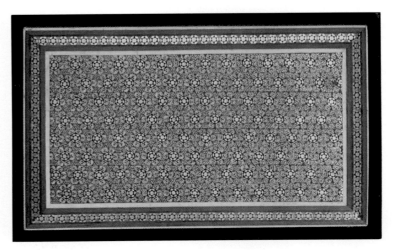

KHATAM BOXES BY GOLRIZ ANCESTORS:

MUHAMMAD, Fifth Generation, *ca.* 1895 (15.2×9.3 cm.)　　MUHAMMAD KHALIL, Sixth Generation (d. 1973), *ca.* 1935 (15.3×9 cm.)

KHATAM-KAR

ISTORICALLY the origins of *khatam-kar* are another of the mysteries of Persian art crafts. To Ustad Muhammad Khalil Golriz, perhaps the greatest of the *khatam* craftsmen, who dominated the art from the opening of the Pahlavi era until his death in 1973, the technique was introduced from China during the Mongol dominion in the fourteenth century. Inlay—carving out a design in a wooden ground and setting in fitted pieces of other wood or material—has been known in the Near East since earliest times. But marquetry—a veneering process in which small pieces are set down on a base and glued or nailed, of which *khatam* is a specialized type—is not of great age. In Europe the oldest samples are almost contemporary with the oldest in Iran. In Italy certosina, minute pieces of bone, ivory and wood, dyed or natural, combined in designs on a thin diaper of wood and inlaid as a unit, dates to the fourteenth century. A century later there is intarsia, pictorial assemblages similar to the work on the preceding pages.†

In Persia in the fourteenth century wood decoration developed "a geometrical linear system wherein complex entrelacs are built up by intersecting polygons" which Bronstein[1] believes stemmed from Hellenistic antecedents, though also known in Outer Iran in Khotan in the third to eighth centuries. By the fourteenth century this technique had developed into the "pure geometry" of such as the ceiling of the main *ivan* in the Masjed-i Jami' 'Atiq of Shiraz,† made of minute intermeshed polygons of wood nailed on. The aesthetic relates to the contemporary brick and faience decoration of the Mausoleum of Uljaitu in Sultaniyeh and the Khanaqah of Natanz.†

Khatam is first mentioned by Dowlat Shah in his *Lives of the Poets*, speaking of Sultan Ahmad ben Avi', *ca.* 1382, "considered a master in several branches of art [including] *khatam-bandi*." In six weeks in 1396 (A.H. 798) Timur built his amazing Palace of Dilkusha in Samarqand with *khatam* doors, probably resembling those in his slightly later tomb, *ca.* 1405.†[2] To Bronstein this represents a "continuity of style fully developed by the Timurids." The work in the Shiraz mosque may well be older, as the building dates to the tenth century.

Other fine old examples are the walnut doors overlaid with bone and various woods, signed by the artist Habib Allah, A.H. 999 (1591), now in the Staatliche Museum, Berlin; the panel from Bukhara in the Victoria and Albert Museum with polygonal panels juxtaposed with floral ornament; and the cedar wood *minbar* in the Masjed-i Lamban, Isfahan, with various polygons and silver detail, dated A.H. 1114 (1702).[3]

357 right

Léo Bronstein
Decorative Woodwork
of the Islamic Period
Survey, pp. 2607–26

Survey, Pl. 1464A

Survey, Pl. 371

Pope—Ackerman
Survey, pp. 1149–50

Bronstein, *above*, pp. 2624–5

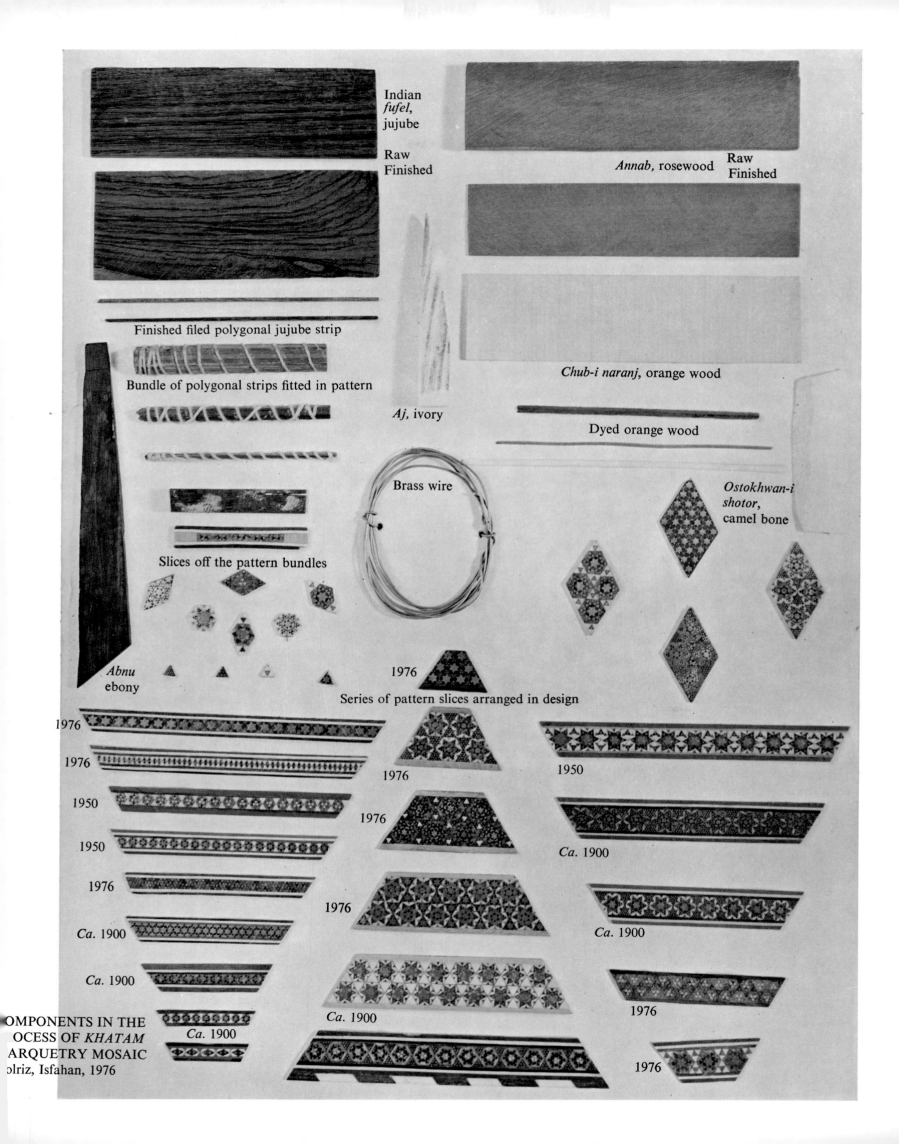

Indian *fufel*, jujube

Raw Finished

Annab, rosewood Raw Finished

Finished filed polygonal jujube strip

Bundle of polygonal strips fitted in pattern

Chub-i naranj, orange wood

Aj, ivory

Dyed orange wood

Brass wire

Ostokhwan-i shotor, camel bone

Slices off the pattern bundles

Abnu ebony

1976

Series of pattern slices arranged in design

1976

1976

1976

1950

1976

1950

1950

Ca. 1900

1976

1976

1976

Ca. 1900

1976

Ca. 1900

Ca. 1900

Ca. 1900

Ca. 1900

Ca. 1900

1976

1976

COMPONENTS IN THE
PROCESS OF *KHATAM*
MARQUETRY MOSAIC
Golriz, Isfahan, 1976

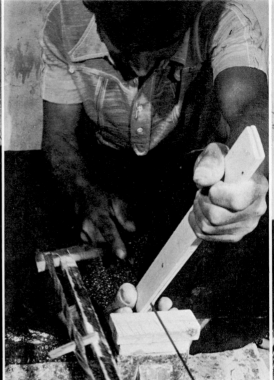

ASSEMBLING *KHATAM* UNITS INTO A LARGE TABLE,
GOLRIZ KHATAM, ISFAHAN

KHATAM, ROYAL STUDY, MARBLE PALACE
Upper left, DADO PANEL, H. 97 cm.
Lower right, DOOR, *Approx. same scale*

CARVED DOORS, MARBLE PALACE, WOOD
Adapted from Sasanian Silver Plates
in *Survey of Persian Art,* Pls. 210, 232A

364

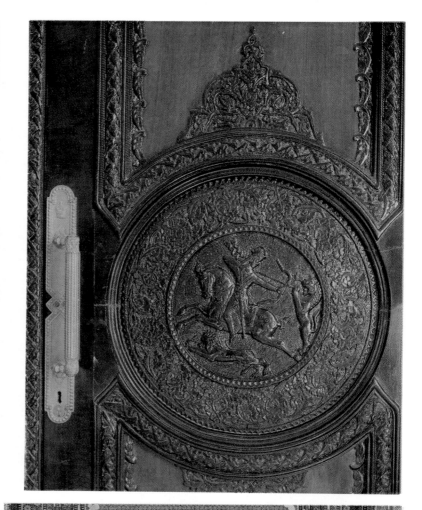

SILVER METAL *KHATAM* DETAILS FROM MARBLE PALACE MIRROR ROOM by GOLRIZ

The early developments in Khotan and the flowering in the Timurid east[4] may be the origins of the idea that *khatam* came from China. Little else supports it. The tradition also says the Chinese original was simple, that what we know today as *khatam* was the Persian development. Whatever the origins, the miniscule mosaic marquetry prospered in Safavid times[5] as well as in Zand in Isfahan and Shiraz. Decline set in under the Qajars when Isfahan was discriminated against. Craftsmen led miserable lives and the few masters who carried on did so out of an almost religious devotion to art as a way to salvation.

In 1811 Sir William Ouseley visited Isfahan and wrote[6] lauding the "minute...mosaick-work" in which "no inequality remains among the hundreds or thousands of the component articles," and that it "ensured considerable profit to many artists of Shiraz and Ispahan." But by 1877 the Persian author of the *Geography of Isfahan*[7] records: "The inlaid works were highly popular in old times and *khatam* worked on old boxes, book racks, chairs, mirror frames, doors of rooms and mausolea involved a lot of hard work and skill, but these old objects are collected and taken away from Iran and foreigners are ever searching for and buying them. The number of people engaged in the craft are now greatly reduced and the low quality of the present product is a reflection of poor sales for there are buyers only in the villages. A small quantity is exported to Rome and Istanbul." By the end of the century the craft had died out in Isfahan and was exclusive to Shiraz.

The turning point came after the lecture to Reza Shah by Pope in 1926. Commander of the First Army, Major General Ayrom, ordered a desk and set of armchairs from Muhammad Khalil Golriz. Reza Shah soon after ordered a plinth in Saadabad Palace done in *khatam*. The Exhibition of Iranian Products inaugurating Avenue Sepah showed *khatam* to acclaim.

Ibid., p. 2608

Ibid., p. 2620, n. 2

Sir William Ouseley
Travels in Various Countries of the East, 1825, III, p. 65

Mirza Hossein Khan
The Geography of Isfahan

THE *KHATAM* ROOM, OFFICE OF H.I.M. REZA SHAH, MARBLE PALACE, NOW THE PAHLAVI MUSEUM

Above

401

401, Facing

With the construction of the Marble Palace in 1934, *khatam* was ordered for the framing in the mirror salon and for the entire royal study.† Ustad Muhammad Husayn Sanie Khatam brought up from Shiraz Gholam Husayn Golriz, Muhammad Malek Muhammadi, Ali Babvieh, Haj Muhammad Sanie Khatam and Ali Akbar Javanmardi. Working at unheard of generous rates per square meter, but giving back even more than they received, the artists drove themselves to peaks of accomplishment creating the finest *khatam* mosaic ever seen. After a year it became evident that if the quality were maintained the mirror room† would take a decade for the trim alone† and the office would take at least a century. The workers were changed over to day wages, for the piecework rate penalized their good intentions. During this period Ustad Muhammad Khalil Golriz was called up from Shiraz to enlarge the crew to eight masters and eighty workers, including the five from the Golriz family. Jali, now fifty-five, sixth-generation head of the family, was a twelve-year-old apprentice. In about five years he will be joined by his grandson, the eighth generation of *Khatam* Golriz.)

367

DOOR, *KHATAM* EMBELLISHED, ROYAL BAZAAR, CHAHAR BAGH, ISFAHAN, RE-CREATION OF 17TH CENTURY ORIGINAL

The Marble Palace was completed in 1937, and the Shiraz artists dispersed. Sanie remained in Tehran, where the family maintains a shop on Manuchehri. Golriz moved to Isfahan to reestablish the craft there and teach at the Honarestan for thirty-six years, so that today there are some fifty masters, each with an atelier, and over three hundred skilled workers in the city. His sons maintain his atelier on Chahar Bagh.

The design for the *khatam* in the Marble Palace was adapted from the doors between the Royal Bazaar and the Madraseh Madar-i Shah, now restored by Golriz. The new massive wooden doors to the recently reopened Royal Bazaar made of *chenar* (plane tree) wood took six months to inlay with *khatam*.† The new parliament building has a *khatam* room by Ustad Ali Nemat of the Honarhaye Ziba workshop.

The harder-than-steel ebony wood of old is now rarely used, jujube replacing it.† For green, camel bone used to be immersed in dye for six months; now orangewood is dipped for half an hour in chemical dye. Mechanization of transport has helped marketing, but hurt the material supply as camels are now so rare that the bone is available only for quality *khatam*, the cheaper using German compressed Galalite C.R. New grinding and sanding machinery promises to reduce the hard labor of hand filing the tiny polygonal strips of bone, wood or metal that fit together to make the starlike larger forms—the best work having some forty bits per square centimeter—but there has been little real success in getting the right machinery. Better cold glues and shellacs make the material more durable and easier to transport to other climes. The art craft thrives again as it has not since early Safavid times, thanks to the initial patronage of the late Reza Shah, and looks forward to even improved work and wider acceptance.

—LUTFULLAH HONARFAR

Above

363

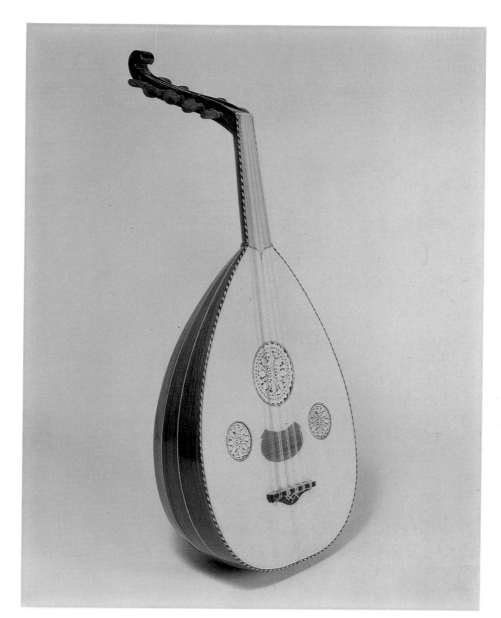

MINIATURE
'UD (OUD)
DEEP-BELLIED LUTE
Honarhaye Ziba workshop,
Tehran
H. 50 cm.

MUSICAL
INSTRUMENTS

THE first references to musicians in Iran are found at Susa, Elam, in the twenty-seventh century B.C. The earliest representation of instruments is on the Elamite relief of Kul-i Fir'awn. An engraved bronze cup from Luristan at the Iran Bastan Museum, Tehran, portrays a double *ney* (reed pipes), *chang* (harp) and *dayereh* (tambourine) in a shrine or court processional, as similarly documented in Egypt, Elam and Babylonia, where music involved the utilization of large orchestral ensembles.[1] The Assurbanipal reliefs (626 B.C.) in the British Museum show Susian musicians.[2] Other "relief sculptures and paintings still extant from early periods...depict instruments as they are today,"[3] except that some, like the *chang* (harp) seen on the Taq-i Bustan reliefs near Kermanshah, have gone out of use.

Music continued to play an important role in the lives of the Persians throughout their history, with its continuity well documented in the Safavid frescoes of the Chehel Sutun in Isfahan, dated, 1647 A.D.

A major revival in Persian music has its inception late in the reign of Nasr-ed-Din Shah, (d. 1896 A.D.) who commanded the establishment of the *Dar'ol Sanaiye*, the "House of Crafts," a center where all important craftsmen could be gathered for making and marketing their instruments. Located southeast of the Sabz-i Maidan, the traditional vegetable market near the old South Tehran Bazaar and the Golestan Palace, there is an extant caravanserai in this area where textiles are sold.

Francis W. Galpin,
Music of Sumerians and
Their Immediate Successors

Henry George Farmer
Survey, p. 2784
Mehdi Forough
Survey, p. 3196

One of the most important makers of instruments at the *Dar'ol Sanaiye* was Ustad Fara-jollah, known for *tar*† and *setar*. He made few of either, his *setar*† being the rarer. Another master maker of *setar* was Haj Tayer.   Making fine *tar* at the opening of the Pahlavi era was Yahya, an Armenian from Julfa in Isfahan, who moved to Qazvin and subsequently to Tehran. Hassan Mashhun notes that his instruments are dated, the last known being 1320 or 1941 (2500). Yahya's father, Khachik, was a maker of *tar* and *santur*, and his uncle, Hambarson, was famous for his *tar*.⁴ Yahya is also known as Yahya the Second, since in former times there was also a Yahya known for *setar*. Yahya the Second took for his model the instruments of Ustad Farajollah. The *tar* of Shahrokh are second only to those of Yahya the Second.

372, Facing

Ruhollah Khalegi,
The Story of Iranian Music
Vol. 1

Seyyed Jalal of Qazvin was another master maker of *tar*† and *setar*. Semiretired Ustad 'Eshqi, a pupil of Seyyed Jallal, worked through the reign of Reza Shah and lived in the back of his shop in Amiriye in South Tehran. The National Iranian Radio and Television's Center for the Preservation and Propagation of Iranian Traditional Music has recently set up a workshop where *santur* and *setar* are made. Ustad 'Eshqi recently joined this workshop.

372 second right

Of many innovators in the history of Iranian instrument design, few were successful. One exception in the Zand Era (1750–1794 A.D.) was Darvish Moshtaq Ali Shah of Isfahan, master of *tar* and *setar*, who added an extra string between the former fourth and fifth strings of the standard *tar*, thus forming a new six-string "*tar*." He added an additional string between the former second and third strings of the standard *setar* (literally "three strings") for a new four-string "*setar*." This was not taken seriously until the master, Darvish Khan, (d. 1945) legiti-mized them, and they are today standard in both *tar* and *setar*. According to Hassan Mashhun, Darvish Khan's own teacher Ustad Mirza Husayn Gholi, however, rejected these innovations and continued to use the old five-string *tar* and three-string *setar*.

The master maker of the *kamanche*† was Hajji Muhammad Karim Khan, who died about fifty years ago. His instruments continue to be among the most prized.

373 right

There has always been a tradition of the so-called "amateur" craftsman. One in the early Reza Shah decade was Ali Muhammad Khan Safa, a finance ministry official, noted for the artistic inlay of wood stripping on the sound box, rather than the usual practice of carving a solid block. However, the sound of his instruments is reported not to be as fine as the more traditional.

Mehdi Nazemi, another amateur in this tradition, again exemplifies Farmer's remarks in the *Survey* that it is especially interesting how many Persians notable in other fields of endeavor have cultivated music as an avocation. This former oil company official from Yazd, now in Tehran, produces *santur*,† which are among the finest ever made. Now sixty-nine, he has been working on *santur* for thirty years since the death of his teacher, the master player, Habib Soma'i. One of his special techniques is to naturally dry and mature his wood in old manure for decades. Nazemi has completed at least fifty *santur*, and his instruments continue to be in great demand.

375 lower

Another such individual, Colonel Heydari, about seventy, who makes *setar*, is an artful innovator in his treatment of inlaid fingerboards in the style of Ustad Safa.

One final example of this proud tradition would be Mehdi Kamalian, a former high official of the Ministry of Health and an accomplished *setar* player. Kamalian is presently working with the National Iranian Radio and Television's Group for the Collection and Research on Iranian Music. He has also made several novel alterations in the *setar*.† He has changed the proportions between sound box and fingerboard or neck of the instrument, and has used various materials for his sound box—walnut wood, dried gourd, and even papier maché for the lower half, and black mulberry and ash wood for the surface of the sound box.

Facing lower

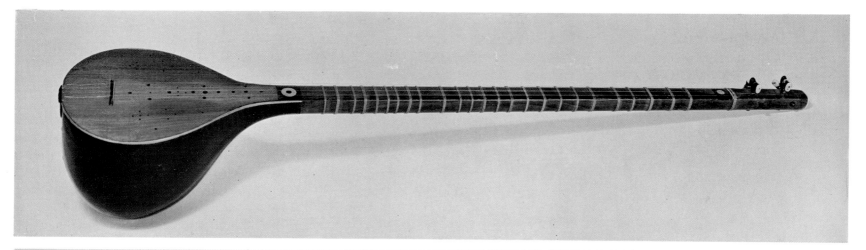

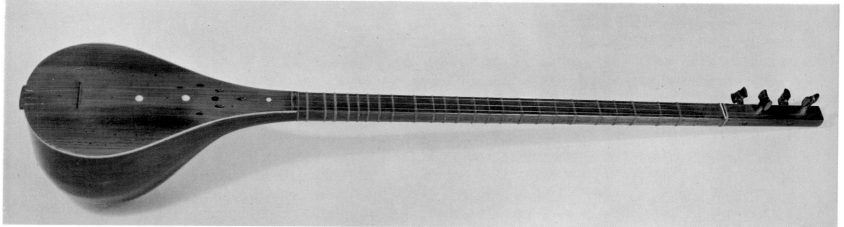

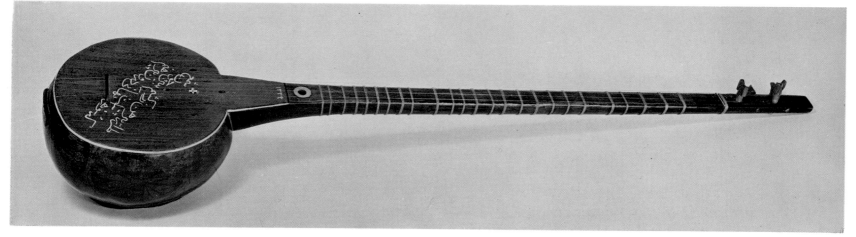

SETARS, 25 FRETS

"Espahbod"
Mulberry–walnut
By Farajollah, Tehran
Ca. 1885   L. 79 cm.

Mulberry–walnut
By Ebrahim Qanbari
1958   L. 85 cm.

Gourd sound box
Inlaid inscription
of Hafez poetry   *369*
By Mehdi Kamalian
Dated 1339 (1960), L. 85

The late Ja'afar Alamir, (d. 1968) an eccentric innovator, developed the unique "*navaz*," with sound box shaped like a *tar* but in the thickness of a violin and a one-piece mulberry wood body with changeable face and strings. It could be used as a *tar* or a violin. Alamir was offered U.S. patents and financing for his creation, but refused to leave Iran. Twelve of these novel instruments are known to have been completed before his death.

Another innovator, Ustad Ruhafza, Tehran *tar* and *setar* maker, is noted for his technique of forming the sound box. Made in two parts, customarily two lateral halves, he makes them of two unequal horizontal units.

Of further note would be Ustad Nariman who has revived the *'ud*,† the deep-bellied lute, after a century of neglect. An Assyrian, he is also known for his *setar*. The devotion of the minority groups in Iran—Armenians, Assyrians, Jews and even *Ghorbat*s (Gypsy)— especially

DOTAR

By Muhammad Husayn Yeganeh
Quchan   1970
Coll. NIRTV Group collecting
and research in music   L. 101 cm.

Scale *ca.* 1/4

Mulberry and jujube
By Ali Askar Afraz
Tayabad of Turbat-i Jam
Recent   L. 118 cm.

TAR

By Seyyed Jallal
Ca. 1926   L. 93 cm.

"YAQUT" (RUBY)

By Farajollah, Tehran
Ca. 1886   L. 94 cm.

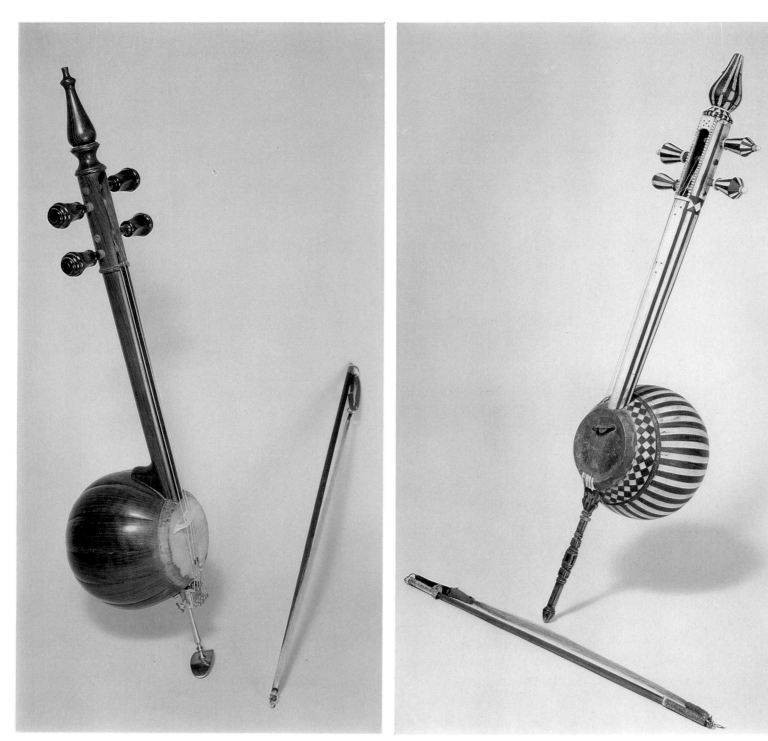

KAMANCHE, SPIKE FIDDLE: Walnut–black poplar, steel strings, Honarhaye Ziba workshop.   Recent.   D. Soúndbox 18 cm.
Walnut, betel nut, camel bone and mother-of-pearl by Hajji Muhammad Karim Khan.   *Ca.* 1880   L. With spike 87 cm.

in the early days of Islam and in frequent recurrent periods of strong orthodoxy, contributed to the preservation of traditional Persian music.

Ustad Ebrahim Qanbari is the most noteworthy instrument maker of the recent era. Responsible for the most important workshop of today in the Ministry of Culture and Art, he is currently submerged in teaching and innovating with his excellent group of craftsmen. Ustad Qanbari has been an employee of the Ministry of Culture and Art since 1955. Thanks to his mastery, a wide scope of activity has been included in his workshop, which not only makes all the instruments related to the music of *dastgah*—the *tar, setar,*† *santur,*† *kamanche,*† *tonbak* (*zarb*) and recently the *ghanun*†—but is also making Western string instruments, like the violin, viola, violoncello, and lately even a harp.

371, 375, Above

375 upper

373

Drums at *taziyeh* performance, Shiraz Arts Festival, 1976   Making *geychak*, Honarhaye Ziba workshop

Since numerous other traditional instruments are used in Iran, although mainly in the provinces, the Ministry of Culture and Art decided to incorporate them into the traditional *dastgah* music, and Ustad Qanbari was asked to remake and adjust them to the demands of both *dastgah* style and the new orchestra medium. This is a most difficult task since these instruments were desired and designed to respond to a particular cultural stylistic media.

In the provinces, the *sorud*, or *geychak*,† for example, historically known to have had only two strings, is currently used with four principal strings and five sympathetic strings. This instrument is used for Baluchi epic and *guat* (exorcism) music. The *tanbur* is used in the Kurdish sect of Ahl-hagh (the people of truth). The *saz* is the instrument of the Ashegs, the epic singers of Azarbaijan. The *robab*, as called in Seistan, *ruh-bab*, literally the Gate to the Soul, still accompanies the *ghazal*, or mystic texts, sung with poems of Khaje Abdullah Ansari, Molana Jallal-ed-Din Rumi and others.

The *dotar*† of Khurasan is a long-necked lute with two strings, still the traditional instrument of that enormous province and of significant historical interest. It is used mainly in northern and eastern Khurasan and by the Turkomans of Gurgan. Research is being undertaken by the authors [Fozieh Majd, Head of the National Iranian Radio and Television's Group for the Collection and Research on Iranian Music, and Mehdi Kamalian] to link the *dotar* with the *tanbur* of Khurasan, as described by Farabi, *Mussighi Kabir*.

There are several craftsmen working with Ustad Qanbari. These include Husayn Sanati, born in Borujerd, with thirty years of experience especially in the making of the violin and the *'ud*; Ali Asghar Zangene Semnani, born in Tehran, with twenty-five years of experience especially with *santur* and *setar*; Mansur Bahranmi Gorji, born in Khansar of Gulpaygan, with eighteen years of experience especially in *robab* and harp; Mahmud Ghorban-Ali, born in Borujerd, a specialist in *tar*; Hessam Moradi, born in Shiraz, a specialist in *ghanun*; Fereydun Salehi, born in Mianeh, a specialist in violin, and Mohammad Hossein Rostami, born in Tehran, a specialist in violoncello.

With the exception of the *dotar*, Ustad Qanbari has made some alterations in all instruments mentioned above. The *sorud*'s or *geychak*'s current five sympathetic strings have been eliminated, and it is made in such a way that a *kamanche* player can play upon it. The *robab*, or *ruh-bab*, the short-necked lute, now has a longer neck or fingerboard so that more frets can be

Above right

372 left

Santur hammers
Mehdi Nazemi

374

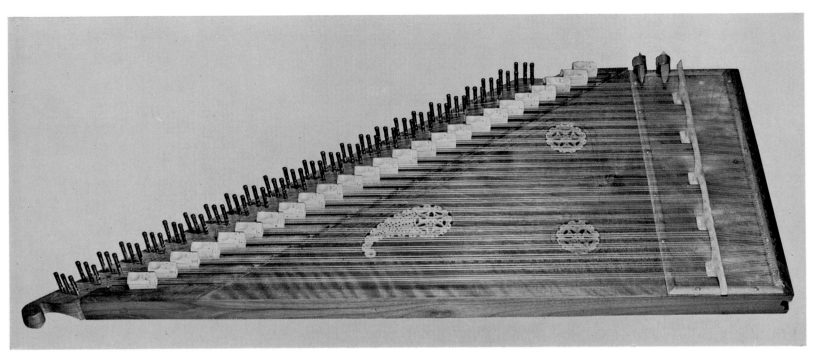

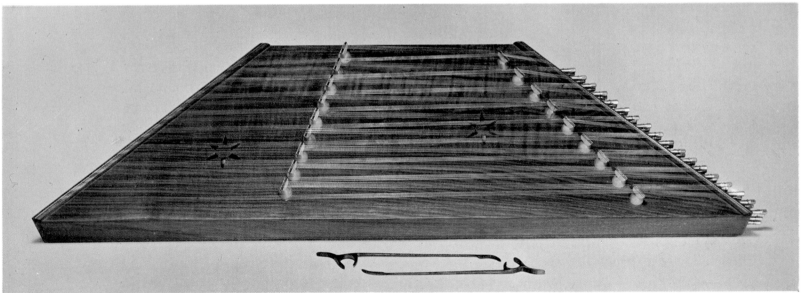

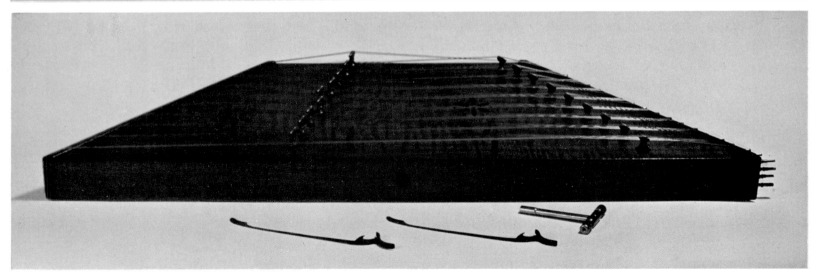

Top, GHANUN, 75 STRINGS
Walnut with sheep-gut strings, Recent
Honarhaye Ziba workshop, Tehran, Front L. 100 cm.

SANTUR, 72 STRINGS (36 BRASS, 36 STEEL)
Center, Walnut and Boxwood, Honarhaye Ziba workshop   L. 90 cm.
Lower, Tuned to *G,* made by Mehdi Nazemi, 1975   L. 90 cm.

TONBAK DRUMS

"ZARB," INLAID WITH *KHATAM*
Shiraz   1900
D. Membrane 23 cm.

WITH TUNING DEVICE, PLANE TREE WOOD
Honarhaye Ziba workshop   Tehran
D. Membrane 26 cm.

added. The *tanbur* has not been altered, but the workshop has produced *tanbur* on the model of the late Elahi, leader of a branch of the Ahl-hagh sect in Tehran, who died in 1975.

Ustad Qanbari has also made certain remarkable innovations in the traditional *dastgah* instruments. The *santur*, the *kamanche*, and the *tonbak* have had certain structural alterations with new devices introduced for tuning. The steel ring device with three key tuning sockets for the *tonbak*† is of particular note, for it is now possible for the player to adjust his instrument to the basic modal tonic of a *dastgah*. Also in group playing, especially in orchestras, the *tonbak* finds a new directional role, since it is now possible to prescribe a particular note for the instrument. These are experimental devices which have been introduced by Ustad Qanbari to make these instruments adjustable to a new orchestral media, and it is possible that much use will be made of these new innovations by the composers searching for expressions within a national unity or identity.   —FOZIEH MAJD and MEHDI KAMALIAN

Above right

376

QALAMDAN PEN BOXES

Painted by Vahab, Tehran, 1854
Museum of Decorative Arts   L. 22 cm.

By Sani Humayun, Tabriz, *ca.* 1910
Museum of Decorative Arts   L. 21 cm.

Cartouche by Ali Kerimi, *ca.* 1970
L. 22 cm.

Artist unknown, *ca.* 1970   L. 25 cm.
with detail of side view

Painting a pushcart, Tehran

PAINTING

Painting a *qalamdan*, Tabriz

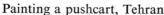

PAINTING as decoration is known from the dawning of humankind and is common to all peoples, but what characterizes Persian painting is its miniature quality. The term miniature was unknown to us until applied by Europeans in the past century in recognition of this. It, of course, developed out of the private nature of our art due to religious strictures. At various times in our history we have known murals and larger paintings: Qajar art is noted for these, Safavid had the great murals of Chehel Sutun and the homes of Julfa, murals have been excavated at Nishapur from tenth century sites and are known in many Sasanian and Parthian remains. Certainly the pictorial tiles of Persepolis must rank as paintings and indicate that murals probably existed then too. But even the paintinglike friezes of Persepolis, almost life-size in their representations, are outstanding for their meticulous, almost microscopic detail.† It is this quality, common to all ages of Persian art, that was particularly developed in painting of recent centuries.

Survey Pls. 90–99
176

With religious considerations restricting figural painting of a public nature, it was natural that the urge to represent life turned to decorating smaller private objects. A notable medium for this work in recent centuries has been the pen box, the *qalamdan,* commonly made of papier maché, as well as book covers, boxes of various types and mirror backs and other personal objects. The Persian term for the medium is literally oil painting, in recognition of the oil— actually a form of lacquer—with which the final watercolor-type pigments are coated.

The origins of the papier maché are not clear. From extant book covers we know that through Seljuq times manuscripts were bound in *zarbi* covers, that is, leather embossed or stamped with a design from a hot iron template and that motifs were pure *eslimi*, the so-called "arabesque," without floral embellishment. In Mongol times, especially in the school of Herat, ordinary books were still bound in leather *zarbi*, but important manuscripts were favored with *sukht*, an *eslimi* cut out of thin leather and glued on the leather binding. The repertoire of decoration included fine calligraphy. Papier maché is not known despite the common empire with paper-producing China.

PAINTED MIRROR WITH DOOR
Exhibited Mashhad, 1976   H. 45 cm.
Above, door opened, *Right*, closed.

Farmer's horsecart, Kashan

In Safavid times book covers and other objects made of papier maché suddenly appear in Tabriz and become common as the art styles and power base move to Qazvin and Isfahan. Decoration favors scenes of the royal hunt, an ancient iconographical motif dating back to at least Parthian times and with influences as far afield as Korea and Japan in Sasanian times. Motifs expanded to include floral patterns, evolving into naturalistic representations of individual flowers as in the almost scientific botanical style of the Zands of Shiraz in the eighteenth century. The latter style continues to find favor, but through the nineteenth century degenerated into mere prettiness.

The manufacture of the papier maché base has not changed. Some objects are made of true papier maché, that is, masticated paper, or compounded of paper pulped, while most are made of layered pasted paper. What has changed and caused degeneration is the change in the paper type used. Originally *khanbaleq*, true Chinese paper, the so-called "rice paper," was used which has the quality of exceptionally long life—millennia at times. Because paper was never successfully produced here on large scale it was expensive, and with the introduction of Western wood pulp newsprint late in the last century, this ever available cheap material came into common use. Its unfavorable quality is that its chemical process is never fully terminated and it continues over the years to literally digest itself in its wood acids, turning brown in several years, and to dust in several decades to a century. But with *khanbaleq* papers now being machine-made in Japan and China, [the new printing of the *Survey of Persian Art* for the Shahbanu Farah Foundation utilizes these long-lived papers in the text volumes, *Ed.*] and thus more readily available and economical, the editors of this volume have started to introduce them to Iran and one hopes the art of papier maché will benefit from this.

The paper board maker sits before a flat polished stone slab some fifty by sixty centimeters and twelve to fifteen thick. For an album binder or book cover a sheet of good quality white paper at least two centimeters larger all around than the final cover is thoroughly soaked in water (so that it can be easily removed from the stone later) and spread on the slab, smoothed to eliminate any air bubbles. Then layers of soaked newsprint—or preferably *khanbaleq*—of the same size are soaked in a large vat of glue and laid carefully upon the base paper. When the desired thickness is obtained, another sheet of fine paper tops it all off. A flat wooden board is placed on top and subjected to heavy weight for twenty-four hours of drying, after which it is removed and cut to size with a *gazan*, a blade originally for cutting leather.

For shaped objects, wooden molds are used. Pen boxes call for two molds, one for the outer slip cover and one for the inner draw box. For the cover a solid wood is heavily soaped and the paper coated as above, beating and burnishing it periodically. When finished and dry one end is cut off in a decorative shape which will be the final draw-cover fit, and the bar of wood is removed. The drawer is built up inside a mold of exactly the same dimensions as the bar's outer size. When dry, this is removed and the previously cut-off end of the shell is affixed over one end of the drawer. Filing and sanding finish off the two parts to fit perfectly.

A single coat of sizing is now applied—for the best, *katireh* or gum tragacanth; for cheaper, the sizing will be *serishom*, gelatin of animal hoof (not to be confused with *serishom* of the bilingual dictionaries which is properly *serishom-mahi*, fish glue), or *angom*, gum arabic. If the ground of the painting is to be dark, then this is added next. Otherwise the painting is done directly on to the single sizing. Colors were formerly mixed with egg white, but now painters use *serishom* or *angom* or *shir-i angur*, the residue from boiling down grapes, also once known as *dush-ab*. A good pigment mixture would be ninety-five percent mineral color, three percent *serishom* and two percent *shir-i angur*. Good reds are made from Armenian clays, the *lajvardi* and blues from minerals. Copper oxides were once used but abandoned as they are lethal. Most colors used today are imported gouaches and British Windsor is preferred.

PAINTED EMBOSSED LEATHER
Signed *Husayn Khata*, Isfahan, 1961   W. 80 cm.

Brushes now are also usually imported, for while the traditional brush allowed for finer work and a characteristic stroke, the economics of the art today make them impractical, for the preparation of a brush could take as long as the painting of a pen box. The old brush was of the hair of the Persian cat, the best being from the back of the neck and down the spine almost to the tail, with only the first growth used off the young adult cat. This is springy, and later cuts would have blunt tips. The hair is cut to half its length and soaked in water, being careful to preserve the orientation. Then they are laid out one by one on paper to dry. They are then "combed" with the thumb and aligned. Then a crow quill—actually a pigeon feather—is placed on a glass sheet and the tip cut off at a slight bias and cut again where the feather branches out. The hairs are then assembled and tied with a thread, dipped in glue to shape the brush head. The thread tying it is led through the wide end of the quill and out the point. The brush head of cat hair is placed point first into the quill top, pulled through by the thread till it emerges from the tip. The wet glue on the hair affixes it to the wall of the quill when dry.

After the decoration is painted, the oil must be applied. The decoration itself is often done by two artists, one doing the main illustrative cartouche, the other adding the bordering floral or *eslimi*. If gold work is done this is usually by a third man. The finishing oil coat must be applied in a dust-free atmosphere. The traditional formula was *bazrak*, sesame seed oil, seventy percent, *jala* oil, fifteen, and *sanderus*, a kind of rosin also used in batik, fifteen. The sesame was boiled and as the other elements were added this had to be covered quickly as it is highly flammable and many artists were injured in explosions. It was boiled to a paste, then cooled in batches to be used over the years. The procedure is similar to Chinese and Japanese urushiol, but here only up to eight applications, each being in a glass box to keep out dust then sunned for two hours. Today Sadolux brand imported oil is applied in three coats.

The ground of the painting is called *bum* and the finest ground *bum-morghesh* indicates stippled gold, the most beautiful effect and most difficult to make. Gold was also used to line the inside of fine *qalamdan*s. This was leaf gold hammered from coins between lime-soaked chamois. A coin would be pressed into a strip, stacked in alternate layers of gold and chamois, wrapped in cow's leather and strapped to an anvil to be pounded four thousand blows with a sledge hammer. This could be used as leaf, or further processed to powder for the *bum-morghesh*. Coins were preferred for their known purity, but the late Isfahan miniaturist, Emami—and his surviving daughter continues—prepared his own gold in this manner using bullion from the mint of equally guaranteed purity. This gold leaf process went to India.

Similar painting techniques are still executed on leather for book bindings—many of which never see a book under them but are framed and hung as paintings.† Papier maché is a tedious process and wood is frequently substituted, especially now that improved techniques for treating woods against warping and cracking are available. Large doors† and panels were always done in wood and the painted door in the Safavid house had the artistic importance reserved in the West for hanging paintings. Its only counterpart is the Japanese door.

These seemingly minor crafts, products of pen boxes and mirrors and today cigarette and button boxes, are an important aspect of fine art, the base of the bridge between craft and art. The almost mass-production painting of *qalamdan*s is training for young artists some of whom may rise to greater heights, and they are finger exercises for the more accomplished masters who do the main cartouches, like daily practice or rehearsals for a musician. Few are signed, for they are just practice, but should a good one or a good batch result from one of those lovely days when everything goes just right, then the signature may be applied and the world of fine art thus enriched. And if not, then at least more beauty has been sent out into the world.

The motifs of modern work are the old scenes, idealized and unrelated to the modern world perhaps, but were they not always so idealized as to be unreal at any true period of history.

—Ali Kerimi

Preceding

Facing

PAINTED DOORS
By Hatifi, Isfahan
Ca. 1973   H. 195 cm.

383

Mosaic
tools

ARCHITECTURAL DECORATION

CARVING
PAINTING AND
GILDING STUCCO
Hotel Shah Abbas, 1976

Upper right,
Stucco partly
carved, pencil sketched

Upper left,
Painting stucco

Middle right,
Gold leaf added

Lower,
Finished ceiling unit

IT is through design in its deepest sense that the Persian genius for visual beauty has found its most adequate and characteristic expression. To the twentieth century Western mind, words like "ornamental" and "decorative" too often suggest something of secondary importance. In architecture, simple and massive forms certainly have independent value of their own, but they also provide the substructure for ornamentation. A genius for lucid and vigorous decoration was already a striking feature of the prehistoric pottery of this region, and sumptuous embellishment, mentioned in the earliest descriptions of buildings, has been archaeologically confirmed. In fact, important structures of all periods in Persia have been aglow with color, from the red-painted brick and daub of the simple structures of fifth or even seventh millennium Sagzabad or the earth-colored painted tiles of second millennium Luristan to the brilliant eye-dazzling enameled polychrome tiles of Susa and Persepolis and the painted stuccos of the Parthians and Sasanians.

The motifs of poetry and visual ornament are deeply akin and both share the same faults, notably the urge for ingenious elaboration in which a *horror vacui* is too great a temptation to overcome and can crowd the theme. Yet, that which to a hurried Western viewer may seem a surfeit of opulence is to the Persian, who values contemplation, an invitation to leisurely exploration, a promise of endless delight.

The primary themes are three: symbolic plants and natural forms (from prehistoric time expressing fertility and abundance); geometric schemes (especially since Parthian times due partly to Greco-Roman and Chinese contributions in repopularizing them, but as we know from recent archaeological discoveries by Claire Goff in Luristan and James Mellaart in Çatal Hüyük with striking parallels in the contemporary painted pottery, continuing on through the modern weaves of the very same areas, never having vanished); and calligraphic compositions (from the Islamic period).

Calligraphy in Persia, as in the Far East, is ranking as a major—indeed elemental— art. The Arabic alphabet, the most decorative of all scripts, was cultivated with a passion and was developed by the Persians into an amazing variety of beautiful forms, which ingenious architects incorporated into every part of the mosques so that the building virtually became the word of God.

The many forms of Persian architectural ornamentation are rendered in different materials: stucco; brick in countless forms; to a lesser degree, wood—especially in exquisite patterns for railings and ceilings; metals, for window gratings and ceremonial doorways—generally repoussé over wood; and polychrome faience, in mosaic fragments or solid tiles.

NARENJESTAN PALACE, SHIRAZ: Cutting brick of Pl. 390 lower, cutting tile, laying brick and tile

Stucco—carved, molded, painted—was for nearly two thousand years one of the major elements in Persian architectural ornament. It is significant that in medieval times, stucco patterns, as well as designs for luster faience, mosaic faience and painted ornament, were made by the same artist. While the design of stucco is extremely difficult, the carving requires little more than a carver's skill.

First, the wet plaster is applied to wall or ceiling in a large mass to form the foundation of the design which is blocked out; then as it stiffens to the consistency of cheese the essential motifs and figures are carved, with small sections of new plaster added as necessary. Finally, after the plaster is almost stone-hard, it is cut and polished until it gains clear and lively contours—all rather more difficult than it sounds as we learned during the restoration of the lively Shiraz rose-pattern stucco on the Narenjestan porches† and in the library.† The final process is a plaster coating as thin as paint that can yield a surface almost like polished marble, or a matte base for subtle polychromy. Floral magnificence and exploitation of its fluid possibilities in this lyrical style of carved stucco was chiefly due to Persian inspiration and workmanship.

Enameled tile rivaled stucco but never completely displaced it, as the century-old Narenjestan testifies. Indeed the shallow carved, gaily painted and gilded stucco murals of Safavid Isfahan were brilliant interior complements to the exterior tilework, their matte finish accentuating the gloss of the tile glaze. Recently revived in the Hotel Shah Abbas in that same city by Mehdi Ebrahimian, the new work is in most aspects every bit a match for the original.

Ebrahimian, however, intelligently controlled his poetic *horror vacui*, which at times defeated the Safavid poet-artists. When several of his carved polychrome murals had reached a point in the coloration where one might cry out "enough," the artists stopped, leaving the ground plain, the painted areas floating lightly above.† It is a highly successful effect which blends with the necessarily modern atmosphere of the hotel. There are also interesting developments of Safavid mirror-mosaic combined with painted plaster,† often simplified to fit better in minor situations and frequently highly successful, yet grown from a solid tradition.

CARVED STUCCO
MARBLE PALACE
Bedroom of Reza Shah
1934–37

NARENJESTAN
SHIRAZ
Porch, re-created stucco
1967

HOTEL SHAH ABBAS
Painted stucco, 1967–68

Facing lower left

403 upper

402

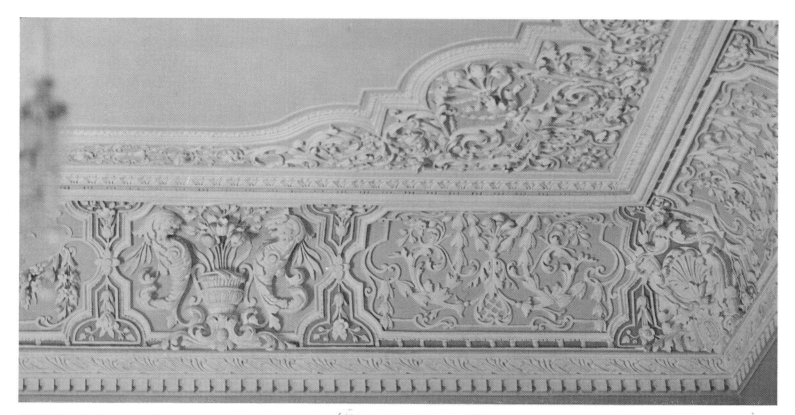

387

MAKING GLAZED TILES IN MONGOL PERIOD-STYLE FOR DOME OF MAUSOLEUM OF ULJAITU, SULTANIYEH
Kneading clay, pressing clay in molds, glazing dried tiles, Mongol-type kiln set up on grounds.

Brick was an accepted building material throughout the whole ancient Near East, for the hand-molded plano-convex brick had been invented in Persia by the third millennium B.C., with large flat bricks in use at Sagzabad perhaps as early as the seventh millennium. Nonetheless, though brick was in general use, its decorative possibilities were not exploited until well into the Islamic period—stucco had been more or less supreme as a surface ornament. But with the Seljuqs, the carving of plaster gave way to the intricate geometry of patterned brick lays and carved brick details in such masterpieces as the Isfahan Masjed-i Jami'.† Here acres of monochrome brick galleries play an architectural solo for the eyes that can only be compared with the aesthetic of the grand pipe organs in the counterpart European cathedrals. It is brickwork carried to a perfection, both aesthetic and constructional, that has perhaps never been equalled since.

Survey, Pls 285-300

SIDE COURT, NARENJESTAN PALACE, SHIRAZ RE-CREATION OF SELJUQ-STYLE BRICK LAY, 1968

Certainly not for lack of trying, for many of the Qajar buildings have charming facades so reminiscent as to be obvious attempts at replicating Seljuq brick lays. And when undertaking the restoration of the Narenjestan Garden Palace in Shiraz deeded to me by His most generous Highness, Prince Shahram Pahlavi, we attracted a wonderful brick mason who performed what Sir Edward Luytens was referring to when he wrote, "Do not speak to me of Persian brickwork but rather of Persian brick magic."

The Narenjestan—which was to house my revived Asia Institute and be a center for the continuation and expansion of the *Survey of Persian Art*—was inspected by Her Imperial Majesty Farah Shahbanu during the Shiraz Arts Festival of 1968. A late summer night under a sparkling Shiraz sky, the building and garden were awash in the daring and ingenious lighting system—totally unobtrusive despite its complexity—with underwater lamps adding visual music to the fountains, theatrical footlighting bringing broader smiles to the "smiling brick" patterns worked by the brick master, and virtual tinkling laughter to the gay mirror-mosaic work of the great *ivan*.

Her Majesty, I am told, paused and sighed, and revealed how she had long dreamed of a revival of Seljuq brick magic, and how here it had been done in Shiraz. Her wish that it be emulated was immediately put into effect in the then newly rising Pahlavi University buildings and in several homes under construction in Shiraz and soon elsewhere in Iran.

**MOSAIC, BRICK AND TILE
DETAILS**

NARENJESTAN, SHIRAZ
Tympanum, inner court
Cut and carved brick

Ceiling, basement gallery
Carved brick with cut tile insets

ISFAHAN, HOTEL SHAH ABBAS
Main entrance facades.
Hassan, Husayn and
Mehdi Mosadeqzadeh
W. Lozenge 147 cm.

**MAUSOLEUM OF
ARTHUR UPHAM POPE**
Safavid-style mosaic in variant colors
In Seljuq-style brick lay (*left*)
Mongol-style carved grillwork (*right*)

Preparing paper pattern and cutting tiles to fit, Ganj Ali Khan complex, Kerman, 1976

It is assembled from pieces cut from solid color tiles. First, clay must be selected, washed, refined and thoroughly kneaded into a smooth consistency of just the right texture.† Only then is *388 upper left* it pressed into square molds.† The clay squares must be sun dried thoroughly, usually for a day, *388 upper right* for a little pocket of moisture left in the bisque could explode in the kiln, or at least warp the tile or prevent the glaze from adhering. A liquified mineral,† finely powdered metal in sus- *388 lower left* pension, is poured on and the tile placed into the kiln† where the heat transforms this glaze *388 lower right* into brilliant color. Each color has an optimum firing temperature with *lajvardi* and turquoise the highest, reds and yellows lowest, while some ripen best under an oxygen-rich flame, others under oxygen reduction. It is this perfection of color tone that accounts for why the considerable extra expense of mosaic is preferred over the simpler *haft rang* painted tiles which must be fired at a lower temperature to accommodate the many colors at once.

The design is outlined in black and white on paper† with repeat patterns often traced from *Above* pinhole-punctured stencils. Small sections are cut out of the paper pattern and pasted on the face of the square tile according to the required color and eventual placement.

The square tiles are then cut into the element of the composition following the paper keys†— *Above, 392, 393* an extremely difficult operation, for the glaze, now harder than glass and more brittle and fragile due to its composition, must not be chipped at the edges, the body not be frayed since the units must fit together like pieces of a jigsaw puzzle. Workers acquire an uncanny skill using an unlikely looking adze that seems ponderously clumsy for such delicate work, much like doing surgery with a butcher's tools, its corner points serve to peck out tiny fretwork. Then tight corner indentations are finished off with a graver or chisellike instrument. In recent years drills and jigsaws have come into use. The best *kashi-kar,* or tile cutters, can cut an intricate *eslimi* design in multiple repeats to fit a specified space without using a pattern or referring to a design sketch or plan.

MOSAIC TILE
WITH GOLD
stad Mostafa Mosadeqpur
58   H. 104 cm.

395

Template for laying Mosaic Tiles for Dome Shell, Masjed-i Jami', Saveh

CEILING
MOSAIC GLASS
with
METAL FRETWORK
LIGHT SHADE
Hotel Shah Abbas
Isfahan

Survey, Pl. 546
393, preceding

392 lower right

The units of the design are now placed face down following the composition on a full-scale sketch plan. For huge flat plaques the myriad of tiny tiles are placed on a smooth floor. One, consisting of some 17,000 pieces, was being made for Doris Duke Cromwell's Hawaiian palace when I noted down the details of the procedure many years ago. Earlier I had seen and photographed the Mosadeqpur brothers working in great ship-bow pie segments to redo the mosaic dome of the Madraseh Madar-i Shah.† A huge flat plaque much larger than the panels illustrated here† cannot be lifted in one piece, so small bits of cardboard are set in to divide it into sections, as they were in the dome segments for the Madraseh.

The back of the tile† is next thickly covered with plaster of paris over which water is poured to help the plaster adhere to the porous raw tile. The mortar is then poured—very slowly at first for if poured too quickly it will knock the bits out of line. Short segments of chopped rope are put into the mortar as it is poured as a binder, much as straw was used in most ancient bricks and earthenware to give greater strength to the backing. The work done today only in Isfahan and in the Gawhar Shad Mosque in Mashhad by potters of Mand, equals the finest of antiquity when the masons are given proper incentive.

It is a brilliant technique of assembly. Were each unit fashioned individually and then embedded, it would be an excessively long and far more laborious process and would lack uniformity and finish. This ingenious method of manufacture, as painstaking and laborious as it is, is a prodigious timesaver, providing a smoother and more elegant finish and giving all the qualities we can ask of a mosaic. It results in more brilliant, scintillating colors than Hellenistic stone-tesserae mosaic and grander and more sweeping design possibilities can be realized than with Byzantine glass-tesserae mosaic. Its slight imperfections of aligning the surface on an absolute uniform plane add to its charm, for the reflections which often dance over a whole surface sometimes have flashing sheets of light momentarily blot out all color and design in the eye of the beholder, sometimes giving a rippling water twinkling effect when the same occurs on single-element surfaces in erratic succession.

Mosaic work has never elsewhere been accomplished in such an exquisitely minute form, yet on such immense facades and voluptuous domes. And it is like the Persians to have used as an architectural technique something as fine and delicate as book illumination.

—ARTHUR UPHAM POPE

Assembling stained glass with wood ribs,
Honarhaye Ziba workshop, Tehran

GRILL WINDOWS, CHEHEL SUTUN, ISFAHAN
Re-created by Roberto Orazi (ISMEO) and Hassan Oshaghi

STAINED GLASS WINDOWS IN GRILLWORK
Caravanserai Moshir, Shiraz, 1969–70
Re-created under direction of Paulette Khodabandeh

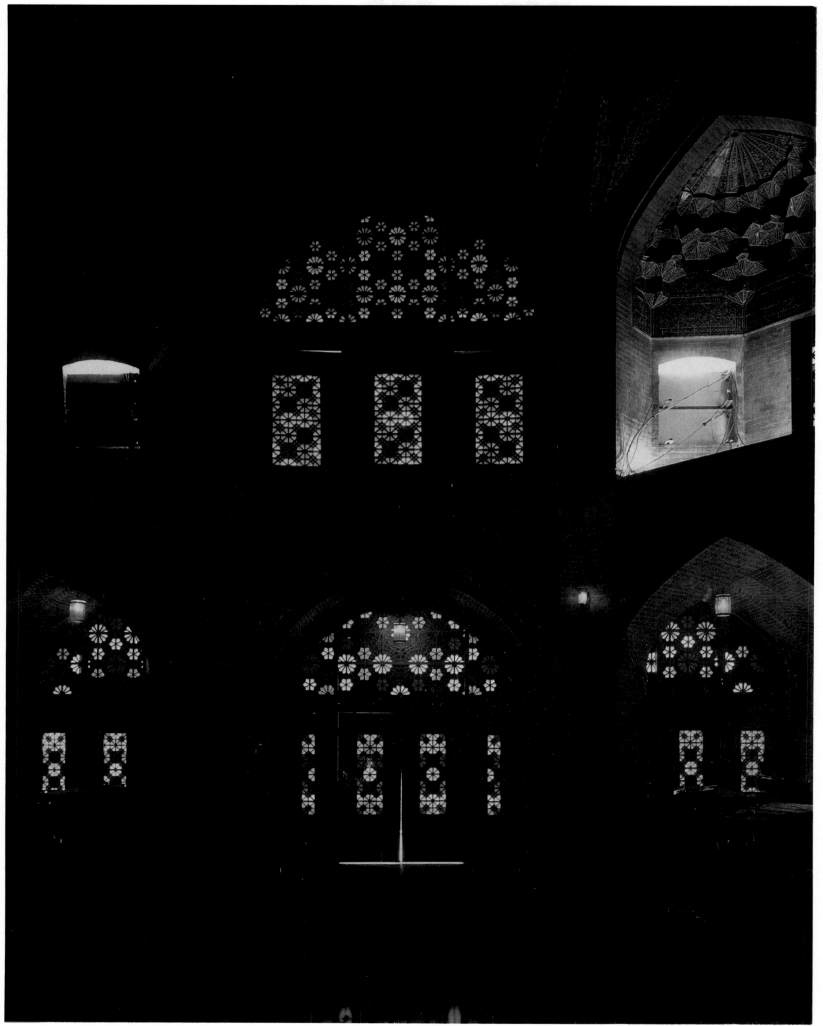

OPAQUE STAINED GLASS AND MIRROR, NEW FRETWORK AND GLASS IN 18th–19th CENTURY FRAME
Hotel Shah Abbas, Isfahan
1968

CARVED,
PAINTED STUCCO

GLASS INSETS,
WOODWORK
Hotel Shah Abbas, Isfahan
Designed and executed by
Mehdi Ebrahimian, 1968–69

Overleaf DOME,
MARBLE PALACE
After dome of
Masjed-i Sheikh Lutfullah
By Heydar Siyah Lurzadeh,
Muhammad Husayn
Khak Negar

That all these architectural crafts are again—or yet—appreciated is obvious from a drive through Tehran: downtown offices sparkle in brilliant mosaic tilework, and there is imaginative woodwork on the carpet bazaar-office building above Ferdowsi Square. Drive through Vanak, Golhak or other rising residential areas of Tehran and outside evidence of stained glass windows and decorative tile panels give a hint of what has been done inside. This, too, is only the decorative aspect of architecture—we have not touched on architecture itself as it is an art apart and no mere handicraft. An art which perhaps more than any utilizes almost all of the finest crafts; it is most important to their continuation and evolution. Possibilities are only suggested in such as the brilliant use of traditional brickwork to produce superb acoustic control as in Moqtader's small theater in Pahlavi University, Shiraz; traditional brickwork and structures as in Ardelan's Graduate School of Business in Tehran; or traditional forms and space concepts built with modern materials as Diba's Modern Art Museum or Majd's palace of the Crown Prince in Saadabad. And there are enough others to be worth more than a mere footnote.

The possibilities are limitless. One need only try them out in Isfahan where the craftsman-power is there to realize them.

406

AFTERWORD

THERE comes a point where a book must be considered finished—not complete, perhaps, but done. William Faulkner said the point was that at which you accepted failure, sent the manuscript off to the publisher and started on your next failure—and failures you could be sure they would be, for the serious artist could never do the subject of his art justice. At the other extreme were, and are, writers like the late Arthur Upham Pope, who revised and rewrote endlessly even rewriting whole galley proofs, till those around him reached a point where someone had to snatch his pencil away, grab the manuscript or proof and cry "Enough!" And by the time his article or book came out he had a manuscript for an expanded edition.

For our many failings, we accept judgment and hope we will be informed so that future editions or future writing can benefit. For what we may have accomplished we are indescribably indebted to too many people for the customary *Preface* so we acknowledge them here.

A book was first suggested to us by Kichinosuke Tonomura of the Kurashiki Folk Museum in the early sixties, who asked us to obtain samples of contemporary weaves for his collection. Mrs. Anoush Kazemi helped shop the Tehran Bazaar in 1963, and the saddlebags bought for personal use in our university residence in Wakayama became the most popular cushions in the house with visiting Japanese students. With Arthur Pope and Phyllis Ackerman in Iran on their state visit in 1964, talks started on new volumes for the *Survey of Persian Art*. Almost immediately Vol. XIV, *New Studies* 1938–1960 went to press, revisions and updatings to the basic volumes were projected and a number of new subjects suggested to fulfill the original title claim of the *Survey* covering *From Prehistoric Times to the Present*. The folk arts and artcrafts were the first in our minds, especially with the richness of the Shiraz bazaar to show us how much there was to work on. Then, and again in 1966 when the Popes moved to Shiraz and we packed to follow, a small selection was taken back to Japan for photographic tests and consultations with the printers on color problems. It was just such preliminary work prior to the reprinting of the *Survey* that taught us the necessity of using letterpress for the color as the offset did not have the range of inks necessary to do justice to the subtleties of Persian natural dyes and the pigments used for the miniatures. And for catching these nuances to the fullest, an especially close cooperation was necessary between photographer and printer. The photographs were made at the Hanshichi printer's studio with the support of the late Patriarch Shozen Nakayama of Tenri, whose Museum of Ethnology now houses some of the material tested. Of several photographers used, the work of Tadashi Yanagimoto was the most successful, both for the dramatic presentation of the material—the least difficult aspect of photography—and the accuracy of his colors. By the time we brought him to Iran in 1976 to take the bulk of large-format color photos for this book he had illustrated over one hundred art books, including most of the *Survey of Japanese Art* (Japanese and English editions).

Pope, on his visits in the late twenties and early thirties, photographed many of the living crafts, but black-and-white film was insufficient to communicate their beauty. Immediately after the war he produced a series of movie films with photographer Steve Nyman dwelling upon the continuity of art in Persia showing traditional craftsmen at work. (Pope later rewrote his script on mosaic tiles for use in the projected book, and it appears herein on pages 385–396.) The color film almost did justice to the carpets, and suggested what could be done under more controlled conditions. Economics forestalled any further work until 1966. The Pope black and whites are also an economic document, when the improvement in the dress of the craftsmen is noted. He also shows beautiful little girls of perhaps seven or eight weaving magnificent carpets in Hamadan, a sad practice ended by compulsory education and child-labor laws. These improvements have also understandably been reflected in the prices of the crafts products—it is not that they are too expensive now, but that they were too cheap then.

Relocated to Shiraz in 1967, first priority went to the restoration of the Narenjestan to be used as the library and research unit of the Asia Institute. Here the team was enlarged as we

Museum of Ethnology, and founder, *the late* patriarch Shozen Nakayama; Tokyo National Museum of Asian Art, Jiro Sugiyama; and The Ura Senke Foundation, Kyoto, Soshitsu Sen. In the *United States*, The Los Angeles County Museum of Art, Rexford Stead; and The Metropolitan Museum of Art's new Islamic wing where *the late* Léo Bronstein dictated the draft of his introductory chapter. In *England*, The British Museum Oriental department's Ralph Pinder-Wilson was particularly helpful in technical background material on Turkoman jewelry and embroideries.

A number of exhibitions were viewed and from several material was drawn for use herein. These include, *outside Iran*: Exhibition of Contemporary Persian Arts and Crafts in Honor of Arthur Upham Pope's Seventieth Birthday, Asia House of The Asia Institute, New York, Autumn 1950; repeated with changes, as part of the series Thousand and One Asian Nights, Asia House of Asia Institute, July 1951; Crafts of Iran, Iranian Pavilion Brussels World's Fair, 1958; Exhibition of Persian Folk Arts, sponsored by *Wakayama Shimbun* (newspaper), Wakayama Castle Municipal Museum, March 1964; Joseph V. McMullan Collection, Metropolitan Museum of Art, New York, 1964; Persian Folk Arts, Tenri Museum Pilgrimage Gallery, Tenri City, Nara, Japan, 1967–68 (one year); From the Bosporus to Samarkand Flat-woven Rugs, Textile Museum, Washington, 1969; World Folk Arts Exhibition Expo 1970, Osaka Japan, with the participation of Iranian Handicrafts Center; Lion Rugs from Fars, Smithsonian Institute Traveling Exhibition, USA, 1974–1977; Iranian Handicrafts, Iranian Handicrafts Organization Showroom, New York, 1976; The Qashga'i of Iran, World of Islam Festival, Whitworth Gallery University of Manchester, 1976; Locks from Iran (previewed), Smithsonian Institute Traveling Exhibition for the U.S. Bicentennial, 1976–77.

Exhibitions viewed in Iran: Persian Tribal Carpets, Iran America Society, Tehran, Autumn 1958; Iranian Handicrafts Center Inaugural Exhibition, Autumn 1966; Iranian Handicrafts (later Organization) Annual Exhibitions 1966, 1967, 1968, 1972, 1975, 1976; Handicraft Exhibition for Shiraz Festival, Shiraz, 1968, 1969, 1970, 1975, 1976; Tribal Animal Covers from Iran, Tehran Rug Society–Iran America Society, April-May 1975; Iranian Handicrafts Organization Tenth Anniversary Exhibition, Pope Gallery, Iran America Society, February 1976; Lori and Bakhtiyari Flatweaves, Tehran Rug Society–Iran America Society, March 1976; Handicrafts Organization Second Annual Awards Exhibition, Mashhad, July 1976; Ministry of Culture and Art Honarhaye Ziba Workshop Products Exhibition, Autumn 1976; Exhibition of Royal Iranian and Kashmir *Termeh* from The Collection of Rahim and George Anavian, Khaneh Aftab, November 1976. Regrettably we did not see the pioneering exhibitions, Gilan by Fahimeh Akbar, and Khurasan, both in 1960, but did benefit from knowledge imparted by friends and informants.

Private collections have been the major source of objects to photograph and of attributions. *In Iran*: *the late* Dr. Phyllis Ackerman (Pope), Reza Alavi, Bahman Amini, Manuchehr Anvar, Nader Ardelan, Ali Askar Bakhtiar, Laleh Bakhtiar, *the late* Yahya Khan Bakhtiar, Assadollah Behroozan, Jannat Bolandgray, *the late* Nurali Burumand, Bijan Darreshuri, Jasleen Dhamija, Mehdi and Violette Ebrahimian, Nasrine Faghih, Monir Farmanfarmaian, Iran Ala Firouz, Farrokh Gaffary, H. E. Ambassador James George, Lutfullah Honarfar, Mehdi Kamalian, Houshang Kazemi, Manuchehr Kazemi, Ibrahim Khalilli, Fozieh Majd, Mohammad Ali Majd, Zaleh Malujeh, Mehri Martinez, Leyly Matine-Daftary, Mohsen and Selma Moghadam, *the late* Mohammad Naraghi, *the late* Mohammad Nemazi, Carl J. Penton, Khosrow Pir, H. E. Issa Sadiq, Hajji Aziz Sanjavi, the Sepenta Collection, H. H. Prince Shahram Pahlavi, Sadre Shayesteh, Parviz Tanavoli, Farangis Shahrokh (Yeganegi), and John Wertime.

Elsewhere a number of items in private possession were photographed, particularly in Japan because of the ready availability due to the early Japanese interest in folk arts, especially among the professional potters and weavers, as well as in the United States. Except for commercial collections of tribal carpets—popular in both England and Germany—there was insufficient time to inspect European collections. However, the Qashga'i of Iran Exhibition included numerous fine pieces from such notable collections as those of Mary Burkett, Jenny Housego, David Marsden and others. *The United States*: Ruth Aley, the late Léo Bronstein, Osborne Hauge, C. Griffin Nelson, Isabel Tozzer and Ruby Zimmerman. *In Japan*: H. H. Prince Takahito Mikasa, Misaki Ando, Giichi Asano, Shoji Hamada, H. E. Abdol Hossein Hamzavi Ambassador of Iran, Takuo Kato, Tokuro Kato, Rokubei Kiyomizu, David Kidd, Michihiro Namba, Houn and Teiko Ohara, Akiko Shimada and Mihoko Yamazaki.

It is the dealers of Tehran who are most often responsible for getting collectors started and who thus establish the first provenance designations, which on occasion is later changed as scholarly detective work narrows down the attribution or discards the occasional dealer misnomer attempting to add antiquity or "import value" to works they fear may not be properly appreciated for their intrinsic beauty if attributed to a living Iranian craftsman. The contributors to this volume particularly wish to express gratitude to: Rahim and George Anavian, Belour, Isaac Cohen, Khodadad Mahgerefteh, Joseph Soumakh, Shokrullah Sakhai and Nejat Rabbi Soleimani, as well as the galleries, Khorshid Khanum, Zinat Sara, the former Maison d'Iran and the indomitable Doky Naraghi's Iranian Handicrafts. The advanced collector is soon deeply involved as well with the pleasant little stalls of the bazaars of Isfahan, Shiraz, Qazvin, Mashhad and the myriad smaller towns in between too innumerable to name, except that we must express our gratitude to Mohammad Meshkat, in the Isfahan Bazaar, for his special work creating the *qalamkar* cover of the deluxe edition limited to 2535 copies, and for much other advice.

In not all instances were objects in the above collections photographed, nor, of course, were all photographs used, but this in no way diminished the value of viewing collections and gaining valuable insights and information. Other collections, some known to us but which we were not able to see because of time limitations in the last hectic weeks, or which we are unaware of (and these must be innumerable) we hope will be encouraged by this book when they see that their own possessions are often equal to, sometimes superior to, representative examples illustrated here.

INDEX

Numerals in *italic* indicate illustrations

Abadeh, *279*, 346, 348, 352: shoes, *261*
Abady, Ustad, *70*, 72
Abbas, Shah, 68, 72, 104, 106, 226, 296
Abdullah, Mirza, vase by, *85*
Abiana, 212
Abu-al-Qasim, 206
Achaemenid, 15, 18, 56, 60, 116, 126, 172, 179, 274, 321: glass, 97
Ackerman, Phyllis, 9, 179, 180, 186, 192, 202, 206, 210, 218, 310, 411
Afghan[istan], 312: invasion, 14
Afraz, Ali Askar, 372
Afshar, 286, *300*, 310, *327*, 332, 336, 340
Ahl-hagh, dervish order, 374, 376
Ahmad ben Avi, Sultan, 362
Ain-e Akbari, 208
ajideh, darvish felt hat, *222*, 222
aklili, gold, bronze printed fabric, 186
alabaster, 30, *38*, *39*
'*alam*, processional standard, *142*, *143*, 144, *145*, 146, 156, 160
Alasht village, 346, *351*
Ali, Rajab, 234, *235*
Alikhani, Ali Naghi, Minister of Economy, 24
Alizadeh, Habib, stone mason, 40
Amini family, *qalamkari*, 192
Anatolia, 265, 296
Anavian, Rahim and George, 214
Andrews, M. and P., 246
animal, motif, etc., 128, *136*, 138, 172, *176*, 230, 273, 298, 336: combat theme, 126, 136
anklets, 172, *173*, 174
An-shi (Parthia), 217
apple tree leaves, 318
applique, 218, 243, 252, 277
arabesque (see *eslimi*), 114, 234
Arbab, Mohammed Mehdi, 190, 208
Archaeological Museum, Tehran, objects in, 30, *62*, *90*, 101, 369
Architecture, 8, 19, 266, 400: decoration, 9, 384–408
Ardebil (Ardabil), 160, 218
Ardelan, [Nader], 406
Aristophanes on glass, 97
Armenians, 128, 275, 310, 352, 371
Ars Islamica, 206
Art and Architecture of the Ancient Orient, 29
art of the people, 17, 18
Ashegs, epic singers, 374
Ashrafdareh, 180
Asia Institute, 8, 9, 389
Assalem, 44, 50, *51*, 80
Assurbanipal relief, 369
Assyria(ns), 274, 371
'*atiq*, stone paste pottery, 56
'*atiq-saz*, potter, 72
at kacheh, felt horse covers, 252
Atrian, *qalamkari*, *190*, 192
Avesta, 212: on carpets, 274
Ayrom, Major General, 366
Azarbaijan, 13, 14, 114, 184, 236, 374: gilim, *307*; pottery, *46*, 60

Babvieh, Ali, 367
Babylon(ia), 97, 369
backgammon, 346, board, *357*
baft-i nakhoni, fingernail weaving, 180, *181*, 182, *183*
Baghai, Afsaneh, 8
bags, various, 9, 184, 236, *238*, 254, 273 *294*, *296*, *298*, *299*, *307*, *308*, 310, 312, *335*
Bahadori, Issa, 94
Bahman-beigui, Mohammad, 292, 336
Bahram Gur, 275

Bakhtiar: Ali Askar, 411; Laleh, 138; Yahya Khan, 411
Bakhtiari [Lurs, Persian-speaking tribe], 25, 174, 184 236, 238, 275, 277, 285, 288, 310, 322, 324, 326, 332: carpets, *307*, *308*, *324*, *326*, 334
balandizi, copper-silver thread, 234
Baluch(istan), 27, 29, 41, 44, 45, 60, 97, 169, *170*, 170, *172*, 172, 176, 218, *265*, 266, 286, 312, 318, *321*, 322, 330, *331*, 332, *333*, 346: epic, 374; needlework, *2*, 27, 254–260, *257*, *258*, *259*; carpets, *314*, 318, *331*, *333*, 340, 342, *344*; pottery, 27, 41, 43–47, *43*, *44*, *45*, *46*, *47*, *49*
Baluchi, Ms. Zarkhatun, 256, *257*
balutt, horse chestnut, 285
bamboo, 265
Bampur, 170, *255*, 258
Bandar Abbas, 48, 169, 170, *172*, 172, *233*, 236, 261, *263*
Bank Melli, 5, 7, 94, 411
barak, fine woolen cloth, 184
barjesteh, raised pattern, *222*
Barnett, R. D., 277
baskets, 265–272, *265*, *266*, *267*, *268*, *269*, *270*, *271*, *272*: carbonized, 265
Basseri, 310
batik, 25, 186, 195–200, *195*, *196*, *197*, *198*, *199*, *200*, *250*: blocks, *196*, *200*
bazaar: Isfahan, 126; Shiraz, 16, 275, 310; Tabriz, 25; Tehran, 124, 369
Baz Bacheh, carpet, *324*
bazuband, armlet amulet container, 170, 282
bazu-bandi, ogive pattern, *210*
beads, 97, 104, 236, *240*, *255*, 258: blue, 56, *57*
bean pots, green glaze, *59*
beast, winged, 148
beehive covers, *84*
Behbahan, 278, 286
Behroozan, Assadollah, 8
bells, camel, *137*
Belt Cave, 177
belts, 170: cotton, 258
bentonite clay, 56
Berasoul, 192
Beshir, Ahmad, Kashmir weaver, 214
Bilish, 246
bird: motif on pottery, *5*, *71*, *73*, *74*, *77*, *84*, *85*; in metal, 146, *147*, 148; -shaped, *128*, *129*, *130*, *139*, *145*, *147*, *149*, *153*; woven, 200, 214, 218, 230, *298*;–and fish, *100*; -footed, 138, *139*
Birjandi brothers, *qalamkari*, 192
Birrell, Verla, 217
black tent, 286
blocks: printing, 186–192, *185*, *187*, *190*, *191*, *192*, 194; –resist (batik), 195–200, *196*, *199*, *200*; 10th century, 186, *196*; carving process, *360*
blue and white, ceramic, 68, *69*, *71*, 72, *73*,
blue beads, *57*, 170
blue glaze experiments, 56
Bokhara, 202, 362: embroidery, *226*
Bolurian, Mirza Assadullah, 128
bone, 362, 368
book covers, 162, 378, 380: –design, 11, 186
bookshelves, from old doors, 402
boqcheh, cloth wrapper, 182
Borghese, gallery, 9
Borujerd, 374
boteh, paisley pattern, cypress or almond tree, *194*, 200, *209*, 210, 211, 214, *215*, 216, 218, *219*, 221, 222, *224*, *231*, 234, 236, *243*, 302, *309*, 310, *326*, *333*, 336

bottles: glass, *79*, *83*, *86*, *88*, *89*, *92*, *102*, 106; cover, 122, *123*
Boulnois, L., 217
Bousheri, Mehdi, 8
bow(ing), 280, *280*, 288
bow-lathe for stone, 34
bowl, *51*, *65*, *73*, *75*, *77*, *79*, *81*, *83*, *85*: –copper, 116, *116*
box, *93*, 164: –*khatam*, 362
boxwood, 352, 375
Boyer Ahmad country, 278
bracelets, 169, *172*, *173*, 176, *176*
braided stitch, 260
Brandow, Mr. and Mrs. George E., item from collection of, *250*
brass, 126, *136*
brazier, charcoal, 50, *51*, *54*,
brick, 384, 388, 389, *390*, *391*: carved–, *390*; cutting–*386*; –patterns, 388; sun-dried–, *386*
bride, 234; –'s coats, 246, *249*, 250, *251*, *252*; –'s shawl, 230, *231*
bridlery, 248
British Museum, 369, 112
brocades, *179*, 186, 210, 212–216, 214, *214*: –figural, 212, *213*
Bronstein, Léo, 17–24, 8, 10, 162, 166, 362, 410
bronzes, 114, 152, 369: ritual vessels, 30
brushes, paint, 382
Buddhist: crowns, 170;–ideas, 338
Bujnurd, 286   217
Bulletin of Needle and Bobbin Club, 186,
bull figurine, stone, 29, *34*, 132
Bulvardi, 336
bum-morghesh, stipled gold ground, 382
Bunat, *329*
Burujerd, 186, 187
butcher, 150, *151*
butter, yoghurt churner, 52, *54*, 80
button, Turkoman, 174
buttonhole stitch, 243, *254*, 258, 260
Buyids, 18: –lion silks, 342
buzu, fine woolen cloth for *aba*, 184
Byzantine, glass-mosaic, 392

Calico, 186, 190
calligraphy, 15, 378, 384, *392*: on *qalamkar*, 194; on tiles, *400*
camel, 137, 330, 334, 368: –bone, *363*, 368; –wool, 318, 322; –bags, 274, 296; –trappings, 252, *253*, *254*; –motif, 226
candy cutter, 152, *153*
canes, 265, *265*, 266
caps: dervish, 222; Qashgai, *285*; Qashgai, Bakhtiari, villager, *288*
carafe, pair of brass, *136*
caravanserai, 9, 369: Moshir, 404, *405*
carmine, 179
carpet, 5, 7, 9, 14, 19, 354: rustic, 273–276; felt, 277–288; flat woven, 289–320; tufted, 321–344: gold-threaded, 274; "high school," 276, 321; lion, 342, *342*, *343*; Winter–, 275; –loom, 273, *321*; –tools, 154; –town, 275
carpets, tribal: Afshar, *300*, *326*, 340; Bakhtiar, *307*, *308*, *324*, 334, 340; Baluch, *314*, 318, 330, *331*, *333*, 340, 342, *344*; Khamseh, *309*, 311, *339*, 340, *343*; Kurd, *301*, 302, *302*, *303*, *304*, 333; Qashgai, *291*, 292, *292*, *293*, *325*, *326*, 338, 340 342, *344*; Shahsavan, 296, *297*, 298, *299*, 342, 344; Turkoman, *275*, 312
carpet weaving school, 292
Caspian, 8, 18, 60, 80, 312, 330, 351
Çatal Hüyük, 42, 177, 186, 217, 265, 266, 274, 384

Caucasus, 10, 14, 18, 186, 290: folklore, 180
Central Asia, 273, 321, 338, 340, 356
centrifugal movement, 126
ceramics, 19: pottery, 41–96; tile, 384–400
certosina, 362
chador, women's full cover, 222
chador-i kamari, scarf draped around waist, *182*, 214, 233
chador shab, in Mazanderan, scarf draped around waist, also hanging or bed cover; *178*, 179, 180
Chahar Bagh, 126, 128, 368
Chahar Shambeh Suri, year-end "last Wednesday" fire jumping rite, 90
Chaichi, 346
chain stitch, *218*, 218, 234, *235*, 242, 242, 252
chair, wooden, *346*
chalgush, earring, 172, *173*; –*baraye bini*, nose ring, 172
challah, finger ring, 172, *173*
chalor, raw stone nugget, *32*, 34
Chal Shotor, 156, 158
chamkali, pendant, *170*
champlevé, 162, *163*
Chardin, Sir John, 6, 104, 106, 124, 162, 186, 188, 218, 226, 322
Chehel Sutun, 369: murals, *378*; windows, *404*
chelle, main warp, 210
chess, 346: –board, 352, *353*, *357*
chest: sea, 354; Turkoman, 354, *355*
chikh, reed screen, 270, *271*, *jacket*
China, -ese, 114, 206, 292, 362, 366: designers, 338; embassy, 217; potters, 72; rulers' gifts of silk, 217
Chinese Art: Recent Discoveries, 217
chini-saz, stone paste potter, *70*, 72, *76*
chinoiserie, 68, *71*, *72*
chir kanni, wooden ladle, *345*, 351
chit, "printed cotton," word of Indian origin, 190
Chitsaz, Hajji Mohammad Taghi Ahavan-i, 192
chlorite, 30, *30*, *31*, *32*, *33*, *34*, *36*, 56
"The Chlorite Trade in the IIIrd Millennium", 32
Choga Zambil, ziggurat, 97, 392
choppers, sugar, 154, *155*
choqa, sleeveless long coat, *184*
chub-i golabi, pearwood, 352
churi, tubular bracelet, 172, *173*
Ciba Review, 206
cloaks, shepherds', 285
cloisonné, *161*, 162
cloth making, 277
cloud motif, 13
Coastal Province, 176
cochineal, 179
cockscomb, stylized, 318
coiling, basket, 265, 266, *267*
College of Decorative Arts, 8
coloring, 286: of silks, *322*
comb, *350*: magical properties of, 180
cooler: water, *53*; drinks, *65*
copper: –wares, 14, 42, 113, 126, *127*, *138*, 166; –oxides, 166, 180; – blue glaze, 56, 90; –smith, 113
Coptic textile, 206, 274
corded sole, 261
cotton, 180, 182, 184, 243, 322: backing, 234
couching, 243: –stitches, 234
court art, 14, 138
cowrie shell, 318
cradles, hammock-style, 234

crossed axe, 302
cross stitch, 246, *247*
crown, 137, 170
Crown Prince's palace, Saadabad, **406**
Ctesiphon, 275
Culture and Arts: Minister of, 26, 40;
   Ministry of, 212, 373, 374
cushion cover, 220, *221*, 222, *224*
cutter: leather, 154, *155*; sugar, 154
cypress tree, 208, 234, 334

Dado panel, 364, *365*
dagger, enameled, *164*
dahyek-duzi, embroidery stitch, gilt
   thread laid and couched, 234, *234*
dandani, tie-and-dye technique, 192,
   193, 196, *232*
dara'i, ikat, 201-205, *201*, *203*, *205*
Darroudi, Iran, 411
Darvish, Ali, 128
Dashtak (village), 246, *251*
Dastajird, 212, 217, 275
Davarpanah (village), 170, 258
decoration, architectural, 384–408
"deep, deep structure," 17
deer, steel, 146, *147*
Deh Bid (soumak weave), 310
deremne, brush for firewood, 106
Dezful, 286, 310
Dhamija, Jasleen, 206, 210, 214, 277-
   288, [J.D.] 290
Diba, architect, 406
Dimand, M. S., 342
divination, 140: –disc, *140*
dizi, stone cooking vessels, 30, 32, *32*,
   34, *34*, *35*
dome: inner shell, *392*, *408*; Marble
   Palace, 406, *408*; of Imam Reza, 14
door, 364, *365*: painted, *383*
double cloth, *184*
doubling and rounding felt, *282*
dovetailing, *290*
Dowlat Shah, 362
dragon, 298; carpets, 16
drapi, shifts, 182
draw loom, 210, 212; harness, 210
drawn work, 228, *229*
dress panels, silk, 192, *193*
dried grapevine leaves, 322
drums, 374; *tonbak*, *376*
dschulchit "bear skin" pile, Uzbek, 273
duck, 180; shapes, stone, *38*
Dura Europos, 124
Durandesh, Salman, 98, *99*, *101*, 106
dyes, dyeing, 280, 296, 322: vegetable,
   214, 322, *323*; namad, 278

Ebadi, *qalamkari*, 190
ebony, *363*, 368
Ebrahimian, Mehdi, 9, 346, 386, 400,
   402, *409*: glass by, 101, 106, *110*
edgings, 236, 261, *263*
Egypt, 186, 188, 206, 274, 369: –ian,
   faience, 56
Ehtemam, Husayn, 128; Muhammad
   Reza, 128
Elam, 18, 97, 177
"elephant's feet" motif, 336
Ellis, Charles Grant, 338
Emami, Karim, 8
Emami, miniaturist, 382
embossing, 113, 126, 128, 174
embroidery: 222, 290; Baluchistan,
   256; Byzantine, 217; Chinese, 217;
   Egyptian, 217; gold, 217, 218, 234;
   Isfahan, 27; Kurdish, 242, *242*,
   243; metallic, 233, *237*; Pazyryk,
   217; Persepolis, 217; spangles, *237*
Embroidery in Persia, 218
Emery, I., 278, 290
enamel, 72, 161–168, *164*, *165*, *168*:
   –ed faience tile, 386, 392
engraving, 113, 126, 128, *136*
'Eshqi, Ustad, 370

eslimi, arabesque, 94, 114, 118, 122,
   196, 214, 234, 378, 382, 392, *393*,
   394, *395*
Estaban(at), *80*, *83*, 90, 285, 286
Esther and Mordecai, tomb of, 156
Ethnological Museum, Tehran, 58,
   144, 156
Europe, 14, 20, 114: Renaissance 15;
   three-dimensionality, 19
evil eye, 170, 236, 340
ewer, *51*, *67*, *101*, 164, *166*: bird-
   shaped, 128, *129*; cock's head, 128;
   Sasanian-style, 101; silver, 128
Excavation Report, 1970, 30
*Exhibition of Royal Iranian and
   Kashmir Termeh*, catalogue, 214
Expedition, 1974, 32

Faience, polychrome, 384
Fakhari, Hossein, *189*
Falahi, Seyyed, 348
family, sense of, 22
fans, *255*, 258
Farah Pahlavi, Shahbanu, 5, 10, 23,
   26, 27, 97, 196, 198, 256, 292, 389,
   410
Farajollah, Ustad, 370, *371*, *372*
farizeh, choker or head band, 170, 171
Farmer, Henry George, 369, 370
Fars, 17, 18, 40, 172, 176, 180, 278,
   280, 285, 296, 332, 334
Farshchian, Mahmoud, 94, *95*
Fazayelli, Habibullah, 166
Fazl Abl, 208
feathers, 218, *283*, 288
Fehzollahi, Gholam Husayn, 165, 166
felt: hats, 277, 285, *288*; horse covers,
   252, *287*; making, 278–285, *277*,
   278, *282*
Ferdows, 261, *263*, 341
figural carpets, *339*, *341*, *343*, *344*
figurines, 62, *63*: steel, 146, *147*
filigree, 124, *125*, 172, 174, 176
fire steels, 152, *153*
Firouz, Iran Ala, 44, 169–176; *177*–
   216; 217–264
Firuzabad, 40, 278, 292
floor coverings, rustic, 273–276;
   see carpets
flower motif, 25, 180, 214, 217, 218,
   226, 230, 234, 246, 312
folk: arts, 14, 17; –lore, 5
Forbes, R. J., 186
Forough, Mehdi, 369
fretwork: metal, 110, *110*, *111*, 112,
   113, 116, 120, *122*, 172, *396*; wood,
   356, *356*, *402*
Frozen Tombs of Siberia, 217, 277, 321
Fryer, J., 188

Gaffary, Farrokh, 9, 106
Galpin, Francis W., 369
game board, 352, *353*, *357*
Ganj Ali Khan, Kerman, *394*
garden carpet, *311*, *326*, 327, *328*
gardens, 14, 19
Geography of Isfahan, 164, 190, 366
geomancy, 140
geychak, stringed instrument, 374
ghanun, 75-strings, *375*
Ghiordes knot, 330, *330*
Ghirshman, Roman, 101
Gilan, 32, 41, 44, 46, 48, *49*, *50*, *51*,
   54, *61*, 62, 80, 104, 114, 179, 180,
   184, 283
gilim, 21, 274, 276: Azarbaijan, 290,
   292, 296, *298*; Baluchi, *315*; Bijar,
   289, 302; Kalat-i Naderi, 317;
   Kurd, *307*; Qashgai, 290, *292*;
   Qassemabad, *307*; Quchan, *315*;
   Sanandaj, 290, *302*, 322; Senneh,
   302; silk, 289; Turkoman, *275*;
   Varamin, *304*

giveh, cloth-topped shoes, 261

glass, 27, 56, 72: Elam, 97; Germans
   imported, 106; Islamic, 104; milky,
   105, *107*, *110*; mold blown, *101*,
   106; mosaic, 392, 396; Sasanian-
   type, *108*, *109*; stained, 406
glasswort, plant ash for a glaze, 56
glazes, 58, 72, 90: alkaline, 68; aubergine, 58; copper, 58; gold, 90;
   green, 58, *59*, 64; lead, 58, 68;
   tin, 58, 68; turquoise, 72, 79
glaze, tiles, *388*, *394*
Gluck, Jay, 8–10, 24, 41–96, 265-272
Gluck, Sumi Hiramoto, 177–209
goats, 177, 184: hair, 289, 296, 318,
   322, 330
Gobelin weave, 290, 320
golab-duzi, chain stitch, 218, 224, *224*,
   225, 226, 227, 236, 242
gold: embroidery, 218; luster, 68, *70*,
   72, 128; printing, 186; -smiths, 124,
   170
Goldaghi, Turkoman, 354
Golriz *Khatam*, 362, 364, 366, 367
Gonabad, 186: pottery, 78, *81*, *82*, *83*
Gonbad-i Qabus, 246, 286
Gosht (village), 170, 258
granulation, gold, 176, *176*
grapevine leaves, (dye), 322   *334*
ground (horizontal) loom, 273, *321*,
Guchan (*see* Quchan)
Guide to Persian Embroideries, 226
gul design, 330, *331*, 336
Gulpaygan, 348, 374
gum tragacanth, 56
Guran, Eskandar Rustami, 322, 410
Gurgan, 104, 106, 184, 246, 330, 374
Guri, Muhammad, 98, 106

Haghighi, Kamran, 124
Hagopian, *130*
Hall, Margaret, 186, 188
Handicraft Center, Iranian, 62, 64,
   106, 322: opening of, 218, 222;
   Emporium, 28; later–Organization,
   9, 10, 30, 38, 192, 296; history of,
   24, 28; *Technical Reports* of, 50,
   169; collection of, 134, 353
Handicraft Excellence Award, 10, 77,
   99, 106, 124, *125*, *130*, 146, *147*,
   182, *183*, *208*, 212, 256, *257*, 346,
   350 *351*, *353*
hand-knit sox, *262*
hand painting, on textile, 186, *188*,
   190
hanging, wall, *see* wall hanging
Hariri, Ustad Kar Sheikh, 192
hasir, woven reed mat, 265, 266, *266*,
   270, 274, *278*: fossil, *274*
Hatifi, painter, 383
hats, *243*, 252, 261: tribal, 277, *288*
hauz, garden pool motif, 286
headpieces, *169*, *174*, *175*
headscarf, 182, *193*, 196
Heraclius, 212, 217, 275
Her Imperial Majesty, *see* Farah
   Pahlavi
Hermitage Museum, 164
Heydari, Colonel, 370
His Imperial Majesty, *see* Mohammad
   Reza Shah
History of Printed Textiles, 186
History of the Mongols, 162
Holt, Eugene—Stefania, 186, 206
Honarfar, Lutfullah, 128, 161–166,
   361–368
Honarhaye Ziba workshop, *136*, 210,
   211, 212, 213, *214*, 233, 358, 359
   368, 369, 373, 374, 375, 376, 404
Honaristan, Isfahan, 94, 368
horror vacui, 384, 386, 402
horse, 180, 252, 333: bit, *148*; blanket,
   285, 287, 290, 296, 298, 312, *313*;
   chestnut, 285; trappings, 184;
   shaped pottery vessel, *312*

Hossein, Hajji Mohammed, 106
Hotel Shah Abbas, 9, 97, 346, 386,
   387, *390*, 402, 406
Ho-tu, cave, 177
Howarth, H.H., 162
Huan Tsang, 212
hunting scene, 126

Idol: clay, 62, *62*; faience, 56; stone
   (Yahya), 30
ikat, 186, *201*, 202, *202*, *203*, *204*, 204
   205, 236: cut velvet, 202, *203*, *205*
Ikat: An Introduction, 202
Ilam, Ostan, 310
Ilya: Abdullah, 68; Abdul Zohad, 52,
   55
incense burner, *49*, *82*
Indian Painted and Printed Fabrics, 186
indigo, 318, 322, *323*
inlay, definition, 362
intarsia, 362
interlacing stitch, 258
Introducing Persian Textiles, 186
Iran Bastan, *see* Archaeological
   Museum
Iranian Handicrafts Organization, *see*
   Handicrafts Center, –Organization
*Iranian Handicrafts Organization,
   Technical Report 1976*, 30, 38
Iranmanesh, Battool, Kerman em-
   broiderer, 222
Irwin, J.—Hall, M., 186, 188
iron-oxide glaze, 90
Isfahan, 72, 113, 126, 142, 172, 186,
   210, 212, 233, 234, 322, 366, 380,
   386; "is half the world," 190
Isfahan Nisf' Jehan, 190
ivory, 362, *363*

Jag, sissoo tree, 346
Jahanbani, Ada, Baluch embroidery
   designer, 256
Jahram, felts, tenth century, 277
jajims, 8; Alamut, *317*; Ziabar, *317*,
   Ziaran, *317*
Jallal, Seyyed, *tar* by, *372*
Japan, 380; tombs, 101; *see* Shosoin
Jarmo, 265, 266
javahersaz, jeweler, 170
jewelry, 169–176: making, *170*; Turkoman, 340
Jews,-ish, 310, 371: in Babylon, 97;
   Kurds, 242
jiggernaut: *banafsh*, purple dye, 186;
   germez, red dye, 186
joak, embroidery stitch, 258
jole, wooden pitcher, 345, 351
jol-i asb, horse cover, 285, *287*, [*corrigen-
   dum*: Shahsavan] *295*, 312, *313*
Joseph, biblical story of, *189*, *266*
jujube wood, *363*, 368
Julfa paintings, 378

Kabiri, Ms. Soghra, Handicraft Excel-
   lence winner, 182
Kahnamu, silk-weaving village, 25
kalagheh, batik, 25, 198
Kalat-i Naderi, 167, 312
Kalegan, Baluchistan village, 286
Kalporegan, painted terra-cotta, *43*,
   44, 45, *46*, 47, 49
Kamalian, Mehdi, 369–376, 370, *371*,
   374
kanaf, hemp, 265, 266
Kashan, 68, 74, 93, 98, 106, 170, 172,
   177, 186, 202, 204, 210, 212, 226,
   234: Museum, 136
Kato, Tokuro, 72, 80, 94
Kazakh(stan), 246, 248
Kazemi, Hushang, 8
Keddie, Nikki, 277–288
Kendrick, A.F., 206
Kerend, 142, 152   383
Kerini, Ali, miniaturist, 25, 198, 377–

Kerman, 14, 29, *29*, 30, *30*, 32, 34, *34*, 42, 45, 62, 97, 113, 126, *127*, 138, 142, 222, 274, 277, 286, 310, 322
Kermanshah, 142, 278
Keyhan International, 24
Khachik, maker of *tar*, 370
Khak Negar, Muhammad Husayn, worked on Marble Palace dome, 406
Khalegi, Ruhollah, 370
khameh-duzi, embroidery work, *260*
Khamseh, 308, 330, 336, 338, 339, 340, 342; *see* carpets
Khan, Darvish, *setar* master, 370
Khan, Hajji Mohammad Karim, maker of *kamanche*, 370, 373
Khan, Mirza Hossein, 164, 190, 366
Khata, Husayn, miniaturist, 381
khatam(-kar), 7, 8, 15, 164, 354, 356, 361–368, *361*, *362*, *363*, *365*, *366*, *367*, *368*
Khayyam, Omar, 122, 242
Khodabandeh, Paulette, 404
Khorshid Khanum, 77, 142, 234, *235*, 236, 238
Khoshkish, Yousef, 6–7
Khurasan, 13, 27, 169, 179, 184, 246, 261, 290, 310, 374
Khuzistan, 18, 285, 310
kiln, 45, 50, 52, 56, 80, 90
Kipling, J. Lockwood, 190
Komeili, Hajji Agha Reza, metal engraver, 128
korsi, heating system, brazier under quilt-covered table, 220, *221*, 222
Kuh-i Kwaja, *265*
Kul-i Fir'awn, Elamite relief, 369
Kurashiki Folk Arts Museum: objects in, 266, 267, 294
Kurd(istan), 13, 25: pottery, 41, 42, 60, 80; jewelry, *169*, 170; textiles, 180; *see* embroidery, carpets

Ladle, wood, *345*, 346
lajvardi, lapis lazuli blue, 102, 166, 378, 380, 394
Lalijin, *41*, *59*, 62, *63*, 64, *65*, 66, *67*
Lamberg-Karlovsky, K., 30, 32
landareh-duzi, patchwork needlework, 226
lantern, *120*: fretwork, *121*; glass, 111; pottery, 60, *61*
Lar(istan), 172, 176
Latifi, Gol Soltaneh, woman potter's work, 50, *51*
Latour, cited, 206
leather: painted, embossed, *381*
le Coq, A.A. von, cited, 217
libation vessel: human form, *62*; horse shape, *312*
lion, 137, 146, 342: capital, 342; carpet, 342, *342*, *343*; faience, Achaemenid, *56*; griffons, 274; heads, 277; hunt, 116, *116*, *117*, 132, *133*; motif, 158; stone, 40; –and bull symplegma, 132, *132*, 137
Lion Rugs from Fars, 340
Lives of the Poets, 362
locks, 140, 156, *156*, *159*, *160*; –making, 113, *158*
Locks from Iran, *158*
loom, 273, 298, *321*, 330: brocade, *212*; double heddle, 180; jacquard, 210, *212*, *214*; treadle, 180, 182
Los Angeles County Museum Collection, obj. in, *250*
Lou Lan, textiles from, 217, 277
Luri, 274, 286, 310, 336: -stan, 8, 14, 18, 62, 114, 128, 148, 172, 179, 180, 310, 384; bronzes, 14, 18, 154
Lurzadeh, Heydar Siyah, dome mason, 406
luster faience, 68, *70*, 386
lute, *369*, 371, 374

Madder, 276, 318, 322
Madraseh Madar-i Shah, 128, 166, 368, 396
maghneh, magnesium oxide, 90
Maghzi, Ustad Ali, mosaic by, *393*
magical powers, 160; of comb, 180
mahout, wool flannel, 218
Mahtab, Ms., Baluch embroiderer, *256*
Maison d'Iran, 9, 62, 63
maize, straw for basket, 265
Majd: Fozieh, 369–376; [Reza] 406
malileh-duzi, metallic thread embroidery, 233
Mamaqan, Azarbaijan, *242*, 243
manganese-black, 68, 90
Maragha, first mosaic tile, 392
marble, white, green, grey, 30; architectural, 40
Marble Palace, 7, 40, 94, 364, *365*, *366*, 367, *367*, 386, *387*, 402; Audience Hall, 398, *399*, *401*
Marguiles, Erwin, 162
Marlik, *62*, 97, *104*, 128
marquetry, 346, 354, *356*, *357*, *359*, 362, *363*
Marshall, Sir John, 177
Marvdasht, town, 278, 286
Mashhad, 28, 208, 330; stone, 30, *32*, *34*, *36*, *38*; Exhibition, 1976, 60, 80, 110, 122, 160, 237, 300, 348, 379
Mashhun, Hassan, music expert, cited, 370
Masjed-i Lamban, Isfahan, marquetry in, 362
Masson, Charles, cited, 318
Mas'udi, geographer, cited, 206
Masulipatam, Persian craftsmen in, 188
Matine-Daftary, Leyly, painter, 8, 9
mats, matting, 273, 277: huts, 266
Mausoleum of Uljaitu, Sultaniyeh, restoration, *388*
Mazanderan, 184, 246, 266, 277, 278, 290
meat cleaver 150, *150*, *151*   *319*
Meibod, pottery, 56, *71*, *72*, *77*, *78*
Meibodi, Reza Aghai, Excellence Award winner, pottery, 77
Mellaart, James, cited, 186, 217, 384
Meshkat, Mohammad, *qalamkar* work of, 190, *191*, 192
Mesopotamia, 38, 42, 68, 97, 266
metal, 384: powers inherent in, 140; threads, 212; -lurgy, 14, 21, 113-160, 126, 128, 146
Meymand, glass of, 106
Mikasa, Prince, Coll. of, 101
Minab, 46: basketry, 266, *268*, *269*, 270
mina'i pottery, 68, 72, 128
minakari, enamel on metal, 161-168
minbar, see pulpit
Ming Dynasty, 48, 58: porcelains, 68, 71, 72
miniature, 14, 15, 126, *148*: -ist, 382
mirror, *14*, 138, 138': work, 254, 258; painted, *379*; -mosaic, 386, *387*, 390, *396*, *398*, *399*, *401*; *sekeh-duzi*, 254
mobility (in art), 17, 19, 22, 23
Mohammad Reza Pahlavi, Shahanshah, 2, 6, 7, 8, 292
Mongols, 68, 104, 186
Moqtader, architect, 406
Mosadeqpur, mosaics by, 394, *395*, 396
Mosadeqzadeh, Mehdi, mosaics by, *391*, *393*
mosaic: faience, 19, 80, 384, 386, *390*, *391*, 392-396, *392*, *393*, *395*, *396*, *397*, 402; glass rod, 392; glass tesserae, 392, 396; mirror, *387*, *396*, *397*, *398*, *399*, 401; stone tesserae, 392, 396
mosque: curtains, blocked, *194*; lamps, 104

Mossaver al-Mulk Ustad Hajji, enamel by, 166, *167*
Muhammadi, Hassan, enamel, 166, *167*
Muhammadieh, weaving at, *180*, 184
Muharram, 144, 146, 150, 200
Muqan, village, produced madder, 276
murals: Chehel Sutun, 378, 386; Safavid-type, 402, *407*
musaif embroidery, 226
Musavi(zadeh), Morteza, pottery by, *80*
Museum of Decorative Arts, Tehran, objects in, *115*, *118*, *119*, 203, 208, *361*, *377*
Museum of National Arts, Tehran, objects in, *93*, 212, *213*, *320*, 356, *359*
music: Baluchi, 374; Persian, 369
musical instruments, 369-376: Western string, 373; innovation, 376
Music of Sumerians and Their Immediate Successors, 369
Mussighi Kabir, 374
mystic texts, 374

Nahavand, 179, 180
Nain, 56, 68, 72, 184, 276   *403*
nakhl, shrine, 144, *156*, *157*, 160, 352, *359*
naksh, tent stitch embroidery, 226
namad felt (mats), 277-288; 8, *278*, *279*, *280*, *281*, *284*, *285*
naqdeh-duzi, metallic embroidery, 233
Naraghi, Mohammad, 9, 77, 106, 111, 196, 198
Narenjestan, 310, 346, *386*, *387*, 389, *390*, *392*, *403*
Nariman, Ustad, musician, revived oud, 371
Natanz, 56, 70, 72, 74, 76, 80
natural color carpets, *326*
natural dye(stuffs), 296, 322 *323*
Nazemi, Mehdi, 370, 374, 375
necklaces, 164, *171*, *172*, *173*, 236
Needle and Bobbin Club, Bulletin, 217
needlework, 217-264
Negahban, Ezzatollah, 104
Nelson, C. Griffin, 321-344
Nemat, Ustad Ali, *khatam* master, 368
Nematian: Abdol Hamid, 246, *352*, *353*; Majid, 346, *350*, *351*, *353*; Nematollah, 346, *353*
New Account of East India and Persia, A, 188
NIRT Center for Traditional music, Noin-Ula, 217, 274   *370*, *372*

Ogee, 162
ogive, 19, 210, *211*
Ohara, Houn, 288
Ohara School of Flower Arrangement, Gallery of Art, obj., *285*, *292*, *312*
Oomoto Foundation, Coll. of, 51
orange wood, *363*, 368
Orazi, Roberto, 404
Oshagi, Hassan, 404
Osku, 25, 27, 186, 198
oud ('ud), 369
Ouseley, Sir William, 366
Oveysi, modern painter, 8
Oxus treasure, 162

Padlocks, 156, 158, *159*, *160*
Pahlavi, 77, 164: Dynasty, 5; era, 362, 370; renaissance, 400; Shahanshahs, 174; (individuals, *see* first name)
Pahlavi Dej, 198, 246, 330
Pahlavi Museum, 7, *367*; *see* Marble Palace
Painted and Printed Textiles, 186
painting, 15, 21, 377-383: on plaster, *385*, 386, *387*, 407; on textiles, 186, *188*, *194*, 261; on tiles, *400*; Qajar, 378; Safavid, 378
paisley, see *boteh*
palm fronds, for baskets, 265

pambeh-duzi, quilting stitch, 222
Parthian, 50, 56, 124, 162, 176, 186, 274
Parthians and Sasanians, 101
Past and Future of Persian Art, The, 15
pateh-duzi, Kerman embroidery, *221*, 222, *222*, *223*, *224*
Pazyryk, 217, 226, 274, 276, 277, 298, 321, 351: carpet, *178*, 179, 180
peacock, *130*, 137, 138 (Sufi symbolism), *138*, 146, 152, 208, 230, 234, 286
pear, 346; pearwood, 352
Peasant and Nomad Rugs of Asia, 342
pen box, 15, 346, *353*, *377*, 378, 380, 382
perivar-duzi, cross and interlacing stitches, *256*, 258
Persepolis, 6, 30, 32, 72, *114*, *116*, 118, 132, *179*, 217, 274, *346*, 378, 384
Piggott, S., 29
Piip, needlework of, *256*, 258
pile voided, 336, *337*; velvet, *207*, 210
Pir, Khosrow, 44, 265-272, 277-288, 322
pitchers, *74*, *82*, *84*, *345*, 346
plaster work, 162, *385*, *387*, 388, *398*, 403, 407
plywood blocks, batik, 200
pomegranate (rinds), 172, 192, 322
Pope, Arthur Upham, 13-16, 273-276, 384-396; 7, 9, 41, 42, 80, 89, 94, 132, 179, 212, 217, 276, 277, 390, 391
porcelain, 56, 68, 94, *95*, 352
potter's wheel, 50, 60, *66*, 70; origins (?), 42
pottery, 13, 18, 19, 21, 41-96, 186: period, prehistoric 5, 310; painted, 5, 14, *42*, *43*, *44*, *45*, *46*, *47*, *49*, 177, 180, 298, 384; Neolithic, 41, 44, *46*, 52; Bronze Age, 46, 50, 52, *58*, 60; Iron Age, 46, 50, 52, 58, 66; Achaemenid, *56*; Parthian, 56, *57*, 64; Sasanian, 56, 58, 186; Chinese links, 58, 62, 68, *69*, *71*, *72*, *73*, 75, 352; Amlash, 46, 50, 62; animal form, 46, 312; as art, 42; black burnished, 60; blue frit, 56, *57*, 58; buff, 52, *53*, *55*; firing, *45*, 50, 52, 80; handles, *46*; incense burner, 46, *49*; invention by women, 41; process, 64, *66*; red, 42, 50, *51*, *54*; Shinto shrine, 50; spouted, 46, *50*; structure, 46; tools, 66; wheel, origin, 42; women potters, 41, *44*, 45, 50, 80
prayer mats, *260*
Prehistoric India, 30
Primary Structures of Fabrics, The, 278, 290
pulak-duzi, sequined embroidery, 233, 234, *235*, 236, *237*
pulpit, mosque, 352, *358*, *359*, 362
puttees, *241*, 243

Qajars, 19, 366; court art, 23; economy, 190; era, 164; motifs, 116; paintings, 378; -style glass, 106
qalamdan, pen box, 346, *353*, *377*, 378, 380, 382
qalamkar, block-printed cottons, 186-192; 166, *185*, 186, *187*, *189*, 190, *190*, *191*, *192*, *194*, *196*, 200, 234; carving blocks, 360
qaleb, wood blocks for *qalamkar* print, 186, 360
qalian, water pipe, *see* water pipe
Qanbari, Ustad Ebrahim, 371, 373, 374, 376
Qashgai, 174, 198, 274, 277, 278, 292, 310: bags, *335*; embroidery, *238*; gilims, pile, *see* carpets; medallion, 336; salt bag, 308; Tribal Carpet Weaving school, 322, *332*, *334*, 336, 342
Qassemabad, textiles of, *178*, 180, 256
Qassemabad-i Aulia, namads of, 288

4l5

Qavam, Hossein, copper form by, *167*
Qavianpur, Hassan, enamel by, *167*
Qazvin, 234, 380
Qoleh Zoh, village, needlework of, *248, 261, 263*
Quchan, work of, 261, *263, 281,* 312, *372*
Qum, work in, 32, *38, 39,* 56, 57, 164
Qur'an: covers, 258; influence of, 354; stands, *354, 355, 361*

Rahbur, namad-making town, 286
Ramsar, 282, 284, 288
Rashid, al-Din, cited, 162
Rasht, 27, 162, 186, 204, 218, 266, 348, 350
Rashti-duzi, chain stitch embroidery, 218, *219, 220,* 226
Rayen, steel products, 142, 152, *153, 154, 155*
Rayy, 72, 106, 124, 202
Read, Sir Herbert, cited, 42
reeds, 265, 270, 274: baskets, *269, 271;* boats, *265, 266;* mats, *265, 265;* pipes, 369
renaissance: in Iran today, 23, 402; Islamic, 18; Reza Shah, 7, 15, 356
resist dyeing, 186, 202, 204; 6th century B.C., 198
Reza, Hajji Mohammad, *qalamkar* maker, 192
Rezai, Mohammad Gholam, Excellence Award, 1976, 212
Rezaiyeh, beadwork in, 236
Reza Shah, 7, 15, (Khan) 15, 94, 106, 192, 274, 356, 366, 368, 386, 400
Ritch, Diane–Wada, Yoshiko, cited, 202
Robinson, Stuart, cited, 186
rose pattern, 302, 386
rosettes, 172
rose water, 274: bottles, 164; pitchers, 236
Royal Bazaar, Isfahan, 166, 368, *368*
Royal Persian and Kashmir Brocades, 214
Rudenko, Sergei I., cited, 217, 277, 321
Ruhafza, Ustad, *tar-setar* innovator, 371
Rural Cooperatives, 319: nonagricultural activities, 296, 322
rush, 265, 288; *hasir* mats, *266*

Saadabad Palace, *khatam* in, 366
Sadatmand, Seyyed Muhammad, *56*
saddle, 273: covers, 218, 273, 285, *329;* cushions, 236, *239;* furniture, 274
Sadiq, Issa, 15
Safavid, 186, 212, 366, 369, 378
Sagzabad, 42, 310, 384, 388
Salmony, Alfred, 217
Sami, Amir, silversmith, 122
Sanandaj, 346, 348, 351
Sanie Khatam, Ustad Muhammad, 367, 368
Saniezadeh, Shokrollah, enamel master, 162, 164, 165, 166
santur, 375: hammers, *374;* makers, 370, 373, 374, *375,* 376
sarv naz, cypress tree, *205,* 234, *235*
Sasanian: decadence, 19; enamel, 162; reconstruction, 18; renaissance, 23; silver, 68, 275; -style glass reproduction, *101, 103, 104, 108;* stucco, 384
Saveh, gilim, *307*
sehna knot, carpet weave, 330, *330*
Seistan, 44, 45, 170, *172,* 172, 176, 179, 260, 266, 374
sekeh-duzi, Baluchi needlework, *254, 258, 265*
Seljuq, 104, 128, 202, 292, 388, 389, 390: brick lay, 389
Semnan, 56, 186, 246, 277, 285

Sergeant, A. B., 206
sgrafitto stone, 34, *35, 36, 37*
Shahbanu Farah Foundation, 15, 380
Shahdad, prehistoric site, 29, 265, 266, 274
Shahin Glassworks, Tehran, 101, 106
Shahin, Hassan, pottery painter, 84
Shah Mosque, 162, *165,* 166
Shahram Pahlavi, H. H., Coll., *29, 30, 34,* 290, 298
Shah Reza, pottery center, 336
Shahsavan, 285, 290, 292, *294, 295, 296, 296, 297, 299,* 332, 342, *344*
Shapley, John, 30, 42
Sheikh Lutfullah Mosque, 7, 94, 394, 400: copy of, 406, *408*
Shesh Buluki, 332
shiluneh, embroidery stitch, 230, *232*
Shiraz, 74, 80, 106, 113, *119,* 172, 261, 278, *282, 286,* 292, 366, 374, 386
Shiraz Arts Festival Exhib., *80, 374*
Shosoin Imperial Repository, 104, 217, 277, 356
siah-duzi, embroidery stitch, 260, *260*
Siakal, red ware pottery, *52*
silk, 25, 179, 243, 246, 340: brocade, 180, 181, 214, 215; coat, Tekke, 249, 250; edgings, 261; growing, 180, 184
Silk Road, The, 217
silver, 118, 122, 124, 125, 126, 166: embossing, *126,* 128; embroidery, 218; engraved, *128, 129, 130, 131;* filigree, *125;* fretwork, *122, 123, 124;* granulation technique, 124; silversmiths, 118, 124, 170, 174
slit, tapestry, 184, 275, 290 (weaving diagram), *307,* 312; *see* gilims
sofreh, cloth used for meals, 180, *181, 182,* 208, 318
sokmeh-duzi, drawn work, 228, *228, 229*
soumak weave, 274, 275, 290, 296, *296, 298, 308,* 310,
sovinuk, polishing stone, 44
spike fiddle, *kamanche, 373*
spoons, sherbet, 346, *347,* 352
stability, 17, 18, 22
steel, 126, 142
Stein, Sir Aurel, 217, 274, 277
stencil-printing, 186, 394
Stocklein, Hans, 162
stone, 29–40: Achaemenid, 30; alabaster, 30, *38, 39;* amulets, 32; bull figurine, *34;* chlorite, *30, 31,* 32, *33, 34, 36;* dizi cooking pot, 32, *33, 34,* 35; figural, garden sculpture, *40;* marble 30; marble architecture, 40; pot making, *32, 34;* prehistoric, *29, 30,* 32, 34, 38; prehistoric mines, 30; sgrafitto, 34, *35, 36, 37;* steatite, 32; tesserae mosaic, 396; weights, *38;* vase, 33
stone paste pottery, 56, *57, 58, 70,* 72, *76, 77,* 80, *82*
Story of Iranian Music, The, 370
stucco, decorative, 384, *385,* 386, *387,* 402, *403, 407*
Studies in Ancient Technology, 186
Sufi, Expressions of the Mystic Quest, 138
Sullivan, Michael, 217
Sultanabad, 352
Sultaniyeh, 362
Sumer: pottery, 56; glass, 97
survey, Handicrafts Center, 26
Survey of Persian Art, A, 8, 9, 15, 24, 30, 32, 38, 42, 68, 104, 106, 114, 124, 132, 148, 162, 166, 179, 180, 186, 192, 202, 210, 212, 217, 218, 275, 277, 278, 289, 310, 340, 342, 362, 364, 366, 369, 370, 378, 388, 389, 392, 396
Susa, 13, 38, 162, 177, 346, 384

Tabataba'i, 8
Tabriz, *73, 79, 84, 122, 123,* 124, 208, 236, 380
Tabrizi, Ustad Abdul Latif, 128
Takhsh, Ustad Yusef, 101, 106
talismans, *31, 140,* 140, 142, 160, 236, *238*
Tanavoli, Parviz, 8, 158, 340, 342, 344
T'ang, 58, 68, 217, 292   302
tapestry, weaving diagrams, *290,* 298,
Taq-i Bustan, 170, 230, 369: garments at, 217
Tarighi, Mohammad, head of Honarhaye Ziba textile workshop, 212
Tavassoli, Hassan, potter, 84
Tavernier, 6
Tayabad (Turbat-i Jam), *372*
teacup holder, silver, *130*
teapot, brass, 114, *115*
Technical Report 1976, 30, 38
Tekke, 174, *174,* 246 *249,* 250, *251,* 336, *337*
template for mosaic, *396*
Tenri Sankokan, museum, 32, 294
tent, 273, 277; tent bands, 252, 336, 337, *354*
Tepe Hisar, 38, *38*
Tepe Musiyan, 177
Tepe Yahya, 29, 30
termeh, 208, *211,* 214, *215, 216,* 222, 233, 236
Textile Arts, The, 217
Textile Museum Journal, 338
textiles, 5, 14, 19, 22, 177–216; fossilized, Susa, Çatal Hüyük, 177
Textiles from Burying Grounds in Egypt, 206
Textiles in Pharonic Egypt, 206
thistle, Russian, 56
three-dimensionality, 19, 20, 21, 23
tie-and-dye, 192, *193,* 196, 230
tikeh-duzi, appliqué work, 218
tile, 72, 86, 186, 378, 384, 386, *386, 388,* 392, 394
Tolmachoff, Eugenia, 186, 217
tongs, charcoal, 152, *153*
tool, 20, 154, 155, *280, 350, 360*
Traditional Crafts of Persia, The, 30, 34, 56, 148, 261, 277, 278, 322
Travels in Persia, 188, 218
Travels in Various Countries of the East, 366
tree motif, 214, 230, 336, 340
trouser embroidery, 226, 230, *232,* 246, *256*
tufted weaves, *see* carpets
Turkistan, 202, 296
Turkmenistan, 246, 250, *250*
Turkoman: jewelry, 169, 174, *174, 175,* needlework, 246–252, *249, 250, 251, 253;* namad, 282, *284, 285, 285,* 288; horse covers, 287, *295, 312, 313, 329;* carpets, 274, 275, 278, 330, *331,* 332; tent band, *337*
Turkoman Needlework, 246
two-dimensional space, 19

Uljaitu, mausoleum of, 362
University Museum, Philadelphia, obj. in, *38*
Ur, Royal tombs, 29, 30
Urartu, 170: pottery, 50
Ura Senke Fdtn., Coll., object in, *283*
urushiol, Japan lacquer, 382

Vafur, opium pipe, 52
vajeh, design detailing, 282
Valiyan, Ali, potter, *89*
vank, flat grindstone, 45
Vaqefi, Ustad, pottery teacher, Honarestan, 94
Varamin, 285: gilim, *307*
Varizi, modern painter, 8

vases, 120, 130, 164: Isfahan, *73, 85, 89, 94, 95;* Kashan, *93;* Meibod, *77;* Ming red, *71;* Natanz, *70, 76;* Shah Reza, *91, 92;* Tehran, *96;* silver, 130, *131, 135*
vegetable dyes, 166, 214, 296, 322, *323*
velvets, 206–210; *203, 205,* 208, *233, 234, 236;* ikat, 202, *203,* 208; voided, *207,* 210
Velvets East and West, 206
Vial, G., Textile Museum, Lyons, 206
Victoria and Albert Museum, 164, 226, 362
villages, oldest known (Sarab, Guran, Buz Hajji-Firuz), 42
viola, 373; violin, 371, 373, 374
voided pile: carpet, 252, *253;* velvet, *207,* 210

Wahab, Ustad, metal engraver, 128
wall hangings, needlework, *219, 222, 223, 225, 235, 237, 242, 252, 264*
walnut: rinds for dye, 322; wood, 346, *348, 375*
water, mosque font, copper, *115*
water pipe, *qalian,* 46, 94, 118, *118, 119,* 164, 236
waterproof coats, 285
weave, diagrams of: plain, twill, 289
Webster's Third New International Dictionary, 212
weights, stone, *38*
Wertime, John W., 113–160
Wertime, J.W. and Tanavoli, P., 158
wheat straw, 265, 266, 267
whistles, toy clay, *52*
whitework embroidery, *khameh-duzi, 260*
window, grillwork, *404*
windows, stained glass, *404, 405, 406*
wine bottle case, silver, 122, *123*
woodblock printing, 186
woodwork, 15, 19, 27, 345–360, 354, 362, 368, 384; inlay process, *358;* products: bowls, 348, *349, 350, 351;* goblets, *348;* plates, *348;* portrait, 353; tray, 348, *349*
wool, 177, 184, 276, 280, 321, 322, 340
women potters, 41, *44, 45,* 50, 80
Wulff, Hans, 30, 34, 56, 148, 210, 261, 277, 278, 322

Xenophon, 274

Yahya, Armenian *tar* maker, 370
yaka, sissoo tree, Persepolis, 346
Yamut, 174, 250, 275
Yazd, 30, 113, 116, 120, 126, 184, 186, 196, 202, 204, 212, 230, 233, 340; pottery *53, 69, 70, 71, 77, 78,* 134; stone, 32; textile, *322*
Yeganegi, Farangis Shahrokh, 9, 24–28, 77, 198
yurts, felt, 285, 312, 340

Zabol, 170, 260
Zagros Mts., 18, 310, 342
Zand, 366: painting, 380
zanjan, silver filigree, 124, *125*
zarbi, embossed leather cover, 378
zargar, goldsmith, 170
zari, brocade, 190, 210, 212, *213*
zarif-duzi, double-braid stitch, 258
Zenderudi, modern painter, 8
zigzag pattern, 180, 302, 340
zileh, embroidery, see *naksh,* 226
zilu, cotton flat-weave carpet, 236, 276, 289
Zoka, Yahya, design by, 233
Zoroastrian: community, 196; costume, *230;* embroidery, *231, 232*
Zovin: village, 180, 182, 261, products of, *183, 263*